MONTANA MURDERS

NOTORIOUS AND UNSOLVED

BRIAN D'AMBROSIO

RIVERBEND
PUBLISHING

Montana Murders: Notorious and Unsolved

Published by Riverbend Publishing, Helena, Montana

ISBN: 978-1-60639-124-2

Cover and text design by Sarah Cauble, sarahcauble.com

Riverbend Publishing
P.O. Box 5833
Helena, MT 59604
1-406-449-0200
riverbendpublishing.com

The book is dedicated to the victims,
and to the hope that whatever unsolved cases featured within
are ultimately confronted and resolved.

Acknowledgments

Special thanks to the family and friends of the individuals who will not be forgotten, including Jon Andersen, Pat Andersen, Arleta Berg, Peggy Berg, Jane Botkin, Chris Broell, Brigit Craig, Cathy Fallang, Sherie Fallang, Eli Fisher, Mary Guana, Chris Johnson, Reilly Neill, Anita Spooner, Dave Stefonek, Mary Todd, Karie Webb, Kari Weber, and Jackson Welker.

A Note on Sources and Selections

Like most nonfiction books, *Montana Murders: Notorious and Unsolved* combines primary and secondary sources. I have used the past tenses when employing trial transcripts, books, newspapers, and other second secondary sources (for example, "wrote" or "said"). If a source is quoted or referred to in the present tense ("says" or "Johnson believes"), he or she spoke to me during the two years of my research on the book.

This book is by no means a full compendium of each and every notorious or unsolved murder in Montana. Inclusion or exclusion shouldn't be interpreted as one case feeling more pressing or one person seeming more notable than any other case or person. Instead, as with all books, the selections reflect the whims, directions, and personal attachments of the author. They include cases the author suddenly became aware of, or ones the author gravitated toward and eventually held closely, or some that the author was directed toward for a wide range of reasons.

CONTENTS

INTRODUCTION

For thousands of years, humans have been gripped by tales of killers in our midst. As long as we have mated, congregated, or foraged the peripheries of the earth, we have also, alas, murdered one another—and written about it.

Fascination with brutality is nothing new. Truman Capote's groundbreaking, controversial true crime masterpiece *In Cold Blood*, first published in 1966, is but part of a perverse reflection that has frightened and warned us for ages. Indeed, true crime publishing started with the Gutenberg press and continues to this day.

Murderer Who Stepped off the Mayflower

No human society or social system is absent of murder. In the U.S., murder arrived with the west-sailing ships that carried the first bundle of refugees seeking freedom from religious prosecution. The first documented case of a murderer in the New World involved John Billington.

Born around 1580 in England, John Billington probably arrived in the New World in 1620, when passage to the Virginia Colony was offered to several families with the promise of a better life. It didn't take long for the Mayflower passenger and pilgrim to end up in front a judge.

In March 1621, Billington was brought before the Dutch West India Company and charged with "contempt of the Captain's lawful command with opprobrious speeches" and was sentenced to have his neck and heels bound. It seems that he pleaded mercy, and such was granted, because it was reported that "upon humbling himself and craving pardon…it being the first offence, he is forgiven."

But Billington couldn't keep free of trouble: in 1630 he killed

John Newcomen, apparently over a lingering quarrel, "they having been enemies for some time." Most reports state that Newcomen didn't see the end coming, having been shot in the back with a blunderbuss. Billington was tried by jury and sentenced to death by hanging, carried out in September 1630.

Centuries later, the heirs of John Billington said that they have endured the stigma of his alleged crime for 389 years and even have sought a pardon on the grounds that he was tried unfairly. "The mere mention of being a descendant usually results in the comment, 'Oh, you're descended from a murderer,'" one of his successors said in 2019.

Early Montana

Montana's history is fraught with tribal and lawless murder. From Native tribes at war among themselves to the organized incursions against tribal people by the cavalry, our state's early history drips with blood. One of the first recorded accounts comes from the annals of an official of the American Fur Company, who noted that on February 18, 1844, a pair of white men who were angry over the killing of one of their slaves by the Blackfeet, fired a cannon ball into a crowd of Indians trading at the fort. More than twenty Indians were killed, and all the corpses were scalped, the official noted.

Indeed, rumors, legends, and bloody campfire tales abound about lawless men such as John Jeremiah Garrison Johnston, or "Liver-Eating" Johnson (1824-1900), an endlessly recounted buffalo hunter and scout of the American Old West who would carve out and consume the liver of some of the Indians that he killed.

Born in New Jersey, Johnson traveled west to try his hand as a gold prospector and wood cutter in Alder Gulch, Montana Territory. The cannibalistic legend begins in 1847, the year that his wife, a member of the Flathead tribe, was killed by a young Crow, which prompted Johnson to supposedly dine on his victim's innards as a further course of revenge.

According to one well-respected biographer of Johnson, "He supposedly killed and scalped more than 300 Crow Indians and then gulped down their livers 'to avenge the death of the wife.'" As his reputation and pool of scalps got bigger, "Johnson became an entity of fear." Feasting on the vitals of one's enemies, apparently, was the most degrading insult to the Crow, who believed that the liver was "essential if one were to advance to the spirit world," according to one historian.

Eventually, Johnson made amends with the Crow, who became "his brothers," and his much-vaunted personal vendetta against them ended after 25 years and scores of slain Crow warriors. Either way, the brutality and the violent rage inside him were compelling enough to be immortalized in the highly fictionalized movie *Jeremiah Johnson*, starring Robert Redford.

From Territory to Statehood: Core Element Violence

Most of Montana's territorial tales, if continued long enough, end in violent death. On January 10, 1864, sheriff Henry Plummer and two other road agents, Ned Ray and Buck Stinson, were hanged by Vigilantes in Bannack. Plummer had been involved in a series of criminal activities and shot and killed a rival named Jack Cleveland in a saloon fight in Bannock one year earlier. Plummer and his men were getting ready to exit town when the Vigilantes arrived. He was hanged from gallows he had constructed as part of his work as sheriff. Grisly epitaphs in Boot Hill Cemetery, near Virginia City, are authentic Americana; some date from days before vigilantes, when "road agents" hàd free rein in territory.

News sources of the Montana Territory are rife with stories like that of Nellie Paget, "a saloon girl" from the Midwest who arrived West in 1862 and two years later, on April 22, 1864, was shot and killed by an enraged miner at Bannack. The jealous miner was incensed by Paget's affections for another man; she is buried in the Bannack cemetery.

There were macabre sights such as Helena's Hangman's Tree, a pillar of territorial justice on the outskirts of town just east of Dry Gulch. There, below the mining camp's version of "boot hill," at least 10 men were lynched between 1865 and 1870, the last taking place when vigilantes hanged Arthur Compton and Joseph Wilson for highway robbery and attempted murder.

Even some of our most notable predecessors met ignominious fates. In the spring of 1867, Acting Governor of Montana Territory Thomas Meagher called for six hundred volunteers to fight the Blackfeet who were the prime culprits in the killing of John Bozeman near present-day Livingston.

Bozeman was murdered while traveling along the Yellowstone River in April 1867. While his partner, Tom Cover, reported they had been assailed by a band of Blackfeet Indians, a number of historians have alleged that Bozeman was killed by Cover himself, or perhaps even by a henchman of a pioneer Montana rancher.

Judged to be motivated for the wrong reasons, Meagher's proposal to wage war on the Blackfeet was on the whole disregarded by the public. But soon afterwards, the greatest potential murder mystery of Montana occurred.

On July 1, 1867, Meagher apparently fell into the Missouri River in the middle of the night from a steamer docked at Fort Benton. He was never seen again—and his body was never found. Some historians speculated that political rivals may have had something to do with Meagher's disappearance. Other persistent rumors suggested that Meagher fell into the river while under the influence of too much gin.

Of course, even statehood in 1889 did not stop violent and volatile men such as Harvey Logan, aka Kid Curry, who committed his famous crime of murdering Pike Landusky in Landusky in 1894, and dark secrets and bloody deeds have lurked for decades in the massive collections of the state's largest libraries and historical societies.

The Butte Archives keeps folders on the most heinous and infamous murder cases in Silver Bow County. The earliest documents recorded murders committed between 1894-1899. The first registered slaying took place on January 15, 1894, with the notation "Ying We Foo shoots and kills Gui Yick Moi." The following day, the body of one Felix Doncel was found in the brickyard and, two months later, Addie Collins killed her newborn infant son by throwing him into the bottom of an outhouse. On the final day of March 1894, Chin Ye Tuck killed Quong Tuck Wing with a knife and a hatchet.

Twentieth Century

Montana's Indian Wars and the most famous early murders have been suitably and successfully documented, which is why this book commences in the early 1900s.

The stories run the gamut of writing genres—the tale of convicted murderer "Turkey" Pete Eitner, perhaps the longest incarcerated inmate in Montana history, has a strong historical bent, while the disappearance and presumed murder of twenty-four-year-old Amy Johnson in Livingston in 1986 reads like modern true crime. The presumed murder—disguised as suicide—of Marion resident Shane Todd carries international insinuations that pulse and thump like plot twists in an espionage novel. Some stories flirt with the surreal: when journalist Edith Colby was arrested in 1916 for killing a politician, her defense contended that the victim had asked for it since he refused to apologize to her for an alleged insult. The insult so preyed upon her mind that she was not responsible for her actions at the time of the shooting.

Notorious

Twentieth-century murder and mayhem in Montana have left as much as an indelible impression on the collective conscious of the nation as the state's fly-fishing and skiing. Perhaps even more so.

More people on both coasts are probably familiar with "The Unabomber" than the Big Sky ski resort or the Blackfoot River of *A River Runs Through It.* The average Montanan might not recognize the name of every Montana town, but they've certainly heard of the name "Kaczynski," the brilliant child prodigy who went on to bomb universities and airlines while "living as a hermit" in an itsy-bitsy cabin (10 x 12 feet) near Lincoln.

Perhaps no two men set back—or, alas, negatively advanced—Montana's image more than Dan and Don Nichols. The father and son "mountain men" had lived by poaching game and growing small gardens at various hidden camps in the mountains near Big Sky. In the summer of 1984, the deranged duo abducted world-class biathlete Kari Swenson with the stated intention of finding a wife for the son. The crimes—the kidnapping quickly escalated into the murder of one of Swenson's would-be rescuers—and prolonged manhunt in the wilderness northwest of Yellowstone National Park finally ended when a sheriff stormed into a winter camp used by Nichols and his son.

Some of the acts in this book, such as the specifics and timeline of serial killer David Meirhofer, are beyond chilling. In 1974 the detestable Meirhofer was arrested and charged the kidnappings and slayings of Sandra Dykman Smallegan, 19, and Susie Jaeger, 7, who was taken from her family's tent while they camped near Three Forks in 1973. Before he hung himself in a jail cell, Meirhofer admitted to randomly slaying other victims, some even younger. May we never again see the likes of someone such as Meirhofer.

Unsolved

The figures are astonishing and discouraging: if you are murdered in America, there is a one in three chance that the police won't apprehend or even determine your killer. Chances are that your case will be resigned to a handful of manila folders in a dusty filing cabinet and, if lucky, an occasional anniversary feature in a newspaper or a "true-crime" podcast, which is a burgeoning cash cow industry.

Incredible advances have been made in investigation techniques, forensic analysis, and DNA testing, yet, paradoxically, the rate of solving murders has steadily declined. Criminologists estimate that at least 200,000 murders have gone unsolved since the 1960s—leaving literally millions who knew and loved the deceased to brood and grind their teeth. To borrow from the FBI's vocabulary, the national "clearance rate" for homicide today is 64.1 percent. Fifty years ago, it was more than 90 percent. And clearance doesn't equal conviction. Clearance can be successfully applied to cases that result merely with an arrest, or cases in which "a culprit is otherwise identified without the possibility of arrest," the most common example being that the suspect has died.

Montana's clearance rate is parallel to the national average, with several baffling cases that continue to defy logic while simultaneously evading legal prosecution, such as the murder of Dexter Stefonek at the Bad Route Rest Stop near Glendive. In the winter of 1985, police discovered Stefonek's burned car at the desolate rest stop. The following spring, Dexter's body was discovered in a private landfill only miles from the last place where he was seen alive.

Several cases, including the unsolved vanishing of Father Kerrigan, a Catholic priest who disappeared in Ronan 35 years ago, have been treated as homicides. Indeed, although his bloody clothes and car were recovered, his body never was. Decades later, Kerrigan's name appeared on a long list of pedophile priests who had been coddled by the Helena Archdiocese instead of being censored, terminated, and prosecuted. Was this the reason for his apparent murder?

There is the ineluctable human impulse to distance ourselves from tragic events. However, whether you encounter the information through the news or social media, most people immediately want to know more. What time of day? Who was the last person to see the victim? Where was the exact location? Did the victim fight back? Did they know their attacker? Was it the decedent's spouse or partner?

Perhaps we ask these questions in hopes that we can distance ourselves from the crime. Perhaps we are looking for information that convinces us we don't have to worry that such a fate will befall us. In truth, such reassurance is specious.

Columbia Falls native and UM graduate Jennifer Lynn Servo was murdered by strangulation and head trauma on September 16, 2002, in her apartment in Abilene, Texas, one week before her 23rd birthday. Sheila Jordan was beaten to death only a few feet from her Livingston apartment one summer night in August 2000, minutes after walking the few blocks from County Market where she worked as a cashier. No amount of positing or question-raising could even remotely rationalize away these crimes as anything other than acts of depravity that should drive the stake of sympathy into our hearts, leaving a gaping wound that will never patch or even heal, regardless of whether the crime is "cleared" or not.

Murder is gritty, heart-wrenching reporting, and while homicide can't be stopped, the lives of the victims must not be marginalized or trivialized or even normalized to the point of any one of them being lost or resigned to history.

One body, one homicide, is tragic enough.

1

"DYNAMITE" IKE'S CAMPAIGN OF TERROR

Helena, 1903
Victim: Deputy Sheriff Tony Korizek
Case Status: Solved

A sketch of "Dynamite" Ike Gravelle, who tried to extort money from the Northern Pacific Railroad by bombing trestles, tracks, and trains. COURTESY MONTANA HISTORICAL SOCIETY.

MONTANA'S MOST INFAMOUS dynamiter-murderer looked the part: dusky, fixated eyes, deep sockets, sneering, pursed lips. Something about his face exuded its own sense of lawlessness. His eyes reflected that he was a lost soul, someone searching for some kind of validation—and a way to fit into society.

Yet the desire for recognition for Ike Gravelle wasn't superior to his desire for money.

In this fashion, his campaign of terror started in July 1903 in the deluxe offices of the Northern Pacific at St. Paul, Minnesota. The letter—and two, similarly handwritten identical copies—had been mailed at different post offices, more than a thousand miles distant.

The writer of the dispatch stated that the N.P. was being held for $25,000 ransom and that railroad property would be destroyed until the sum was paid. Fifteen days. That's the grace period the N.P. was given to meet the terms of the payment. In part, the letter read:

> July 16, Board of Directors,
> N.P.R.R. Company.
> Dear Sir: We write you this letter to notify you we hold the Northern Pacific Railroad company for twenty-five thousand dollars ($25,000) ransom and if necessary we will destroy your railroad property until the same is paid.
> We will give you 15 days from date to think this matter over and if at the expiration of that time you have decided to comply with our demands, you can notify us of your decision in the following way: Tie a piece of white cloth to the drawhead of the last coach of each of your passenger trains running between St. Paul, Minn., and Spokane, Wash.

The threat implied the shared zealotry of "us," assuring the railroad company that "we" mean business, followed by a discursive rant about the workingman's blues:

> Hereafter give the working man more justice and you will avoid this kind of trouble. If we have to go to extremes in this matter, we will increase the amount

```
of ransom. This letter must be delivered
with the money. Yours truly.
```

The letter was not signed. Officials, believing that the missives emanated from an idle crackpot, tossed them aside.

Dynamiter Strikes

The first blast perhaps played no small part in convincing skeptics. On August 1, 1903, a section foreman living near Livingston was awakened in the early morning by an explosion believed, at first, to be a clang of thunder. He investigated and found that granite piers of the N.P. bridge over the Yellowstone River had been blown apart. The tattered bridge now supported only by a pinnacle of stone. A freight train and a passenger train by some means had passed over the bridge without incident after the blast.

More mayhem ensued. According to contemporary news accounts, on August 5, 1903, at a point about one mile west of Bozeman, "approximately 26 miles from the site of the Livingston bridge attack," a freight train rolling across Montana struck explosives tied on the track. The freight crawled into a roundhouse with its headlight blown away, pilot shattered, and its front entirely demolished.

On September 8, 1903, a streetcar on the Butte car line was demolished by dynamite just a short distance from the point where the tracks crossed the Northern Pacific. The motorman was knocked off his feet. Several passengers were dumped on their backsides.

The dynamiter then stepped up the frequency of his bombings. On September 22, 1903, an engineer named John Brown, running a passenger train between Helena and Logan, struck dynamite on the tracks. At Birdseye, a few miles west of Helena, there were three successive explosions that ripped apart rails. And twelve miles east of Helena, "a quantity of dynamite was found between the rails," according to one contemporary account.

N.P. officials, at first dismissive, understood that the letter writer was no idle prankster. Now, convinced that the extortionist was a thoroughly dangerous man, they displayed the white signal as he had demanded. Then, a second letter arrived from the dynamiter, mailed from Butte. It expressed approval that the N.P. had decided to comply with the extortionist's orders. It instructed the railroad to "leave the money at a point along the right of way where a red lantern would be displayed."

When the railroad disregarded the order, other blasts followed. The N.P. was notified yet again, but this time the writer upped the ransom amount to $50,000.

Railroad officers from St. Paul to Spokane must have been feeling increasingly anxious. There was no possible way to protect every stretch of railroad from an act of sabotage, they thought. Railway officers, sheriffs, and the police of many cities sought the dynamiter. They were spurred on by a large $5,000 reward offered by Governor Joseph K. Toole of Montana, who issued a proclamation "denouncing the criminals" and offering on behalf of the state of Montana a reward for their capture. Other rewards proffered included $5,000 by the Northern Pacific and $500 by Park County, Montana, for an extravagant total of $10,500.

Suspicious Man in the Snow: "The Dynamiter"

One day in October 1903, a suspicious man was reported digging in the snow on the railroad tracks, near Blossburg. A group of ex-sheriffs and men "experienced in hunting criminals" took up the trail on their saddle horses.

Footprints in the earth were followed from Blossburg to an adjacent hill, where the suspect, who was wearing high-heeled boots, mounted a horse and rode to Priest's Pass. At Priest's Pass, the thirty-mile chase ended, and the elusive rider was captured. The accused was brought from Priest's Pass to a local livery stable; he was persistent in the claim that his name was Plummer.

"The Dynamiter," as he came to be known, was identified as Ike Gravelle. Born in 1869 in Canada, his father was a Frenchman, who, according to one 1910 pulp reader, "emigrated to Canada from France, where it is said he participated in the Franco-Prussian war," and, the pulp continued, "there is a legend that he acquired renown by reason of the great courage he displayed at one of the memorable battles of that war."

Gravelle, already an ex-convict, was tried and convicted on the extortion charge and was sentenced to ten years in the Montana state prison and fined $5,000.Gravelle also would be tried on the theft of the dynamite from the Holter Company, and there was a good probability that he would be sentenced to life under the "habitual criminal act."

Escape and Murder

While awaiting the theft of dynamite charges, Gravelle was kept in the Lewis and Clark county jail in Helena. Authorities intercepted a letter he had written that began, "Friend Myron." This became known as the "scratch letter," as it was written with invisible ink and became readable only when heated. Gravelle, it appeared, had surreptitious plans in mind.

On August 11, his case was fixed to go to the grand jury. According to later accounts, as Gravelle and Deputy Sheriff Tony Korizek left the courtroom for the noon recess, "the criminal whispered something to Korizek," and the two went into the lavatory of the courthouse. A short time later the two men emerged and then crossed the lawn to the jail, where Gravelle was placed in a cell.

Later the jailor, Ed Jones, went to Gravelle's cell, where Gravelle flashed a revolver and thundered, "Put up your hands!" Gravelle ordered Jones to unlock the cell door. (Where Gravelle obtained the gun was never learned, though it was most likely planted for him in the bathroom.) Gravelle forced Jones to walk ahead of him down the jail corridor, where they met Korizek.

Jones silently tried to warn Korizek but was unsuccessful. Gravelle forced Jones and Korizek to turn to the wall. It is believed that at this moment Korizek reached for his gun, but Gravelle fired three shots in rapid succession, inflicting fatal wounds upon the deputy. Korizek staggered and fell to the floor, and Gravelle seized the officer's pistol, "a big .44 caliber revolver."

Gravelle ran to the street and toward Governor Toole's mansion, at 304 North Ewing Street. A posse of lawmen fired shots, wounding Gravelle in the arm, and, according to one news account, "a woman caught in the line of fire ran to the front door of the governor's mansion." The governor's wife, Mrs. Lily Toole, heard the shots, rushed to the door, and let the woman in, before re-locking the door in a panic. Seeking escape, Gravelle darted to the rear of the Toole residence, but there was no outlet.

As the rabid pack of lawmen closed in, Gravelle found himself trapped by high, brick walls. He took shelter in an enclosed alleyway that led into the cellar. His ammunition was nearly exhausted; his situation looked hopeless. Desperation steeled his determination. They would never take him back to prison.

Closing in for the kill or capture, his pursuers heard a shot. They came to the steps of the areaway, and looking down, saw the limp frame of Gravelle. The man was lying with his head toward the cellar door, his right arm bent under his body. With one of his few remaining bullets he had fired the gun at his head—dying instantly.

The escapades of the Montana dynamiter and murderer were over.

2

REPORTER SLAYS POLITICIAN

Thompson Falls, 1916
Victim: A.C. Thomas
Case Status: Solved

The mug shot of newspaper reporter Edith Colby, who shot and killed a prominent Montana politician on the main street of Thompson Falls after the man allegedly insulted her. COURTESY MONTANA HISTORICAL SOCIETY.

PERHAPS EDITH COLBY'S MURDER of A.C. Thomas could not have been scripted much more surreally: a newspaper reporter claimed she murdered a prominent politician because he offended her with a lewd comment and, worse, refused to apologize.

Born in New Hampshire, Edith Colby came to Montana from Spokane, where she worked as a "copyholder" for *The Spokesman-Review.* At some point, she was engaged to one Dr. Hilscher and "endured a traumatic breakup," which may have led her to pursue a fresh job and circumstances in Thompson Falls.

Colby, either 43- or 44-years-old, depending on which account one sources, seemed to be adjusting well to her new employment as a reporter and proofreader by *The Independent Enterprise*. The newspaper was established four months earlier, and both Colby and the fledgling publication would be growing together.

A dispute on the main street of Thompson Falls on the morning of September 28, 1916, turned Colby from citizen to assassin, and thrust the young reporter and her place of employment in the clutch of a scandalous trial that *The Missoulian* referred to as one of "an extremely sensational nature."

The disturbance occurred in front of the Ward Hotel. The victim: A.C. Thomas, a chairman of the county Republican Party. The genesis of the murder: the day before, Colby claimed, Thomas had called her "a red-light woman." The alleged insult took place, she said, when she "reprimanded him for withholding news" when she visited Thomas looking for information on a story she was preparing to file.

On that fateful day, Colby confronted Thomas and insisted on an apology; Thomas, she said, would not heed to her demand. In fact, Thomas paid no attention to her. He casually passed on, inflaming the reporter, who took a gun out of her handbag and demanded a response, "Now you must apologize!"

Finally, Colby fired four shots at Thomas. Two took effect. One of the bullets only cut into Thomas's right arm, but the other created a wound that soon proved fatal. At first, the doctors held out "a slight hope for recovery," until they discovered that the bullet ricocheted through the liver, "the fatty tissue that encases the liver, intestine and stomach, and twice through the colon," according to Thomas's death certificate.

The murder of A.C. Thomas was rumored by some to be a political act. After all, *The Independent Enterprise* had opposed Thomas, a top county Republican official, and recently published a series of strongly worded political attacks against him. On top of this, Colby was a politically minded Republican. She had once served as assistant labor agent in Spokane and unsuccessfully vied for a city commissioner job there.

Suspicion of a conspiracy further intensified after Colby asserted to police that John L. Manire, the editor of the paper, and A.S. Ainsworth, its publisher, had urged her to make Thomas apologize, and that they even incited her to kill him. After the coroner's inquest found that Ainsworth and Manire shared the blame with Colby, all three of them were arrested.

Burton K. Wheeler (1882-1975), later a vice-presidential candidate under progressive candidate Robert M. "Fighting Bob" LaFollette, was named special prosecutor. However, he had a hard time supporting charges against Colby's superiors: their behavior was instigative, even reckless, alas, not criminal. Thus, the court dropped all charges against Ainsworth, and the judge directed the jury to find Manire not guilty.

Colby's action, however, were clear-cut and patently prosecutable.

Colby Defense: "Mentally Deranged"

Edith Colby was placed on trial for second-degree murdering Thompson Falls on November 27, 1916. The defense did not deny the particulars of the actual shooting but contended that Colby was "mentally deranged," an unhinged, anguished (and thus blameless) person triggered by the callous insults heaped upon her by Thomas. The testimony introduced by the state, however, sought to depict that Colby had "calmly and calculatedly" planned the murder.

Spokane attorney John T. Mulligan in his opening statement for the defendant said Colby "had suffered extreme mental anguish" and that "in a fit of insanity partly hereditary, and induced by mental suffering," had shot Thomas as the result of an "irresistible impulse."

The opening witness called by the defense was Colby's aged mother, Jane F. Coolidge, of Worchester, Massachusetts, who testified to her daughter's mental health defects and to "indications of hereditary insanity. "Jane listed a series of events in her daughter's life likely to have caused her "mental derangement."

Colby's lawyer conceded the obvious: she was a killer. However, he portrayed her as the "victim of a factional political quarrel," easily influenced and eager to please, a low-level newcomer "driven" to her murderous act by the authoritative men who "incited" her.

"Miss Colby will be cleared when the facts are placed before a jury," declared John T. Mulligan. "The sentiment has already swung around in her favor since the truth has begun to leak out. Public feeling at Thompson Falls is running high against men believed to be involved in the case. The first night I was here, I heard talk of trying to lynch some of these men who are believed to have incited Miss Colby to the killing."

Colby, continued Mulligan, was working and living in the capacity of "a defenseless woman, trying to make an honest living. "The real criminals are those who took advantage of her by carrying to her manufactured stories reflecting on her character."

Prosecutor Wheeler did not reject the possibility that Colby had not acted alone. Indeed, he even insinuated it, referring to the likelihood of a "master hand" behind a larger plot to remove Thomas.

"It is improbable that he ever insulted that woman," Wheeler said. "No life is safe in Sanders County, if a woman can be brought in from Spokane to kill on this pretext. Always the 'master hand.' She was going to get Thomas under its guidance."

Before the state rested, Opal Harris, a printer at *The Independent Enterprise*, testified that when Colby returned to the office after her initial meeting with Thomas, she was fuming with anger. Harris repeated Colby's allegation that Thomas called her "a red-light woman," and introduced a scenario that confirmed that Colby had in some sense been goaded into the deadly act.

"Miss Colby said she was so mad she could kill Thomas," Harris said. "She was so mad she was shaking. She said he had called her a red-light woman who ought to be kept on a side street. Mr. Manire (editor of the paper) said, 'Why don't you do it?' He told her no jury would convict her."

The following morning, Colby returned to the office with a pistol in her handbag. According to Harris, Colby planned to bluff Thomas into apologizing.

"'Don't worry, dear,' she said to me, 'I'm not going to shoot him. I'm just going to scare him into apologizing.'"

"High Drama" as Edith Colby Takes the Stand

Finally, Edith Colby took the stand in her murder trial—and "high drama ensued," according to one contemporary account. At one point, "the strain had become more than she could bear," wrote a news correspondent. The jury, consequently, was excused while Miss Colby "recovered her equilibrium."

Colby, downplaying her role as the aggressor, offered up the killing as a self-defense response to the menace of Thomas. "He sneered at me and doubled his fist like he was going to strike me," she testified. "And I shot, but don't remember how many times. I pointed the gun down."

Colby stated that she was unaware that she in fact struck Thomas with the shots until "the sheriff arrested her later that evening." She didn't hear him scream. She didn't see blood.

Colby also depicted her mental condition the night before the confrontation. Distressed, she unsuccessfully attempted chloroform to lull her to sleep. She said she "did not sleep an hour" that night. (She had earlier testified that she "hadn't been able to sleep for two years," and that she routinely used chloroform "two or three nights a week" to induce sleep.)

No matter her intentions, Colby couldn't deny that she pulled the trigger. After all, Thomas was shot twice in front of "half a hundred people" and, as a result, expired soon after he was taken to St. Patrick's Hospital in Missoula.

Guilty Verdict

Colby was found guilty of second-degree murder. Her sentence for slaying Thomas was meted out on December 6, 1916. It called for a penalty of 10 to 12 years in the state penitentiary. She entered the state prison at Deer Lodge on December 14, 1916.

Her attorneys appealed, claiming that prosecutor Burton K. Wheeler "maligned" Edith Colby's character during the trial and made "public remarks" that affected the verdict. The Supreme Court of Montana denied a new trial.

Edith Colby served only two full years at Deer Lodge. In July 1919, Governor Sam V. Stewart commuted her sentence and she was paroled from the penitentiary on August 19, 1919. She was required to report once each month to the state board of prison commissioners until March 14, 1924.

Colby left Montana for her former home at Franklin, New Hampshire. She returned to newspaper work as a proofreader and died in Los, Angeles, California, in 1942.

3

THE LYNCHING OF LABOR LEADER FRANK LITTLE

Butte, 1917
Victim: Frank H. Little
Case Status: Unsolved

Vigilantes abducted firebrand labor leader Frank Little from his Butte hotel room in the middle of the night. The next morning his body was hanging from a railroad trestle. No one was ever held accountable. PHOTOGRAPH OF LITTLE COURTESY JANE BOTKIN.

FRANK H. LITTLE began making speeches as soon as he arrived in Butte. In all of them he condemned the government and in some he angrily attacked the administration of President Woodrow Wilson while the nation was at war.

On July 19, 1917, before a mass meeting of miners at the baseball park, Little—a former miner who was now officially identified with the Industrial Workers of the World (I.W.W.)—referred to the United States soldiers as Uncle Sam's "scabs in uniforms." In the same speech he said: "If the mines are taken under federal control we will make it so damned hot for the government that it will not be able to send any troops to France."

Little was familiar with the Pacific Northwest, having spent several weeks in the county jail and notorious Franklin School jail annex in Spokane in November 1909 for labor agitation. He was part of an organized "free speech fight" in Missoula, an I.W.W.-instigated series of meetings and rallies from approximately September 28, 1909, until October 8, 1909. Little was arrested when he stood on a soapbox on the corner of Front and Higgins Streets on September 29, 1909. His speech was titled "On Temperance." Authorities never let him speak beyond the words "Fellow Workers and Friends." He spent the night in jail, then left for Kalispell to unite lumber workers. He was in northwest Montana when he was ordered to visit Spokane.

Less than two weeks later, he was dragged through Butte streets behind a car and hung from a railroad trestle. A note pinned to his body said, "Others take warning."

Little Arrives

On July 17, 1917, Frank Little left Salt Lake City, arriving at the Front Street Depot in Butte the next day to discuss an I.W.W response to threats against workers in Arizona and Montana mining camps. In one of his first addresses, he referred to the telegram he had sent to Governor Thomas A. Campbell of Arizona, telling him, "Governor, I don't give a damn what your country is fighting for; I am fighting for the solidarity of labor."

Thirty-nine years of age and single, he was peripatetic, with connections and fleeting residences in Fresno, California, Oklahoma, and Chicago. At the time of his death, his address was listed as a post office box in Miami, Arizona, a mining camp near Globe.

"When Frank arrived in Butte, he was really bitter and he was totally embarrassed as to how the government was in cahoots with the copper company, and the labor fight was intensely on his mind," says Jane Botkin, Frank Little's great-grandniece and author of *Frank Little and the IWW: The Blood That Stained an American Family.*

He took his case to the miners in Butte.

On Friday night, July 27, 1917, at Finn Hall before the Metal Mine Workers' Union, Little said: "A city ordinance is simply a piece of paper which can be torn up. The same can he said of the Constitution of the United States."

United States District Attorney Burton K. Wheeler asked if prosecution could be brought against Little "on the ground of his unpatriotic utterances." Government men worked on the Little case, according to Wheeler, "with a view to possible prosecution."

Little was murdered before a case could be made.

Death of Frank Little

In the dark morning hours of August 1, 1917, several men broke into room No. 30 on the ground floor of Mrs. Nora Byrne's boarding house at 316 N. Wyoming in Butte. But the men—possibly in uniform—found it empty.

The noise awakened Mrs. Byrne, who heard someone say, "a mistake somewhere," as the men rummaged the adjoining room. Then they came to her room and pushed the door ajar, but she held it shut. "Wait until I get my clothes on," she told them.

"We are officers and we want Frank Little," one of the men told her.

Mrs. Byrne got into a bathrobe and opened the door slightly. One of the men poked a revolver into the opening and said, "Where is Frank Little?" She told them he was in room 32 and they kicked its door open. Mrs. Byrne later said she believed "that police officers had arrested Little."

Byrne saw the men "half lead and half carry him across the sidewalk" and push him into a waiting car, which went south on Wyoming Street. Bernard Byrne, son of the landlady, was sleeping across the hall from Little's room. He said he heard "the battering of the door," the sound of men running down the hall, and then his mother arrived and exclaimed, "They have taken Little!"

"Whether there were six or seven men there that night abducting Frank is conflicting," says Botkin. "So many parts of the narrative still have conflicts."

One issue is indisputable

As the sun crested the Continental Divide and flooded Butte with summer daylight, rumor spread that a dead man was hanging from a railroad trestle.

The letters written at the bottom of the note "L-D-C-S-S-W-T "are believed to have represented the initials of several union organizers. Courtesy Janie Botkin.

The ties on the trestle were about 14 feet above the roadway. Little's feet were approximately five feet from the ground. On the back of his head was a bloody blotch.

Attached to the clothing on Little's right thigh was a pasteboard placard, about six by ten inches, bearing in red crayon letters the inscription: "Others take warning. First and last warning—3-7-77-

I.D.C.S.S.W.T." The series of letters were inscribed at the bottom of the card with a lead pencil. The figures "3-7-77" have long been attributed as a sign of the vigilantes in Montana. The custom of the vigilantes was to send two warnings to a marked man, the third and the last warning being written in red. On Little's body, the same card also bore these words: "First and last warning. Others take notice. Vigilantes."

"The detective wrote in the memorandum that he thought 3-7-77 was the measurements of a grave," says Botkin. "I've been told all my life that 3-7-77 was a vigilante code, but I set out to find the alternate proof of what the numbers meant, and I did. This detective, S.W. Kelly, wrote that it was meant to be the measurements of Frank's grave. As to all other speculations about vigilantes being responsible for Frank's lynching, I think that the first person was wrong about that and everyone else started copying the idea."

"They Got Little"

Responding to the murder of Little, *Solidarity*, the official publication of the Industrial Workers of the World, wrote:

> With carte blanche from the federal government, the minions of corporation power will proceed to glut their vengeance against organized labor to their heart's content. That is, if drastic steps are not taken and if the political representatives of Wall Street in Washington do not do this the I.W.W. will. The I.W.W. has stood all it can stand of such atrocities and all it is going to stand. Let them gloat over their victim, we have learned a lot of their method of fighting. This is by no means the end.

"The action of the men in Butte in hanging Frank Little will cement the loyalty of the Industrial Workers of the World throughout the country," said Fred H. Moore, attorney for the I.W.W.

"They got Little. He was the first man marked to go. We had received warnings and were told that Joe Shannon was the second in line, Tom Campbell third and another man fourth," William Sullivan, attorney for the Metal Mine Workers' union, said on the afternoon of August 3, 1917. "I cannot tell you how we received the warnings, but we know they were marking some of the men."

Attorney Sullivan only shrugged his shoulders when questioned if he were the fourth marked man. "We used every precaution and even had the marked men change rooms every so often," added Sullivan. "I cannot give the names of the other men who were supposed to be designated as victims."

Sullivan declared that there "would be no outbreaks (of violence) in Butte, although the temper of the men is much tried.... We have taken steps to provide against trouble....The men will not cause riot or other disturbances. We are going to the bottom of this thing, but in a legal way."

Sullivan said he had a good idea who the murderers were. "We have practically proven who five of them were, we are uncertain as to the sixth. We soon will know who they all were," he said.

"It is the most unwise thing that has happened in Butte," Wheeler said on the morning of August 2, 1917. "The men who perpetrated the affair should be brought to justice." Wheeler told the media that government officials would work "ceaselessly on the Little case."

"It is a cold-blooded murder and every effort will be used to apprehend the men who did it," Silver Bow County Attorney Joseph R. Jackson vowed. "If they are caught, they will be prosecuted to the full extent of the law."

The volume of people who participated in Frank Little's funeral procession showed his support among Butte's miners and union members. Little's advocacy is still embraced by workers around the world. Courtesy Author's Collection.

U.S. Congresswoman from Montana Jeannette Rankin and others pushed hard for a federal investigation.

But nobody was caught. Nobody was prosecuted.

One Hundred Years of Speculation

One hundred years later all that remains is speculation and theory. Alleged eyewitnesses failed to testify or produce substantive details at several hearings and investigations. Both Nora Byrne and her son, who spoke afterwards to several newspaper reporters, suddenly developed powerful cases of amnesia.

Little, a doctor's son, had been identified with the I.W.W. since 1906. He organized and personally led the so-called "free speech campaign" in Fresno in 1910 when several hundred I.W.W. members were arrested for violating a city ordinance. Little refused to work on the municipal rock pile and was placed on a bread and water diet in a murky cell. Eager to give oxygen to the fire, Little eventually imported agitators from all parts of the nation.

Botkin believes Little's death was orchestrated by Butte's Anaconda Company, and that he was killed not just to finish the strike in Butte but to prevent his budding anti-war sentiment from festering.

"I think there were some people who were riled up and angry at Frank for his alleged seditionist statements and they may have been offered money to kill him," says Botkin. "I believe it was well-organized, and not something spur of the moment. After his first speech [on July 19, 1917], he received a warning, and he was told that there was some plotting against him the night before he died. It's possible that all five or so of the gunmen worked for the Anaconda Company or were on its payroll, and that the murderers were young men who were enlisting, who felt ruffled that Frank had said all of these terrible things, in their minds, about soldiers."

Little's Rallying Cry Legacy

Beyond a legacy which is still fully embraced by the I.W.W. and people worldwide of varying political persuasions who often co-opt him as a symbol for their movements, few relics or remnants remain of Little's life. The city of Missoula once placed a marker on the spot that he proclaimed "Free Speech Corner" in 1909, but that plaque is long gone. Both Mrs. Byrne's boarding house and the adjacent Finlander Hall, on North Wyoming, were demolished in the early 1940s.

Butte, however, remembers Little with an annual graveside commemoration, a sculpture, and several references at the Labor History Center. His headstone in Mountain View Cemetery has become a destination for visitors from all parts of the world. On the August 1 anniversary of his death, I.W.W. members congregate at Little's grave, toast him, and sing old I.W.W. songs.

Botkin believes that Frank Little's legacy retains influence beyond a few labor groups and a smattering of extremists.

"Frank Little stands as a soldier for free speech," says Botkin. "His death in Butte was merely the denouement to a life dedicated to leading a non-violent approach to protest, encouraging hardy, weather-beaten faces to hold fast, despite receiving inhumane treatment at the hands of their employers."

4

FIFTY-YEAR SENTENCE FOR "TURKEY PETE"

Deer Lodge, 1918
Victim: Joseph Nugent
Case Status: Solved

"Stone walls do not a prison make,
nor iron bars a cage."

—Richard Lovelace

Six months before WWI ended in 1918, a manacled prisoner entered the stone barricades of Montana State Prison. He died there in 1967—two world wars and almost half a century later—but not until he proved that humanitarianism can be found in harsh places.

Born in Germany, Paul G. Eitner saw precious little of free America. Four years after arriving in the U.S., he was behind bars, doing life. Eitner, only five feet tall and still a fresh immigrant to this country, left New Jersey in 1914, hoping the dry Montana prairie could ease his tuberculosis. At the age of 37, he wandered into Miles City and found work as a cook in a downtown restaurant, stayed at a boarding house, and might have worked on a ranch for a while.

While the precise details are lost, Eitner's life took a dark turn after four years in Montana: he was accused of murdering Joseph

Nugent, either another boarder or perhaps a hotel operator, who allegedly had tried to court a woman who Eitner desired. He pulled a .38 caliber pistol from his bureau drawer and shot Nugent to death.

Eitner said it was self-defense but later changed his plea to guilty. He was sentenced to life in prison.

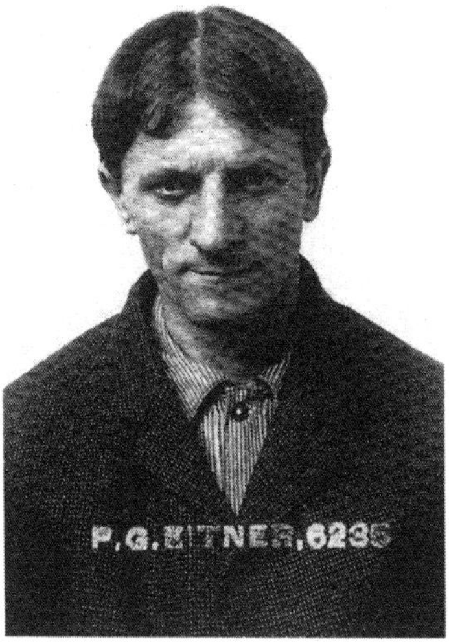

Born in Germany, Paul Eitner's life took a dark turn after four years in Montana: he was convicted of murdering a man who allegedly tried to court a woman Eitner also desired. MUG SHOT OF EITNER COURTESY DEER LODGE HISTORICAL SOCIETY.

Delivered to Deer Lodge

On March 6, 1918, Eitner was delivered into the hands of prison warden Frank Conley. He was 40 years old when the steel doors shut on him the first time. He came up for parole in 1931, 1934, and 1956, and each time it was denied, perhaps because of a stunt that earned him the nickname of "Turkey Pete."

In 1922, he was sent outside the walls to work on the prison dairy farm near Galen and was put in charge of raising turkeys with the instruction to treat the birds "as if they were his own."

He did—and got in trouble.

The prison farm was near a heavily traveled gravel road and prisoners sometimes passed part of their meager daily wages through the prison fence to town-bound motorists. On their way back from town, the motorists would drop off cigarettes or snacks to the prisoners. Eitner concocted a small twist to the commercial arrangement. He started selling prison turkeys for 50 cents apiece, a successful trade he plied for years.

Eitner went back inside the main prison walls in 1932 for a "rules" infraction. Warden Ed Ellsworth, Jr., later said there was only one black mark on Eitner's record and that it wasn't very black. "Pete was sent to the state hospital at Warm Springs to look after a bunch of turkeys," Ellsworth told *The Montana Standard* newspaper in 1965. "He started selling them to neighboring farmers for 50 cents each. The hospital superintendent didn't find out about it until the flock was almost depleted. He returned Pete to the prison."

By the time Eitner's last chance for parole was denied in 1956, Pete had accepted his fate as lifer. When asked about a parole plan, he shrugged it off.

"Where would I go? This is home."

By then, his years inside had earned him the status of trustee and a few special considerations. But Eitner found further escape, into a world of fantasy.

Fantasy World: "Eitner Enterprises"

Eitner became convinced he owned a firm called "Eitner Enterprises," and he reportedly thought nothing of writing million-dollar checks. Everyone at the prison went along with Eitner's fantasy. Prisoners drew up scrolled stock certificates for the spurious company and Eitner had a checkbook imprinted with his company's name. To safeguard his company's funds, Eitner required his personal secretary to countersign any check. (Mrs. A.D. Lightfoot, a social worker at the prison, played this role.)

One of the wardens remembered a typical transaction: one of

In prison, Eitner escaped into fantasy by concocting a fake business called "Eitner Enterprises." Other prisoners and staff went along with his imagined world. Courtesy Deer Lodge Historical Society

the guards would tell Eitner he had a good herd of cattle that he wanted to sell. Eitner would ask where the cattle were and then say he would send some of his people to look at them. A few minutes later, he would come back and say his people had looked at the cattle and they were a little skinny. Eitner and the guard would haggle about the price and Eitner would write out a check. A few minutes later, he would sell the cattle to another prisoner at a profit and his bookkeeper would enter the transaction in the checkbook.

Eitner pored over newspapers, seeking backsliding companies to buy, and rejuvenating them for millions in profits. Prison guards and other inmates said they received checks when Eitner thought they had been especially kind to him.

"He even sent millions to (Fidel) Castro when Castro was still considered a good guy in this country," Montana State Prison deputy warden James Blodgett said at the time of Eitner's death. "And once he sent $3 million to free an Arabian sheik's harem." Once, when Eitner's interest in his business deals dulled, his friends arranged a sham telephone call from President John F. Kennedy.

"He hadn't talked very often on the telephone and he was really thrilled that the 'president' called him to thank him for all the help he had given people," said Blodgett.

Men convicted of murder, rape—the entire scope of criminal

activity—played along with Turkey Pete's game. "Everything was said in respect and in fun," said Blodgett. "They knew that here was a guy that had been here 49 to 50 years and it wouldn't be fair to make fun of him. Then, too, I think everyone looked on it not as an act of insanity but a means of survival."

Some in the prison called him "Champ" because he believed he was training for a fight with heavyweight champion Cassius Clay. He would shadowbox in circles around the guards and speak of a potential bout with Clay.

In later years, Eitner served as mascot of the prison band. In that capacity he once traveled to Helena where the band gave a concert for the residents of the Vocational School for Girls, and Eitner wrote them a check for $1 million.

He died April 4, 1967, at age 89, entering his 50th year as an inmate at Montana State Prison, the most time anybody has ever

Eitner was nicknamed "Turkey Pete" after he was caught selling prison turkeys to area residents. He eventually became a prison favorite. Here he blows out candles on his birthday cake. Courtesy Deer Lodge Historical Society.

"Turkey Pete" died in 1967. He was 89 and had been in prison for 49 years, the longest time of any Montana prisoner. When he died, his Cell No. 1 was retired. Late in life he refused parole, saying, "Where would I go? This is home." COURTESY DEER LODGE HISTORICAL SOCIETY.

served there. Warden Ed Ellsworth Jr. said he had no records to cite but believed Eitner's imprisonment was one of the longest in the nation. Research showed the prisoner had a nephew and a niece. They wrote to Pete, but he had no memory of them.

Funeral services were held in the prison auditorium—the first time, so far as it is known, that funeral services had been held inside the walls of Montana State Prison. Administrators and correctional officers served as pallbearers. He was interred in the "Isle of Forgotten Men," the prison cemetery three miles west of Deer Lodge.

Death brought Eitner to the end of a trail that led only to a patch of land surrounded by stone walls.

"Stone walls do not a prison make, Nor iron bars a cage," wrote English poet Richard Lovelace in the poem "To Althea, from Prison," in 1642. Turkey Pete Eitner found a way to prove it true.

5

"WORK OF A MANIAC," THE BILLINGS AX MURDERS

1924
Victims: Nels and Anna Anderson
Case Status: Unsolved

BLOODY FINGERPRINTS on a water faucet and washboard supplied the only clues to the murderer who killed Mr. and Mrs. Nels Anderson by splitting their heads with an ax.

The couple was killed in their combination barber shop and beauty parlor, and Billings police were "hopeful" that the fingerprints on the washbowl, a few feet from where Mr. Anderson was slain and where the murderer washed his bloody hands, would serve "to aid in the apprehension of the murderer." The murderer seemed a curious mixture of mad (for obvious reasons) and methodical (the ax handle apparently had been wiped clean of blood).

The *Billings Gazette* summarized the police department's belief that the heinous crime was solvable: "Police are clinging to the theory that the murders were committed by an insane man with a desire to avenge some real or fancied wrong, and are hopeful that the fingerprints may prove a valuable aid in their search."

THE BILLINGS GAZETTE

EARLY MORNING EDITION

COUPLE MURDERED WITH AX

$10,000 LIMIT PLACED ON NEW ISSUE OF BONDS

Backers of Republic Carry Election at German Polls

LUDENDORFF'S GANG AND REDS WIPED OFF MAP

SEVEN WINGED IN GUN FIGHT WITH BANDITS

PARIS POLICE RAID REDS AND JAIL HUNDREDS

BARBER, HIS WIFE, KILLED IN SHOP

HOLDS UP BANK TO CASH CHECK

BANDITS LOOT TACOMA BANK'S MONEY TRUCK

LIGHT BRIGADE SURVIVOR DIES

YELLOWLEY SAYS WASHINGTON IS TO BE DRY CITY

HOUGH, SLAYER OF SWEETHEART, IS GIVEN LIFE

Found with the blood-smattered ax lying nearby, Billings police discovered the bodies of Mr. and Mrs. Nels M. Anderson on December 7, 1924. A newspaper called the gruesome murders "the work of a maniac." Courtesy Montana Historical Society.

"Work of a Maniac"

"The dual murder is believed to be the work of a maniac," announced the *Decatur Herald*.

Billings police discovered the bodies on December 7, 1924 after the couple was reported missing, failing to come home to their four children. Anderson and his wife were found at 4:30 in the afternoon at 2911 Minnesota Avenue. The body of Mrs. Anna Anderson was found with the ax laying by her side. She apparently had been killed in the beauty parlor (referred to in contemporary accounts as "the marcel," a wave made in the hair made from a heated curling iron) and her body dragged to the rear of the shop. Copious amounts of blood stained the heavy steel hair-styling equipment and "a quantity of groceries she (Mrs. Anderson) had bought to take home."

The *Great Falls Tribune* spared no graphic detail: "His head was split from crown to the roof of his mouth, while that of his wife bore at least three ax wounds, the deepest of which almost split the skull in twain."

Nels' body, dressed in his overcoat and one glove on, was found sitting in a barber's chair. One hand, "dangling over the arm of the chair," was seen by police as they looked into the window of the shop. The cash register was not "disturbed" and the pockets of both victims reportedly "contained money." Outside the shop, the Anderson family auto was standing at the curb.

A young woman who had passed by the shop at about 9 p.m. the night before told police that she heard loud talking, "as if any argument was under way," between Mr. Anderson and "a dark man, of Mexican resemblance."

"But as Mexican crimes run to the petty and their killings are usually with pistol or knife, the police are not satisfied with any hypothesis that a Mexican slew the couple," said the *Billings Gazette.*

According to the *Billings Gazette*, police estimated that the ax belonged to the Andersons and was stored in the shop: "Whether or not on the night of the killing it was in the front part of the shop where the murderer first used it in the slaying of Anderson has not been determined. Ordinarily, however, the police say the ax reposed in the shed at the rear of the shop and was used there for splitting kindling wood."

Billings officers failed to agree on a murder suspect theory. Two sisters and a brother of Mrs. Anderson arrived in Billings to assist investigators, but they could shed no light on the background of the Andersons that would suggest a motive for the murders. The possibility of "enemies at Miles City" being linked to the crime, a theory advanced by Anderson's sister, Anna Erickson, was discarded by the police.

When other theories failed to develop substantial clues, the police and sheriff's office centered their attention "on suspicious characters, lawbreakers and drug addicts" for a possible solution "of the most atrocious crime in the criminal history of Billings." Such "suspicious characters" were gathered by the police and their fingerprints taken, after which they were held as "vagrants" for additional investigation.

The coroner's inquest was no less beneficial, simply concluding that the Andersons were murdered with an ax wielded by the hands of a person "whose identity is not known at this time."

While an effort was made to preserve the blood-stained fingerprints on the faucet and washbowl, the forensics available at the time were too crude to identify a perpetrator. No person was ever arrested or charged for the crime, and the Billings ax murders will most likely forever remain unsolved.

6

FIENDISH MURDER OF A WEALTHY WIDOW

Butte, 1930
Victim: Christina Wilson
Case Status: Solved

A RICH WIDOW OF BUTTE was the victim of one of the most brutal murders known to Montana police.

Christina Wilson's body was found in the second-story room of the Paragon Hotel, 107 West Broadway, on March 11, 1930. Her arms and legs had been lashed to the four corners of a bed with ropes tied in hangman's knots, her head battered, and a hand towel apparently tamped down her throat with an iron pipe. The hangman's knots "are pointed to by officers as evidence showing the brutal crime was premeditated," said the *Montana Post*.

The woman's body was completely covered by a quilt. Her false teeth were found in a pool of blood on the floor, a pillow placed over her face. The bed and floor of the room were inundated in blood, apparently from the wound to the head.

An examination of her apartment showed that it had been thoroughly ransacked. Drawers were pulled out, clothing thrown about, and a security box containing personal papers broken open. An attempt had been made to pry open the window, and the glass was cracked.

Wilson was a wealthy widow. She owned the entire Paragon Block. According to media accounts, "Mrs. Wilson was last seen about 5:45 p.m. in her own room by two girls and she was missed at 7 p.m." A back window of room 6, adjoining Wilson's apartment, was found opened when the police searched the building. There were marks of rubber heels on the bed clothes, indicating that a man had stood there while tying the body to the bed.

One Man Implicated

That evening, shortly after friends started searching for the missing woman, the lights in one side of the hotel shut off in a mysterious manner. Montana Power workmen were called and reported to have found some dead fuses. Officers later discovered that the iron pipe with which the woman was apparently killed had been torn from some fixtures on the ground floor.

"It is believed that the murderer had paraded the halls of the building with the iron pipe in his hand before committing the crime," Butte police informed the media. From the start of the investigation, police told city residents that they believed "that only one man was implicated in the murder." A mysterious young man who had been seen with the rich widow before she died emerged as a suspect.

If the murder wasn't macabre enough, another bizarre incident happened when an unidentified man attempted to make away with the "vital organs" of Wilson's body, which was in the office of Dr. J. F. Lhotka. According to the police report, "The youth came to the doctor's office posing as a messenger from Chief of Police Murphy, saying that the chief wanted the vital organs sent to his office." Suspicious, Dr. Lhotka told the stranger that he would accompany him to the police station. As they reached the street by the Owsley Block, the young man fled. He was never identified.

Killer: "I Needed the Money for Food"

Christina's husband, Ralph Wilson, former contractor, had died several years earlier. She was uniformly described by tenants and relatives as a kindly, lovable soul who showered the underprivileged with warmth, respect, and at times, even money. In fact, her generosity and her willingness to aid all in need factored into her fiendish murder. A torn letter (later pieced together by the police) was discovered in the murder room. It led to the culprit.

Wilson, according to the subsequent printed confession of 18-year-old Melvin Payette, was killed "because I needed the money for food." He had 20 cents, no job, and said that he didn't know where to get one.

On the fatal evening, Wilson came into her room to fix the bed, and Payette said that he had been "sitting in a rocker reading a murder story in one of these confession magazines."(Why Payette was in the room in the first place was never specified, but it's safe to speculate that, considering Wilson's tendency to take in stray youths, her benevolence was a contributing factor.)

Payette said he had "thought about robbing her for a couple of days before," but when he found the pipe and the rope in the closet, he'd figured that he'd go through with the murder. Payette said as Wilson bent over the bed to fix a pillow, he "struck her several times with the pipe, grabbed a towel, and tied it over her mouth."

Payette's Escape and Apprehension

According to Payette's confession, after leaving the woman dead and taking the money from her apartment, he left the Paragon Block through a rear window and made his way to the Panama Hotel, where he changed his clothing.

With a suitcase full of clothing and a gun, he made his way to the Northern Pacific railway yards at the same time that the first tip of his whereabouts was received by the police. According to available press accounts, he is thought to have taken one of the Northern Pacific eastbound passenger trains to Billings. Before police could scour Billings, Payette had already left the city on a motorcycle.

He purchased the motorcycle with gold and silver, and the garage owner reported the peculiar transaction to Billings authorities.

Twenty-five miles south of Hardin the motorcycle broke down. Payette returned to Hardin, taking a room in a hotel. The Billings garage man, suspicious of the man, kept a friendly, continuous dialogue with Payette as a pretext to track him, which gave police an opportunity to trace the killer's movements in Colorado and then Missouri. Authorities speculated he zigzagged by passenger trains.

At Denver, Payette sold his cap and shoes at a loan store. The cap and shoes were the ones he wore when he murdered Wilson. From Denver he went to Kansas City and then direct from that city to El Paso. A phone call to the Billings auto dealer in which he agreed to dispose of his motorcycle for $300 gave officers an opportunity to arrest Payette at the El Paso side of the US-Mexican border.

Lawmen transported Payette to Salt Lake City and then to Butte, his one leg weighed down with an "Oregon boot" to guard against his escape. Payette's mother, "a woman of 40, stout and of Polish descent," took her son in her arms while he was in transport. "I'm glad we're on the last leg of the trip back to Butte," Payette told the *El Paso Times* as he left his mother. "I'll be glad to get this thing off my foot...It's a long tough trip, a whole lot tougher than it was going down. But I want to go back and get it all over with."

Two weeks after he had killed Wilson, the youth was arrested and shipped back to Montana to face prosecution. Tributes were given to Butte's police chief J.J. Murphy "for his clever work that led to the capture of Melvin Payette."

Sinister Details Emerge at Trial

Sinister details of the murder and the life of the slayer emerged throughout the criminal trial. He had served two terms in the Idaho State Reformatory at St. Anthony. Both times, Payette had been sent up for theft from Mackay, Idaho. He was received at the institution the last time on June 25, 1927, and after his eventual release on parole, he was sent to his home in Salt Lake City. He had learned to tie the hangman's knots with which the body was tied to the bed while at the Idaho reformatory. Payette had been in Butte several times during the previous few years.

Police Chief J.J. Murphy gave this account of the murder: Payette registered as Mr. W. Nolan in the hotel "where that woman was killed, and struck her with a pipe from the electric light connection. You took the fuse plug out to throw one side of the building in darkness while you killed the woman. You tied a bath towel around her neck and stuffed a pillow slip down her throat and tied her feet with a hangman's knot.

"A roomer saw you unlock the door and prowl down the hall to Mrs. Wilson's apartment. You unlocked the door with a key stolen from the dead woman and prowled among the papers. Then the noise came of a window in the rear being raised, a window opening onto a high dirt bank across a vacant lot."

Payette's defense was that he had hit Wilson "but didn't mean to kill her." Perhaps sensing that such an argument was too unsatisfactory for even him, he eventually pleaded guilty. Payette escaped the gallows but was sentenced to life in prison for the crime of first-degree murder of Mrs. Wilson.

Life imprisonment satisfied the county attorney. "I think the ends of justice will be well served if this boy is sentenced to life imprisonment," the county attorney concluded. "I would not want to be the one who pulls the rope to send him into eternity."

Judge Lynch, "a veteran of the criminal bench," cited a half dozen murders in Butte in the previous two years in which the "scoundrels deserved hanging more than this boy" and had escaped with life sentences.

After the sentencing, Payette was led away, "tears streaming from his eyes." According to the *Montana Post*, in the patrol car on his return to the county jail where he was held a few minutes before starting to Deer Lodge, "he was again surly and taciturn, refusing to speak, declaring only, 'I talked too much already. If I'd kept my mouth shut I wouldn't be where I am now.'"

On the hour and a half trip to Deer Lodge, according to the *Montana Standard*, Payette said, "All I hope is that it ain't as bad as the reformatory." He also "discussed the murder freely with" Sheriff Angus McLeod, who was transporting him. He reportedly asked scores of questions on the penitentiary, the customs of the facility, and the work given prisoners. "I won't be very old when I get out anyway, will I?" was his parting question as he was taken in through the big steel gates that clanged shut behind him.

Once inside, he was given the regular "entrance bath" accorded all prisoners as they entered, a suit of convict dungarees, and placed in the receiving cell for the night.

Life Sentence; Paroled in 1942

A lifetime behind prison walls was the sentence, but Payette didn't remain behind closed walls for too many years. He was paroled in 1942 after serving twelve and a half years. He had a good prison record and some time knocked off for good behavior. Governor Sam C. Ford wrote a letter to the State Board of Pardons stating that Payette was "not armed, nor did he have the intention of committing murder." In perhaps a somewhat perverse justification, Ford claimed that Payette "only intended to rob the victim" and didn't realize the consequences which might result from it, since he had placed "a gag upon his victim's face for the purpose of enabling him to escape the scene of robbery."

At his parole hearing Payette pleaded for his release and said that he desired his freedom so he could support his widowed mother, living in Salt Lake City.

Payette's release from prison concluded the final chapter to one of Butte's most sensational murders.

7

FIFTEEN-YEAR-OLD MURDERESS—OR VICTIM?

Great Falls, 1937
Victim: Gust Anderson
Case Status: Solved

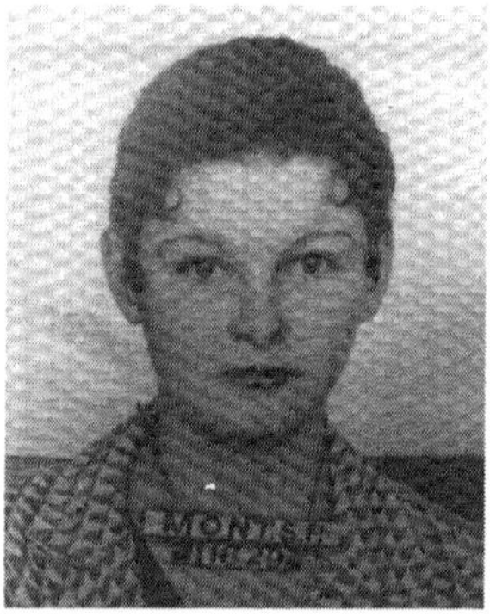

Perhaps Montana's youngest convicted femme fatale, Muriel Murphy was only 15 years old when she was sent to prison for her part in a Great Falls murder. She was found guilty of luring an older man to his beating death. COURTESY MONTANA HISTORICAL SOCIETY.

MURIEL MURPHY, 15, and William J. (Buddy) Newman, 18, were charged in 1937 with murdering "elderly carpenter" Gust Anderson of Great Falls on Dec. 17, 1936. Anderson was alternately pegged in various accounts as 58, 59, or 61 years old.

The two teenagers stood accused of luring Anderson into an alley. There, it was contended, Newman struck Anderson, took a small sum of money from his pockets, and left him unconscious, bleeding on the ground. Anderson died two days later in a hospital.

Murphy declared that Anderson made improper advances to her after offering her money in the Elkhorn beer parlor, and that Newman was defending her from Anderson's attempted assault. The salacious story drew a large crowd "that surpassed any in the history of a trial in Cascade County."

First-Degree Murder Trial

At 15, Muriel Mae Murphy was reported to be the youngest person in the history of Cascade County and probably Montana to be charged with murder in the first degree.

Buddy Newman, three years older, appeared on the stand first, and according to the media, under direct examination, answered questions "in a clear cut and calm manner." He testified that he had known Muriel and her family for about five years. Pressed under cross-examination, however, "he answered questions heatedly, indefinitely and with qualifications."

Sheriff Guy Palagi related facts of a conversation with Newman and Virgil Murphy, 18, Muriel's brother, regarding a gold ring that was said to have been in possession of Anderson. Both defendants disclaimed any knowledge of the ring. Sheriff Palagi testified that Newman was aware that his assault of Anderson was the cause of his death. "Yes. I did kill him," Palagi recounted Newman stating.

According to the *Missoulian*, the opening statement of the defense counselor "declared that the implication of the male co-defendant in the case" was to a degree due to "misguided chivalry."

The defense counselor said that Newman went to the Murphy home about 7:00 or 7:30 on the evening of December 17 and remained there between 15 and 30 minutes. Later, Newman and Muriel and Virgil Murphy went downtown, both boys being "in possession of money derived from the sale of Christmas trees and employment by the national youth administration." The trio, the attorney said, went to the Rainbow Theater and saw the picture *Scar Face*, and left there about 10 or 10:30.

Shortly after that, they walked down Central Avenue and turned south, entering "the Pastime beer parlor" on First Avenue South. Newman said that he had been served there previously and that "there were usually persons there that he knew and liked." Newman had been given a couple of drinks of illegal "moonshine liquor" earlier and "felt effects of the liquor but was not intoxicated."

A table was obtained in the Pastime but the management or the help refused to serve the beer, and they then crossed the street and entered the Elkhorn beer parlor. Anderson, Newman's attorney continued, "who had made himself obnoxious," came in later.

Proposition

"We were sitting there drinking beer and I saw an old man, Gust Anderson, running around and raising Cain," said Newman. "He was running around, enjoying himself and was boisterous.... He was offering girls money to dance with him and looked several times at Muriel. I could imagine that he was wishing that he could dance with her. He came over later and said, 'Don't I look 35 or 40? She said, 'Yes, you look 35.' He threw a silver dollar on the table and seemed pleased. She refused the dollar."

Anderson, of "the Home Hotel," then was said to have gone to the bar and some patron challenged him to buy a round of drinks for the house. Newman testified that Anderson pulled out several bills, saying, "Maybe you think I can't."

Anderson returned to a table and purchased several drinks. When the "aged man" made an offer of $10 for a dance with Muriel, Newman admittedly suggested that the offer be raised to $15. Anderson, however, "danced with some other person." Newman and the girl, the testimony indicated, "discussed the matter" and came to the conclusion that if Anderson wished to give the Murphy girl $10, "It was advisable to accept it."

But Muriel, according to testimony, did not wish to accept the money while in the beer parlor. She would accept the money down the block or outside of the establishment.

Murphy, it was stated, left the beer parlor with Anderson through the front door. Newman followed, and Virgil Murphy sat at the table and consumed his drink.

Premeditation, or Act of Protection?

The defense attorney declared that the evidence would show that Newman hit Anderson when he observed Muriel struggling with the "aged man in the alley." Newman, according to his testimony, reached the entrance to Second Alley south and observed the girl arguing with Anderson. The latter was said to be swearing and Newman testified that he heard Anderson say, "How far is it to your room?" or "Where is your room?" Muriel, Newman asserted, was held by the arm and said. "Let loose of my arm!"

"I walked up and I don't know whether I told him to let loose or not," Newman said. "He would not, however, and I got close to him and hit him. She was then loose and going up the alley. I hit him to make him let loose of her arm and he did not let go until I hit him." Newman declared that he "merely hit Anderson with his fist," probably targeting the jaw, and that he could not say what happened to Anderson after that time.

The counsel further said that Newman was "inclined to be somewhat of a braggart" and told others that he hit the man, evidently with a view of boasting or trying to show "that he was as tough as other fellows."

"Improper Advances" Alleged by Murphy

Muriel Murphy's story corresponded to that of Newman's: the victim made "improper advances," had refused to release her, and Newman's aggressive response neutralized the escalating predicament.

The "diminutive" Murphy corroborated Newman's testimony about events earlier in the evening, including most incidents in the Elkhorn. She said that Anderson was "noisy and boisterous" and approached her table. Anderson's purported conversation as to his age was also related. "I said he looked 35," said the girl. "He seemed pleased and offered me a dollar."

She then told of Anderson's alleged attempts to induce her to dance with him, including his offer to pay her $10. She declared that the offer was "refused," and that someone said it was worth $15. Anderson later approached the table again and engaged the girl and Newman in conversation and once more left.

According to the testimony, Anderson suggested that the girl accompany him outside, and Newman and Muriel decided "that he was foolish to give his money away but I might as well take it as anyone else."

Muriel declared that she had decided she was not going to ask for the money but would take it if offered to her. She said the reason she didn't take the money inside the beer parlor was because she was "ashamed" because Anderson "was drunk" and it would "have been cheap."

At one point during their walk outside the bar, Muriel said Anderson allegedly stopped and asked if she was not going to his room with him. "I said I was going up the alley," the girl said.

"Anderson tried to embrace me and put his arm around me." Muriel testified. "We were then in the alley. I struggled with him and asked him to leave me alone." Muriel said that Anderson swore and grabbed her tightly. She said she demanded that he let her go, and Newman arrived and made the same command.

Then Newman struck Anderson. "I realized then what Anderson was going to give me the money for," the girl testified. After Newman struck Anderson, Muriel allegedly broke away and ran up the alley, joined later by Newman. Finally, the two met Virgil Murphy at a different bar.

Newman declared that he did not take anything from Anderson and expressed the opinion that if Anderson, "a large and well-developed man," had gotten hold of him, "I'd have been on the wrong end of the rope."

Newman testified further that after Anderson was dead, he became "scared" as he thought officers might charge him with the killing. He further asserted that he had "done a lot of lying to officers and others," admitting that he signed statements of implication but asserted they were "untrue" and coerced. He signed them, he said, in a belief that if he did so he would be prosecuted as a juvenile delinquent rather than a criminal.

Muriel admitted under cross-examination that she went into the alley with Anderson "because she thought she might get some money." She said that she thought he would hand her the money on the street. Muriel asserted that she had "never been in a beer parlor before that night" and "never drank beer before." She admitted that after drinking six or eight glasses of beer that it began to work its effect on her.

Conviction, Pardon

Murphy and Newman were convicted in Cascade County District Court on May 23, 1937, of responsibility for the death of Gust Anderson. The girl was found accountable of luring Anderson outside, where Newman struck him and inflicted injuries which proved fatal.

A jury convicted them, and Judge H.H. Ewing sentenced them to life imprisonment. Defense attorneys for Murphy and Newman appealed their convictions on the grounds of juror prejudice. The defense attorneys said the affidavit signed by the prejudiced juror read: "I voted to convict the defendants because I had known Anderson for so many years and because I had herded his cows as a boy and liked him." The defense counsel's request for a new trial was denied.

Post-trial, it was revealed that at the time of her conviction Murphy had been married for three months to Herbert N. Owens of Augusta. Muriel's parents, Mr. and Mrs. C.C. Murphy of Great Falls, filed an application for a conditional pardon, hoping to have the girl released into the custody of her husband.

Governor Roy E. Ayers received many petitions asking clemency for the couple, and in May 1940, the Montana Board of Pardons approved a conditional pardon for Murphy and Newman. Ayers, at the request of many petitioners, including the attorney who prosecuted the case and the sheriff, recommended the pair be given10-year conditional paroles.

Unfortunately, Muriel Mae Murphy and William James Newman, central figures in one of the most sensational murder cases ever tried in Montana, couldn't steer clear of the law after their release. In September 1949, the twosome was held for trial at Anchorage, Alaska, on felony charges, with Newman charged with assault with a deadly weapon. They were convicted, imprisoned, and later released to, considering their checkered pasts, relatively normal, or murder-free, lives.

8

BUTTE PASTOR KILLED BY KOREAN ARMY

Korea, 1950
Victim: Jimmy Maginn
Case Status: Unsolved

On the day of his First Communion in Butte, Montana, neither Jimmy Maginn or his parents, nor his classmates, envisioned that a monument to the young communicant would one day exist in distant South Korea. Nor would anyone have suspected that the young man would eventually die at the hands of North Korean communists who accused him of being an American spy.

Ireland to Butte to Ireland to South Korea

James Maginn was born in Butte, Montana, on November 15, 1911. His parents, James and Annie, had emigrated from County Down, Ireland. James was the second of four sons.

Maginn was baptized at Sacred Heart Church. His father, James Maginn, was the officiating priest. At the altar rail there, he received his First Holy Communion. His family returned to Ireland when he was nine years old.

In 1929 James began his preparation for priesthood in the Columban Seminary in Galway, and after ordination in 1936, he left for the Missions in Korea.

Father Maginn was placed under house arrest when Japan invaded Korea in World War II. Released in 1945, he was appointed pastor to a new parish in Samcheok, South Korea, in 1949.

"I was privileged enough to meet Father James in County Down in 1948," says Teresa Maginn-Dillon, first cousin of Father James Patrick Maginn. "I met him several times at his father's house and our house. I remember one party my parents gave him before he left for the United States and then his return to Korea. He stopped each person individually gave them a blessing. His advice was the route of peace and prayer in whatever was asked of him."

Return to Butte in 1949

While en route to Korea in 1949, Father Maginn returned to Butte for the first time since he was in the fourth grade. He enjoyed a reunion with classmates. At that time he was recuperating from malnutrition and mistreatment received while "a prisoner of the Japs." According to the *Montana Standard*, he was captured by Japanese forces "when the Nips" overran parts of Korea during World War II. During his stay in Butte in 1949 he attended the Friendly Sons of St. Patrick banquet held at the Hotel Finlen on March 16 and was honored at a reception at the Sacred Heart parish hall by his former classmates. At that time, according to a later press account, "he expressed fear that the Communists would overrun Korea and that missionaries from his order, including himself, might suffer imprisonment and possible death."

Regardless offers for his safety, Maginn returned to Korea where he felt his services were needed. When the Korean War broke out on June 25, 1950, Father James was the pastor in the Parish of Samcheok. About one month later, the Communists invaded the village and Father Jim, one of some 35 Columban missionaries in Korea at the time, was arrested in his church.

Maginn was interrogated at the police station for two days. Authorities, suspicious of his American birth, pressured him to confess that he was an American spy. Finally, the Korean army marched him through rugged mountain terrain, weakened, browbeaten, and barefooted, to his execution.

Maginn, 39, was estimated to have been killed between July 4, and July 7, 1950, near a swamp outside of Samcheok village. His body lay in the open for several days until parishioners found him; his corpse was soon buried under a tree on a close hillside.

"We had a huge stack of Far East newspapers and magazines, where the family would look through to hear communication from Father James," says Maginn-Dillon. "But there was no communication from Father Jim. I remember the day in '50 when my brother Frank came to our house and delivered the news. It left such a terrible sense of loss and grieving."

Following Maginn's execution "some of his former classmates of 40 years ago on Butte's East Side," according to the *Montana Standard*, started a movement to help financially with construction of the church to be built in Samcheok, South Korea, as a memorial to the Butte martyr.

While the construction of the church never came to fruition, a couple of years later, in March 1952, Maginn's body was exhumed and reinterred alongside Father Patrick Reilly and Father Anthony Collier behind the Cathedral in Chuncheon, South Korea.

Collier, a native of Clogherhead, County Louth, had been placed under house arrest by the Japanese from 1941 to 1945. When he was executed by Communists on June 27, 1950, Fr. Collier was the first Columban and, according to some printed materials, "the first non-Korean" to be killed in the Korean War.

Father James Maginn has been referred for Beatification.

9

TEEN COUPLE EXECUTED ON LOVERS' LANE

Great Falls, 1956
Victims: Lloyd Duane Bogle
and Patti Kalitzke
Case Status: Unsolved

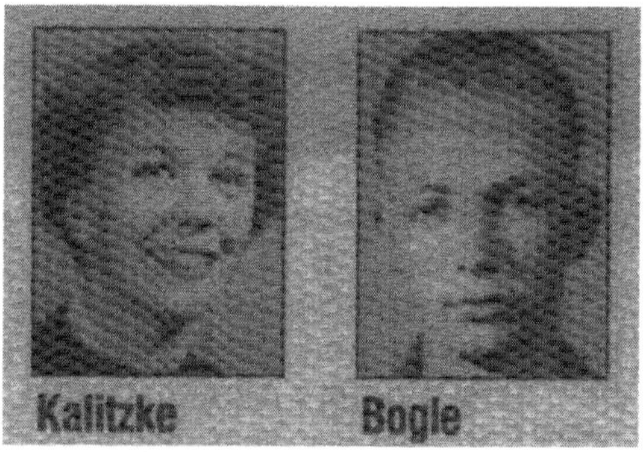

Patricia Kalitzke, 16, of Great Falls, and young airman Lloyd Duane Bogle, 18, of Waco, Texas, were executed one night in January 1956. The killer or killers apparently forced the young girl to witness the execution of her boyfriend before they shot her. The double murder remains unsolved. Courtesy Montana Historical Society.

Young airman Lloyd Duane Bogle, 18, of Waco, Texas, and Patti Kalitzke, 16, of Great Falls, were killed Monday night January 2, 1956. The young couple had gone to a drive-in for hamburgers and later parked in Bogle's car at Wadsworth Park.

On, reportedly "the last day of the Christmas vacation," January 3, 1956, Bogle's body was discovered by three young boys ambling along a little-used dirt road near Wadsworth Park. At night, the gravelly side road was used as a "lovers' lane" for older youths. The boys kicked a couple of cans, and, at times, one another. They talked about the fast speed of the vacation, their wishes for another week of waking late, even another day of freedom would be fantastic. Up ahead, near the Great Falls Trap and Skeet Club, the boys spotted a car parked between two trees. Progressing further, the boys saw a body lying face down beside and partly underneath the car.

Dressed in civilian clothes, he was apparently the victim of a "Chinese execution," according to a spokesperson for the Great Falls Police Department. Apparently he had been ordered to kneel down, his hands securely bound behind him by what was believed to be his own belt. His wallet containing $5 in currency and an "expensive camera" were left in his car.

A .45 caliber bullet had been fired through his head. An examination failed to identify if a second hole in the skull had been caused by the bullet or by a piece of bone. The second hole was in the left temple.

Bogle's car had been left in gear with the emergency brake on. The ignition switch, radio, and headlights also had been left on.

Bogle had been stationed at Malmstrom Air Force Base for 82 months. Described as "quiet" and "reserved," Bogle was just one of the thousands of men who came to Malmstrom throughout the years. He was punctual and ambitious. He even met a local girl who he was spending much time with. Her name was Patricia Kalitze. She was sixteen.

Kalitzke Found

The pair was not engaged but had been dating steadily for the past several months. After Bogle's body was found, Patricia's parents notified police that their daughter was missing. She had been last seen leaving with Bogle for a westside drive-in restaurant the preceding evening.

Kalitzke's body was discovered on a steep road embankment seven miles of Wadsworth Park on Wednesday afternoon, January 4, by a county maintenance worker as he graded the county road. Her body was found fully clothed—blue coat with a wide belt in back, red scarf, and gold-colored skirt and blouse. As with Bogle, she had been shot in the head.

The killer or killers had apparently forced the young girl to witness the execution of her boyfriend and then took her on another road to shoot her. Sex and robbery were discounted as motives. Cascade County Coroner C.E. Magner said the girl had not been molested.

Police: "Mad Killer on the Loose"

"We are grabbing at every straw we can find," said Sheriff D.J. Leeper. "We have a mad killer on the loose." Leeper said there was little doubt the same person killed both teenagers. The sheriff said there was no indication the girl or the airman put up a struggle, indicating the killer could have been known and trusted by them. Police had little details to provide other than indications that Bogle and Kalitzke were forced to kneel before their killer, who then fired a bullet into the back of their heads.

Bogle's car was examined but no clues were found. A car found abandoned on the Belt highway with a bullet hole in the door proved to have no connection with the slayings.

Detective Sgt. Jack Anderson of the Great Falls Police Department, assigned to the case along with Sgt. Fred Peres, said, "We've questioned a lot of people and gathered a lot of information. Now we just hope some of it will help lead us to the killer." Within days of the killings, Anderson said that nothing definite had been established and it appeared the killer was "very lucky" or "planned it very carefully." The mother of the murdered airman, Mrs. Albuquerque Bogle, arrived in Great Falls from Texas and tried to provide authorities clues or leads as to whether her son mentioned being afraid of someone or of having been threatened.

Police left no proverbial stone undisturbed. Officers questioned friends of the victims on the theory the shootings may have climaxed some type of love triangle. Shortly after that, officials detained an airman at the base who allegedly argued with Bogle a day or two before the shooting. Officials questioned Kalitzke's parents and her school friends and other associates of Bogle on the base. None of these conversations yielded a clue to the killer's identity.

Havre police reported that they had held "an Indian who had scratches on his face and first told them he had been in an automobile accident." The police were alarmed because the man later changed his story about how he received the facial cuts. He claimed that he'd gotten into a fight with a girl who scratched him up. The man was released.

With no new information, the double murders soon slid from public recollection. On the anniversary of the killings, there was a blurb here or a short account there, most of which alluded to bits of information that had been investigated or to the lack of current activity in the case.

The biggest spark of interest in the case took place in 1989 when authorities cut down a 150-year-old cottonwood tree in hopes of finding a bullet that might shed light on the unsolved double murder. The tree, described as "80 feet tall, with a trunk 4 1/2 feet in diameter" was cut down and, according to one investigator, "33 growth rings were shaved off its lower section."

"The tree ... has always been of major interest to law enforcement officers because that's where he was killed—right at the tree," Cascade County Sheriff Barry Michelotti said to the Associated

Press in 1989. Unfortunately, the recovered slugs—the police did not disclose how many of them were recovered—could not be matched with any previously seized weapons.

Possible Suspect: A Serial Killer

In 2014 Great Falls Police Detective John Cameron posited that, based on his whereabouts, the culprit was most likely the serial killer Edward Wayne Edwards.

Edwards, who died in prison in 2011 at age 77, had claimed responsibility for five similar, execution-style homicides in Wisconsin and Ohio.

Cameron, who according to an Associated Press summary, "worked 24 years with the Great Falls police force and the last 14 years were as a detective focused on cold case investigations." The article noted that he retired in 2005. As he looked into the Bogle and Kalitzke double homicide, Cameron, stubborn as John Wayne, discovered something in Deer Lodge Prison records that alarmed him; reports indicated that Edwards and his wife had arrived in Great Falls in January 1956 before being arrested in Billings in March for a robbery charge. Cameron, a quiet, private man of quiet, private knowing, worked on a number of different cold cases as an independent researcher after retirement. The despicable theft of these two blossoming lives reserved a special sorrow in him that only galvanized his relentless examination over the years.

"You have an admitted serial killer who was in town on the day that we have a double murder of a couple on lovers' lane in 1956," Cameron said to *USA Today* in 2014.

Despite Cameron's compelling hypothesis, the double murder of the young couple remains uncleared.

10

DOUBLE MURDERS AT MCGREGOR LAKE

Kalispell, 1963
Victims: Mr. and Mrs. Richard P. Easton
Case Status: Solved

THE BATTERED AND BLUDGEONED bodies of Mr. and Mrs. Richard P. Easton were discovered shortly before 3:15 p.m. Tuesday, February, 19, 1963, at Paradise Camp, a resort on McGregor Lake 33 miles west of Kalispell on U.S. Highway 2.

Not too many details were initially released to the press, except that the Eastons operated the resort. "One of the bodies was found by a daughter, Mrs. Roy Norman of the Evergreen District of Kalispell," explained the Associated Press.

Mrs. Norman went to Paradise Camp after her parents failed to answer telephone calls Tuesday afternoon, and when she arrived, she found the premises locked. She and her son, Marcus, forced their way through a basement door. She found her mother's body lying in a pantry-way in a pool of blood at the end of a 40-foot-long trail of blood from a chair adjacent to the fireplace in the main lodge. Mrs. Easton, 66, had apparently been attached there. She suffered from Parkinson's disease and was dreadfully crippled, unable to walk.

Mr. Easton's body was not found until after the arrival of investigating officers. Sheriff's officers forced open a garage door and found his body, also lying in a pool of blood, just inside the door.

The 65-year-old man was apparently bludgeoned to death, and the murderer padlocked the garage door.

Undersheriff Robert Wills said both victims had been beaten to death with some type of blunt instrument. Flathead County Deputy Coroner Harry Campbell said both victims had been "struck savagely" about the head. There was blood smear all over the walls and on the concrete floor. The couple's cash register was taken and Richard's wallet too. Richard was known to keep most of his money in his wallet, authorities noted.

"A macabre note" was discovered less than 100 feet from where the bodies laid. Police did not disclose the details of the note.

Deputy Coroner Campbell tentatively set time of death as sometime late Sunday or early Monday. Neighbors told investigating officers that they had not seen nor heard anything unusual in the past two days.

Richard Easton, "a stubborn former Iowa farmer" had moved with his wife to western Montana from the Midwest. The Eastons had lived in the McGregor area since 1949 and had operated the Paradise Lodge since 1954.

"He very well could have fought with somebody trying to rob him," said one of the Eastons' daughters, Eleanor Norman, who found their bodies.

Leads Turned Sour

Officers traveled thousands of miles on horseback, and in cars, trucks, and boats, and went to several states questioning people about the case. Leads developed and then leads were shelved to wait for more evidence that would make them fit into place. Leads developed and then turned sour.

The proverbial "blunt instrument" was never recovered. Mr. Easton's wallet was found two and a half years later near an old logging road west of Kalispell by a Christmas tree cutter. When authorities explored what they described only as "a wooded area," they found the cash register hidden under a stack of bark next to a cliff. Authorities carefully put the register in a car with ropes, packaged it, and sent it to the F.B.I. crime lab in Washington, D.C.

Flathead County Sheriff Ross Wilson told the *Daily Inter Lake* four years after the murders that the problem with the case, "is obtaining enough admissible [evidence] to convict a person of murder. At the present time, we are trying to gather further factual evidence to tie in with information gathered previously. "Wilson explained that under the new "no confession" ruling by the Supreme Court, law enforcement officers now had to rely on "factual data rather than information gathered through a confession."

Kenneth Pendleton: A life behind bars, on the run

For almost four decades, Arlena LaPierre harbored a dark secret: she believed she knew the man who murdered the Eastons. Though she couldn't recall their names—only that the killings were at the McGregor Lake resort—she would never forget the name of the Boisvert Cabin Camp about three miles away (since torn down), where she and Kenneth Pendleton lived in 1963.

Kenneth Pendleton spent much of his adult life either behind bars or on the lam. Raised on a strawberry farm outside Ferndale, Washington, from the onset of his youth Pendleton was stealing cars, breaking into homes, and blowing things up with sticks of dynamite "he carried with him all the time," according to press accounts.

Arlene married Kenneth Pendleton in November 1959, a few months after they met while in their senior year at Spokane's Rogers High School. Immediately, Arlene learned that physical assaults and death threats were a part of the wedding vows. She was "held hostage" by Kenneth, usually in "backwoods cabins with no phone or way to escape." In approximately three years, Arlene and Kenneth lived in more than 20 places. Kenneth told Arlene that if she ever left him, he would go to Spokane and kill her parents. Wisely, she never doubted the validity his threat.

Arlene said the scariest part of Kenneth was that he presented a sparkling face to the world, invariably coming off to strangers as charming and likeable.

There was one bitterly cold evening in February 1963 when Kenneth returned to their cabin covered with blood. When she asked what happened, Pendleton said "he had hit a deer" and "didn't want to talk about the incident," she recalled to the Associated Press. Then, according to Arlene, he burned his clothes and the incident was never mentioned again.

Pendleton would get friendly with people so he could learn when they were on vacation. Then he'd break into their homes. He above all enjoyed stealing chainsaws.

About a year after the Easton slayings, LaPierre fled with her two daughters, returning to Spokane to live with her parents. Still, he continued to threaten her and her family with letters. She was so frightened of Pendleton that she requested a police escort to her new job as a waitress at the Davenport Hotel.

"I think he was a sociopath with no conscience," Arlene said to the *Spokesman Review* in 2001. Arlene divorced Pendleton in January 1965, remarried in the late 1970s, and moved to California where she worked as a clinical hypnotherapist.

Pendleton, however, continued to lead a life of material crime. In 1967 he was arrested for counterfeiting but escaped from the Spokane County Jail a month later by cutting through the bars with contraband blades.

According to the Associated Press, "he escaped from three prisons," including McNeil Island, in south Puget Sound, southwest of Tacoma, Washington, in 1968, where he buried himself in a ditch to escape guards and search dogs, who walked over him. About 62 shots from guards whizzed at him; seven bullets even penetrated his clothing during his escape.

In October 1983 Pendleton was sentenced to 15 years in prison for robbing a bank in Priest River, Idaho. This punishment brought his cumulative sentences for additional heists to 101 years. Despite the lengthy pronouncement, he was paroled in June 2001.

Law enforcement officers believe Pendleton, yet again, went straight back into a life of crime. According to the *Spokesman-Review*, he most likely was involved in four Spokane-area bank robberies from November 10 through December 26, 2001, in which the description of the robber "generally matched Pendleton." All total, Pendleton was estimated to have robbed as many as 80 banks in at least eight states.

Closed the Books; Likely Killer Identified

Arlene LaPierre had been terrified to tell anyone about her ex-husband's activities until she learned in February 2001 that Pendleton was dead. He had been found beaten to death in Canada on January 11, 2001. Thirty-eight years after the double murder of the Eastons, investigators reopened the books on the investigation, and Flathead County Sheriff Jim Dupont said interviews with Pendleton's former wife convinced investigators that he was responsible for murdering the elderly couple.

Although no physical evidence ever linked Pendleton to the murders, records confirmed that he and his wife were in the area about the time of the murders in 1963. Additionally, Pendleton was booked into the Kalispell jail on an unrelated theft charge a few months after the murders.

"We are fairly confident that he was involved, and it looks like he acted alone," Dupont said to the Associated Press in 2001. "Needless to say, we could not prove that short of getting a confession, and we're not going to get that." He said the case would be "considered closed" unless new information materialized that indicated someone else's involvement in the murders.

Released from a federal prison in Oregon in the summer of

2000, Pendleton's 6-foot, 200-pound body was found in a frozen creek north of Edmonton, Alberta, less than a year later. Authorities said the 59-year-old career criminal had been beaten and stabbed. No suspect was ever identified.

When notified by the *Seattle Tribune* that her father had been implicated in the seemingly random murder of an elderly couple in Montana, Pendleton's daughter Robin LaPierre did not respond with surprise or even attempt to defend her career-criminal father.

"He was definitely someone to be locked up from society," she said.

11

SEPTEMBER SLAYINGS AT THE SUPER SAVE

Great Falls, 1964
Victims: James and Lois Arrotta
Case Status: Unsolved

September 4, 1964, was a chilly day in Great Falls, the skies leaden and dull. Duane DeMars, 27, a salesman at RJ Reynolds Tobacco Company, was a newcomer to the city. He and his family lived about 10 blocks from the East Side Super Save.

DeMars and two other men arrived to purchase groceries a few minutes shy of the store's 8 a.m. opening. As one of the men rested on the front door, it creaked open. At the same time, the assistant manager arrived for work.

Inside the grocery, something was amiss. The courtesy counter had been ransacked, and there were bloody footprints among the items strewn over the floor.

The assistant manager stayed at the front of the store while the three men searched the aisles until they reached the glass coolers at the rear of the store and the entrances to the back room.

Store employee Lois Arrotta, 35, was the first victim to be found. She lay face down near the produce section, her head in the direction of the coolers. The white sweater she was wearing was stained red; her feet were tied with clothesline to a big steel door. A long-bladed knife from the produce department lay next to her body.

Lois had been gagged with an apron and stabbed 13 times. Some of the wounds were so deep they nearly penetrated to the other side of her body. Her blouse was riddled with puncture wounds, the material on the back side of her body sliced to ribbons.

Store manager James Arrotta, 43, was discovered in a back room about 25 feet from his wife. The former Marine lay on his back, his feet and one arm bound with a length of the same clothesline used to tie up Lois. He had been gagged and stabbed in the back nine times.

The killer displayed undeniable brutality: both victims were found gagged with apron strings cut from the store aprons. Both had been struck in the head with glass bottles. The killer used such force in clubbing James Arrotta that the bottle shattered.

Phone calls were made to the Arrotta home and to police. DeMars and the other men were questioned by the police and sent home. The bodies were removed.

Shockingly, by 11:30 a.m. the store was open for business, and customers entered and shopped at the fresh crime scene. Officers later admitted that the initial investigation was contaminated and comprised because the store opened only hours after the bodies had been discovered.

The Super Save store owners were widely denounced for their decision to open the store. In contemporary news accounts, the owners were derided by some as greedy, but considering that such indignation came from the very same customers who were shopping in the milieu of a fresh, morbid crime scene, their declarations were moot.

Three days later, DeMars returned to the store for groceries, where "trace amounts of dried blood" could still be seen on the floor and walls. When he opened one of the middle doors in a cooler, only feet from where he found Lois, DeMars told the *Great Falls Tribune* that the spotted "what he believed to be a smudge of blood on the door."

According to one initial account, "the only thing missing from the Super Save store was $32, taken from a till set aside to collect fees for hunting and fishing licenses."

Newspaper accounts depicted James and Lois Arrotta as a well-liked couple, a civic-minded pair who had called Great Falls home for more than 18 years. They were two people, it was said, with a close bond to family and community. James was a World War II veteran and active in the American Legion and VFW. Both he and his wife were devout Christians and "deeply involved in their church, Sts. Peter and Paul Parish."

On September 4, 1964, the brutally murdered bodies of Great Falls Super Save store manager James Arrotta and his wife were discovered in the back of their store. Thirty-eight years later, a well-known Great Falls man was arrested for their murders but found not guilty, a verdict disputed by law enforcement. COURTESY MONTANA HISTORICAL SOCIETY.

The Arrottas left behind seven children, ages 6 months to 12 years, at their home in east Great Falls. Additionally, James Arrotta had fathered two children from a previous marriage.

When police searched the Arrotta home, they discovered that James Arrotta's coin collection had been stolen, indicating that the murderer had at some point been in the home with the sleeping children.

The Arrottas' car, a 1959 Plymouth station wagon, was found parked in an alley between 37th and 38th streets about a block and a half away from their home. A pair of bloody elk-skin gloves was discovered in a garbage bin across the street.

Super Save Employee Alan Reavley

A few hours after James and Lois Arrotta's bodies were discovered, Great Falls police went to the home of Alan Reavley, a 18-year-old former box boy who had been fired by Jim Arrotta two weeks earlier "for stealing more than $1,100," according to police and news accounts.

Reavley was not home but his mother, Barbara Reavley, gave police the clothes her son had worn the night before. His pants had already been washed and hung out to dry.

According to published police and media reports, Reavley's family told police "they had all been up playing Monopoly on the night of the deaths," and "that everyone had gone to bed around 10:30 p.m." No physical evidence linked Reavley to the crime, and about six weeks later, detectives bumped Reavley's name down the suspect pool ledger. He wasn't cleared as a suspect, per se.

Indeed, no arrests were ever made because the physical evidence found at the scene did not match any suspects. Despite periodic efforts to reopen the investigation, the case faded away—at least in terms of a criminal resolution, certainly not in the minds of the survivors—for nearly 40 years.

Reavley Charged in 2004

Briefly questioned by police in 1964, Alan Reavley went on to become "a respected civic figure" in Great Falls, heading up the food bank. Nearly everything about Reavley seemed bland and retiring, the details of his appearance falling somewhere in the middle: average height, average weight, average build, average age. The cumulative effect of all these qualities made him strangely forgettable. Tellingly, Reavley was never officially cleared as a suspect; there simply had never been enough evidence to support murder charges against him.

On September 4, 2001, Reavley was re-questioned about the homicides. According to a later legal appellant briefing filed by Reavley, the interview lasted approximately four and one-half hours. During the interview, Reavley said that he had asked his parents and a psychiatrist if he could have killed the couple. To investigators, Reavley's behavior seemed suspicious, wary, and watchful, if not outright paranoid.

The following evening, September 5, 2001, Mary Klesh, Reavley's high-school girlfriend, met with Reavley at a local hotel. According to Reavley's legal filing, "Unbeknownst to Reavley, she had agreed to assist the police in their investigation by wearing a wire."

Klesh, carrying a police-issued recording device in her purse, attempted to get Reavley to admit he stabbed the Arrottas—and to divulge unique details of the crime scene. He did not cop to it and mostly maintained his innocence, but at times his defense weakened, his voice quaked, and his explanations were erratic and oblique, even incriminating. "I don't think they have any evidence, any proof, and I didn't do it," Reavley was heard to say on the recording.

Police doubled down on the theory that James Arrotta may have been drawn into the grocery by a phone call from a familiar source, or that he may have had reason to believe the store was being burglarized. According to court documents, investigators believed Reavley "hoped to rob the safe" and "didn't realize even the manager couldn't open the time lock."

On the night of March 15, 2002, Reavley was volunteering as a bid spotter at the C.M. Russell Museum's annual art auction. Late in the evening, as the event was nearing its culmination, a phalanx of police popped into the main ballroom of the Western Heritage Center and arrested Reavley, reading him his Miranda rights. The site and timing of his arrest "sparked widespread outrage throughout the community," according to the *Great Falls Tribune*.

Jim Arrotta's oldest brother, Bob Arrotta, coincidentally happened to be at the auction at the same time. Bob and his wife were part of the stunned crowd of art connoisseurs that watched with their mouths agape as Reavley was notified of his rights, handcuffed, and led away.

On March 18, 2002, Reavley, 57, was charged with two counts of murder in the first degree for the killings of Jim and Lois Arrotta.

Alan Reavley's trajectory appeared to be a decidedly unsuspicious one. After leaving Montana for several years, Reavley returned to Great Falls in the early 1980s. According to the *Great Falls Tribune,* "For nearly 20 years he'd worked for a number of community service organizations including the Montana School for the Deaf and the Blind and the St. Vincent de Paul Society."

At the time of his arrest, Reavley, married with five children, was employed as the executive director of the Great Falls Community Food Bank. Reavley, according to the *Great Falls Tribune,* was "an active member of the Ad Club, active in his church and viewed by many people as a pillar of the community."

But there were other signs that Reavley wasn't the clear-minded, jovial innocent that he projected to others. After his arrest for the Arrota murders, he was charged with stealing $121,000 from the Great Falls Food Bank, where, it was suspected, he abused his position as executive director to siphon money to cover his credit card debts.

During the murder trial, prosecutors said that Reavley killed the Arrottas in a botched robbery attempt and that he needed the money because he thought his girlfriend was pregnant.

According to witness testimony, Reavley explained during religious retreats about "having to kill some people when he was younger." One witness stated Reavley swelled with emotion when he spoke about discovering the bloody bodies of the couple.

"He talked about he was the person, how he was the person that had walked in the store and found the Arrottas," said John Ball, a retired fire chief. "He said he walked in and found the bodies and it was a bloody mess."

Reavley's mother, however, defended her son and provided the young man's alibi, asserting that he "did not leave the house the night of the murders." She said she woke him up "at 6:30 a.m. that morning" and he went to work with his father, "learning about the murders around noon."

Prosecutors also played a tape of Reavley's conversation with his former girlfriend, Mary Klesh, in which he said he didn't kill, "or didn't remember killing," the Arrottas.

In this, Klesh stated that shortly before the murders she told Reavley that she was pregnant. Police believe the news motivated Reavley, one year out of Great Falls High, to rob the grocery store where he worked.

Prosecutors noted that a short time after he'd learned that Klesh was pregnant, Reavley was fired for suspicion of theft. In this fashion, the motive for the murder of the store owners was clear, they said: the Arrottas were most likely stabbed to death after finding someone trying to get into the safe.

A daughter of the Arrottas testified that she saw a man fitting Reavley's description in their house on the night her parents were killed. During further inquiry, she said that she didn't see the intruder's face.

Defense attorneys hammered the point to jurors that there was "no physical evidence linking Reavley to the crime." The deputy county attorney who earlier handled the Arrotta case testified that Reavley was minimized as a suspect about six weeks after the murders because of a lack of proof against him. Forensic witnesses insinuated that more than one person could have been responsible for the murders.

Reavley Acquitted

In the end, Alan Reavley was found not guilty. District Judge Thomas McKittrick returned the verdict about 24 hours after closing arguments in the two-week bench trial.

While exonerated of the murders, he was by no means a free man. One year earlier, in March 2003, Reavley had been sentenced to 20 years in the Montana State Prison for the theft from the Great Falls Food Bank.

Reavley admitted he had cashed donation checks at his personal credit union for five years. He minimized and self-righteously justified the nature of the theft, explaining away his larceny as an act of alms.

"These were checks from people who said they wanted their money to buy food," he said to the *Great Falls Tribune*. "Ninety-nine percent of everything was used to buy food…There was some stuff at the end, at the very end. Money was used to pay credit cards."

Alan Reavley was paroled in June 2013. Justice, some believe, wasn't served in his acquittal.

"We took a 40-year-old case and we put on what we believed to be the best possible case we could put on," said Cascade County Attorney Brant Light in 2004. "I thought things went pretty much the way we wanted them to go. Obviously, the judge didn't think we had enough."

Light's belief in Reavley's culpability in the double murder was unambiguous. "He should get down on his knees and thank God for getting away with a horrendous crime," Light said to the *Missoulian* in 2004.

Ace Hardware on 10th Avenue South is the site of the former Super Save and Arrotta murders. Alan Reavley, who still resides in Great Falls, turned down multiple offers to be interviewed for this book.

12

DOUBLE HOMICIDE, PLUS ONE

Butte, 1965
Victims: Marjorie McQuiston,
Nancy McQuiston, JoAnn Kankelborg
Case Status: Unsolved

On Tuesday, April 13, 1965, Marjorie McQuiston, 51, and her daughter, Nancy McQuiston, 25, went missing from their home at 945 17th in Butte. Concerned relatives and friends could not find the pair in the small McGlone Heights house where they lived, but they found bullet holes, blood stains, and other evidence of violence and possible murder. And missing was the tan 1960 Comet automobile owned by Nancy and ordinarily kept in the garage at the house.

The women were first reported missing one night earlier, Monday, April 12. Police determined a .22-caliber pistol had fired the bullets which left holes in a door and in a stack of phonograph records in the home. Copious blood stains and spots of blood provided ample physical evidence.

Come Tuesday, April 13, a break appeared in the baffling case. About 8 p.m. Tuesday, four boys from Walkerville found a billfold near the Alice Pit on Butte Hill, about one-half mile from the McQuiston home. It contained Nancy McQuiston's identification papers and numerous photographs. Police did not disclose whether there was money in the billfold.

On Wednesday, April 14, a man told deputies he noticed a purse beside the road leading to the county dump. According to available media accounts, he said papers, including a state liquor license, were scattered near the purse. The papers, it turned out, identified Nancy McQuiston.

The bodies of Marjorie McQuiston, 51, and her daughter, Nancy McQuiston, 25, were found in a dump less than a mile from their Butte residence. The double murder remains unsolved. Courtesy Butte Archives.

Bodies Found in Dump

Their bodies were found Wednesday afternoon in the Big Butte dump area, west of the old Walkerville city dump. They were stuffed into McQuiston's car, which was off a side road that ascended Big Butte, not far from their residence.

Evidence indicated that one of the bodies was crammed into the trunk, the other into the back seat. Official police reports noted that officers believed the car "was pushed down an incline leading northwesterly off the side road, and into a gully." The car was discovered in the gully, about 400 feet from the side road, at the foot of a sharp incline. The only damage to the car was "a broken left front wheel."

Slaying of JoAnn Kankelborg

The body of JoAnn Kankelborg, an attractive 17-year-old high school student, was found by "a volunteer worker" on Thursday, April 15, about 14 miles southeast of Butte, "face down in a small creek under a bridge in the Roosevelt Drive area," according to the *Montana Standard*. Kankelborg's death was particularly grim: she had been slashed to death with a broken bottle.

Kankelborg had been missing since the previous Friday afternoon (April 9). The McQuiston women were also last seen the night of Friday, April 9. Officers said they had not ruled out the possibility that the slayings might be related.

Gerald Van Nuland, 24, a 6-5, 250-pound Butte athlete, "a tall and husky Butte warehouseman," according to one newspaper account, was charged in the death of Kankelborg. Van Nuland had been in custody since Tuesday, April 13. A rifle, identified by officers as the property of Van Nuland, was sent to the FBI laboratory.

Authorities revealed their belief that the McQuiston women were shot on April 9, 1965, and stated that some medical evidence indicated that Nancy probably survived several hours, probably into April 10. Later, the gravestone of mother and daughter reflected this opinion—April 9 as the date of death for the mother, April 10 for the daughter.

Everyone known to have been acquainted or associated with the McQuistons, however remotely, was questioned. Lie detectors were used during the investigation. An inquest by coroner Andy Aleksich on May 5, 1965, provided, as one *Montana Standard* reporter wrote, "a glimmer of something on which hope might be founded." Undersheriff William L. Duckham testified that the sheriff's office had information which it could not release at that time without jeopardizing the investigation.

For a long time, that statement remained the last word from either the Sheriff's office or any other official connected to the investigation. Coroner Aleksich did not close his inquest. He recessed it, for some time keeping seven jurors on call, and keeping the inquest open indefinitely. Coroner Aleksich, it was reported, had a general theory "that someone known to the victims shot them to death and that the slayer was and is no stranger to Butte."

Investigation "Simmered Officially to Nothing"

Countless leads were chased down, all to dead ends. Rumors swirled. Butte-area citizens deluged the police department with reports of abandoned cars, parked cars, prowlers, and what seemed to be suspicious behavior wherever noticed. Three months after the murder, Sheriff William L. Dalling assured the community that he and his deputies were still digging and intended to keep digging. "We have sent 250 articles to FBI laboratories for analysis and are still awaiting reports on the last batch shipped. This is a tough case to crack but we have never thought of quitting it." Six months later, *Standard-Post* Staff Writer Lewis T. Poole described the harsh impact that the unsolved murder had taken on the faith of the community: "Butte has had other slayings which have gone into the records cloaked in mystery, apparently forever. None was quite like these in brutality, in boldness, in impact upon the community. What seemed at the time to be a wealth of physical evidence in the house on McGlone Heights where the two women lived, and the lonely hill nearby where their bodies were discovered, has simmered officially to nothing, or near it."

Butte authorities seemed to take all the right steps, having all the evidence reviewed by experts. In November 1965, Martin T. Mangan, state criminal investigator at the time of the McQuiston murders, commended Sheriff William L. Dalling and his deputies on their investigative efforts into the murder mystery. He wrote Sheriff Dalling: "I have reviewed the investigative reports and evidence obtained by your officers and wish to commend you and your department for the logical and thorough investigation you have conducted in this case, in view of the difficult circumstances under which you were working at that time."

Yet, the double murder still turned into a divisive political issue. Sheriff Dalling, a candidate for reelection in 1966, encountered criticism from a Democratic opponent, Bronco Manovich, who cited lack of a solution to the case as grounds for a "change." Manovich noted that a year had passed since discovery of the bodies: "The lack of results in the McQuiston investigation points up need for change in our law enforcement setup."

Sheriff Dalling responded in the press: "We can't very well issue daily news bulletins on an investigation of this kind. That doesn't mean with aren't doing anything. We are working hard and have no intention of letting up. We are working under certain handicaps. No one wants a solution more than I do."

The unequivocal solution to the JoAnn Kankelborg murder stands in sharp contrast to the McQuiston case. Van Nuland confessed to killing Kankelborg, and after several delays in district court proceedings, pleaded guilty. He was sentenced to a life term in prison.

For a short time the McQuiston and Kankelborg investigations had run concurrently, but authorities ultimately decided that with no clear connection to Van Nuland, the two crimes were related only by coincidence.

Murder in all its grotesque ugliness dominated the Silver Bow County news in 1965, so much so that *Standard-Post* editorial staff members were unanimous in one choice as far as the city's top story of the year: the unsolved murders of the McQuiston women. The solved slaying of JoAnne Kankelborg was adjudged the second story of the year. Still another murder was considered to the be the fourth most important news story, the slaying of Robert H. Henningsen, 44, a Butte businessman shot in his furniture store.

The McQuistons murderer remains unknown.

13

A REIGN OF HOMEGROWN TERROR

Manhattan, 1967-1974
Victims: Bernard Poelman, Susie Jaeger, Michael Raney, Sandra Dykman Smallegan
Case Status: Solved

THE FOUR SLAYINGS occurred over seven years, and none of the victims was older than 19. The murder method fluctuated, and there was no evidence that a lone demented mind was behind the murders. But in the small town of Manhattan, panic and speculation reigned.

On March 19, 1967, Bernard Poelman, 13, was the first to be victimized. The sun shone brightly as Bernard and a friend relished in the thawing harbingers of spring. While his friend watched, Bernard climbed the supports of the Nixon Bridge spanning the West Gallatin River outside Manhattan. Suddenly a rifle shot rang out, and Bernard's body plunged into the river. His buddy fled in terror.

Fourteen months later, violent death struck again at a Boy Scout encampment in Headwaters State Park, a popular tourist spot near Manhattan where the Gallatin, Madison, and Jefferson rivers merge to form the Missouri. Michael Raney, 12, son of a Bozeman doctor, was in a tent with several other scouts the night of May 5, 1968.

According to available published police reports, "At 5:30 a.m., one scout awoke to find Michael's sleeping bag soaked with blood. The tent had been slashed open, and Michael had been stabbed under his left arm." He died in the Bozeman hospital of a punctured lung after slipping into unconsciousness. No weapon was found, no fingerprints.

The circumstances of Raney's death paralleled those of Susie Jaeger, 9, a Farmington, Michigan, girl, who disappeared from her family's tent at the same park on the night of June 25, 1973. An intensive search for the girl continued for months, but no clues were found. The Jaegers, who were in Montana to study a possible move there, told the press that the family would refuse "to give up hope that Susan would be found alive until her body was found."

On Monday, February 11, 1974, Sandra Dykman Smallegan, 19, was reported missing from her flat over a garage on Main Street, Manhattan, by her father.

Smallegan, a waitress in a coffee shop, had grown up in Manhattan and had briefly been married. She was last seen Friday night in Belgrade at a basketball game and later that evening in Manhattan's American Legion clubhouse. About an hour later, she was spotted walking to her apartment200 feet away. There was no indication of a struggle in the teen's apartment, but her 1969 white Ford Cortina was missing.

A week after Smallegan went missing, an investigator searching the Horseshoe Hills, 12 miles west of the campground where she was abducted at Headwaters State Park, spotted a pair of woman's underwear dangling from a fence post. Nearby at the abandoned Lockhart ranch, Smallegan's automobile was discovered under piles of straw in a dilapidated barn. An open-pit fire near one of the outbuildings at the ranch yielded several human teeth and about 1,800 bits of human bones.

Phone Calls Lead Investigators to Focus on Suspect

According to the Associated Press, "around the time of the search for Susie Jaeger," a man phoned the Denver bureau of the FBI and said that he had Susie and wanted a $25,000 ransom. He provided no instructions, nor did he offer evidence he had the girl. Apparently, sometime in the summer of 1974, another call came to the sheriff's office in Three Forks doubling the requested ransom amount. That call was traced to Cheyenne, Wyoming. No further calls were received.

Indeed, the killer might never have been caught had not his conscience bothered him—not about Smallegan or the others, but about Susie. On June 25, 1974, a series of phone calls were made to the Jaeger home in Michigan. "Exactly one year to the minute after he had taken Susie from the Jaeger's tent, the kidnapper called," said the *New York Daily News.*

The caller said he had earlier phoned Denver and Three Forks and, for the first time, disclosed a unique detail that confirmed he had seen Susie. The called mentioned Susie had a small deformity, one of her forefingers was missing, and that was something the public didn't know about.

Susie's mother, Marietta Jaeger told *ABC News* in 2006 that she spoke to the caller with compassion and patience. "You know I've been praying for you ever since you took her," she told the man on the phone. According to her account to *ABC News,* "She asked him how they might help him and what they could do—both for him and to be able to see their little girl again.

The caller remained on the phone for more than an hour; the long conversation provided investigators with ample clues to track him down.

Manhattan serial killer David Meirhofer, 25, the son of a pioneer family, was arrested at a parade he helped organize in his hometown. He later confessed to four murders over seven years and was suspected of others. COURTESY MONTANA HISTORICAL SOCIETY.

ARRESTED AT PARADE

On July 27, 1974, David Meirhofer, 25, the son of a local pioneer family, was organizing a parade in Manhattan, his hometown. As the parade concluded, he was arrested on two charges of suspicion of murder and kidnapping.

Meirhofer had served five years in the Marines. He had never been in trouble with the police. Outwardly speaking, there was nothing noticeably aberrant about him. One might even have described him as good looking. All four victims were slain not far from his birthplace.

Investigators, according to Marietta Jaeger's later accounts, asked Marietta to go to Montana to confront Meirhofer face to face. "We were totally convinced that the only thing that would crack him would be a strong female confronting him with the crime that he committed," said Patrick Mullany, a psychologist who was called on the case, to *ABC News* in 2006.

Marietta met Meirhofer, and he described kidnapping, molesting, and choking her daughter to death.

Meirhofer, who had once worked at the Lockhart ranch where Sandra Dykman Smallegan's auto was located, said he would confess to all four slayings on one condition: that his taped confession is not made public.

Gallatin County Attorney Thomas A. Olson said he would not recommend the death penalty on the condition that Meirhofer make a "full and complete statement" concerning the deaths of Susan Jaeger, Sandra Dykman Smallegan, "and any other cases" which might be brought into questioning.

Meirhofer admitted firing his rifle at Bernard Poelman from 150 yards away and watching the boy plunge into the river. He knew the boy and "liked him." Of the Raney boy's slaying, Meirhofer said: "I went to the park where the Boy Scouts were camped, and I was going to get somebody. I opened this tent and I saw this little boy, and I couldn't force myself to take him, I guess, so I stabbed him in the back." He talked about once dating Smallegan but that she had ended the relationship.

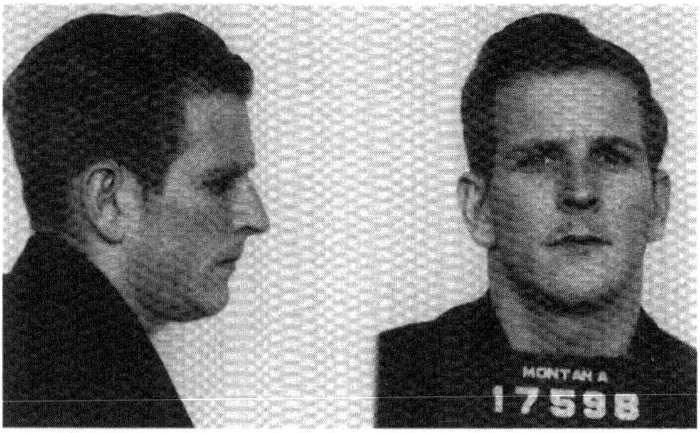

Two weeks after being arrested, Meirhofer was found dead in his cell, hanging from a towel hooked to a ceiling light fixture. Courtesy Montana Historical Society.

Transcripts of a Demented Mind

A partial transcript of the taped confession was published in newspapers nationwide in October 1974. In the excerpt that follows, "PD" is FBI Agent Pete Dunbar and "DM" is David Meirhofer:

> PD: Being very blunt, very truthful, cutting this to the bare essentials, did you, on June 25th, take Susie from a tent? Susie Jaeger, in the Headwaters State Park, at Three Forks, Montana?
>
> DM: Yes
>
> PD: Did you cause Susan to be hurt, and if so, how?
>
> DM: Yes, I had to choke her.
>
> PD: Was she killed when you choked her?
>
> DM: No.
>
> PD: When was she killed?
>
> DM: Uh, a little later.

Meirhofer described how he took Susie to a ranch owned by Bill Bryant, undressed her, and then choked her and "cut her up" with his hunting knife.

> PD: And where is the body located?
>
> DM: Well, not much left of it.
>
> PD: What's left? Where? Where did you put the pieces?
>
> DM: I put her head in that outhouse

```
behind the ranch and all the rest of it
was burned."

PD: And, what did you burn it with,
David?

DM: Just wood. It was done in different
places on the ranch.

PD: And where did you spread these
pieces?

DM: Well, the, uh, the main part of the
torso, upper torso, was burned alongside
a culvert on the road between the
Lockhart Ranch and Menard.
```

The conversation eventually steered toward the murder of Smallegan.

```
DM: Well, I went up to her apartment
at 2:00 o'clock in the morning of the
10th...And, uh, I, she was sleeping and I
jumped on her and choked her, and then
tied her up and put a piece of tape
around her mouth and then I was gonna',
while I was putting some of her clothes
and stuff in the car she evidently died.
She couldn't get any air through the
tape."
```

Meirhofer Suicide; Victim's Mother Writes Book

On the morning of September 29, 1974, the detestable David Meirhofer was found dead in his jail cell, hanging from a towel hooked to a ceiling light fixture. He had hanged himself two weeks after being arrested. (After Meirhofer committed suicide, a Bozeman judge ruled his confession a public document.)

Marietta Jaeger wrote a book about Susan's kidnapping and murder, titled *The Lost Child*, published in June 1983. She became an active member of the Catholic Mobilizing Network, a national organization mobilizing all people of goodwill to, among other things, end the practice of the death penalty.

"I came to realize that the kidnapper's life was just as precious as my Susie's," says Jaeger. "That might seem like a big stretch, but that's the kind of God in whom I believe. That's a God who is in love with all of us, despite who we are and what we've ever done."

Smallegan's Possessions Found in 2005

In 2005, Smallegan's wallet, identification, and a small wire-bound notebook were found in the wall of a building believed to have belonged to Meirhofer. A work crew was remodeling the building for current owners and found the item when they ripped into an inside wall. Contained within a plastic bag, covered in plaster, the ghoulish mementos of Montana's home raised horror.

The Gallatin County Sheriff's Office processed the evidence with "our ultimate goal here is to return them to the family," Sheriff Jim Cashell said to the Associated Press. "This is going to be something that the family is going to have that was really close and personal and that I think they really deserve to get back."

Cashell said that he spoke to both the Meirhofer and Smallegan families about the discovery and told the AP that "this is the first time" he recalled evidence from a Meirhofer case being found.

The sheriff said it is difficult to rationalize, but about "every four or five years" someone will bring up Meirhofer's name and his heinous acts and want to learn more about the sick details of his reprobate mind. "I'm not sure why, and I wouldn't want to hazard a guess," he said.

14

BRUTAL BLOW PUTS EX-BOXER DOWN FOR THE COUNT

Missoula, 1969
Victim: James F. "Spider" McCallum
Case Status: Solved

IT TOOK A VICIOUS AND BRUTAL blow with an ax to do what hundreds of fists could not—put James F. McCallum down for the count. It was a robbery slaying that ended the life of the popular ex-boxer and Missoula nightclub owner nicknamed "Spider."

NUMEROUS TALES PRECEDED THE ONE ABOUT HIS DEATH.

McCallum's first professional fight most likely took place in a gym in Livingston in 1932. His opponent was Jimmy Tate of Billings, and Spider knocked him cold. It was a successful start to a long career that lasted about a quarter of a century. His early fights were held in a curious lot of opera houses, social clubs, temples, theaters, and athletic clubs across Montana.

Among Spider's legendary feats: two 10-rounders he fought in one night, his epic battle with Tiger Bob Noonan at St. Regis on July 3, 1948, when both were more than twice the age of most mature fighters, and his still climbing into the ring for another run

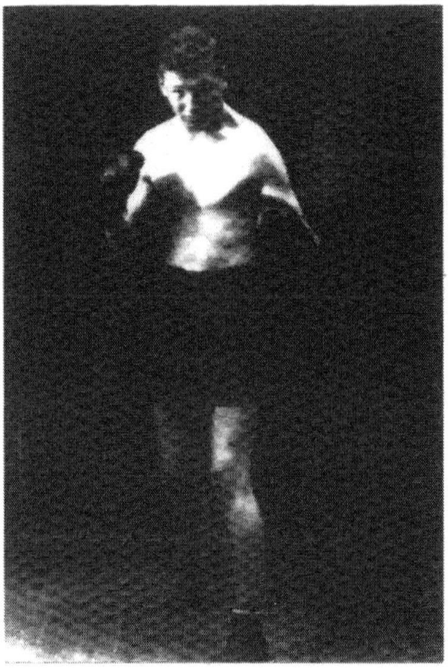

At age 12, James "Spider" McCallum won his first boxing trophy. The welterweight was reported to have appeared in more than 100 amateur and professional boxing matches, though he never contended for a major boxing title. COURTESY ANITA SPOONER.

when he was 50 years old. Following retirement Spider owned a saloon in Missoula, and it was his technique of vaulting over the bar to stop disturbances that impressed spectators.

LIFE OF "SPIDER"

McCallum was born November 23, 1912, at Dobson, Montana. James and his two siblings were all adopted out of an orphanage at one unknown point in time, according to Anita Spooner, McCallum's daughter and only living descendant. At age 12, "Spider" was an amateur boxer and won his first trophy from the Intermountain Amateur Athletic Association.

Spider moved with his family to Bozeman when he was 14 years old in 1926, where he attended local schools. The McCallum family moved once more in 1935, this time to Missoula.

Spider had his eighth professional bout in 1935 in Missoula. At the time he was with the Civilian Conservation Corps Company #1998 at the Thompson River Camp. His boxing ability kept him traveling to camps and cities in the Northwest and Montana. In 1938-39 he was a boxing instructor for the CCC in the Fort Missoula CCC district. Spider kept at professional boxing while trying a number of other jobs, including security guard, Northern Pacific Railroad switchman, sugar beet processor, and even boxing promoter.

The welterweight McCallum was reported to have appeared in more than 100 amateur and professional boxing matches, though he never contended for a major boxing title. One his final fights in Montana on November 9, 1955, was an 8-round decision over Ron Milne of Spokane, at Missoula, in which he reportedly "showed marvelous physical conditioning."

Ten days later the Montana State Athletic Commission banned McCallum from participating in any professional boxing in Montana because he was more than 38 years old. Commission chairman Sonny O'Day quoted Montana codes to the newspapers as stating: "that a boxer cannot box in a Montana professional ring after reaching the age of 38."O'Day said the decision was made in the interest of the sport and the protection of McCallum, who had fought and won four bouts since coming out of retirement in the summer of 1955. Nonetheless, it appears that he kept fighting in Montana—he had one more fight in Great Falls in 1956—before wrapping up his career with fights in Washington, Oregon, and even Edmonton, Alberta, Canada.

The Maverick Bar

The Maverick Bar, located on 633 Woody Street, formerly known as the Helena Hotel, started operating in the 1940s. Spider stayed active in boxing but in his spare time, he liked to cook and bake. He even enjoyed writing poetry, and his handwriting was said to be impeccable. But the bar occupied most of his attention. Spider was known to give "graduation parties" for university students who had made his place their hangout during their academic tenure.

"Spider" McCallum (right) became a popular tavern owner in Missoula. It took a vicious and brutal blow with an ax to do what hundreds of fists could not: put James F. McCallum down for the count. Courtesy Anita Spooner.

It was a notoriously rough bar, especially in its earliest days. In fact, McCallum was dangerously wounded early one morning in October 1947 while attempting to break up a fight between two patrons. McCallum was slashed in the stomach as he wrested a knife from one of the men. According to the *Missoulian*, "McCallum was reported in a satisfactory condition by the physician who operated upon him to repair tissues of the stomach, penetrated by the long, dagger-like knife wielded, police said, by (Sammy J. Mercer)." McCallum refused to sign a criminal complaint against Mercer.

Spider opened the Maverick Bar in tandem with his wife Edna, and the bar outlasted the marriage. (Spider was once arrested for assaulting Edna.) He later married a waitress from the Main Spot Café, and they started a home at 1901 South 13th Street West. When that marriage also faltered, Spider and his brother Oren and his brother's wife Dorothy shared a house at 817 N. Ryman Avenue.

McCallum's Murder; Arrests

On February 28, 1969, Spider McCallum's body was found by Missoula police at his Ryan Avenue residence following an anonymous phone call. Police said he had been dead about a week. The autopsy report disclosed "3 lacerations on left side of head. 1 being an extensive crush with a blunt instrument, (probably an ax)."

Three men were charged with the slaying: James Roark, 33; Gene Maddio, 25; and David Tamietti, 26. Roark was arrested in a Helena rooming house; Tamietti and Maddio were apprehended in Idaho Falls.

On March 28, 1969, homicide charges against Roark and Maddio were dismissed after the men were able to prove they were not in Missoula at the time of the murder (determined to be the night of February 21, 1969).

However, Spider's electric razor, electric toothbrush, and hair clippers were found in a tan suitcase that Tamietti was carrying. Tamietti's first question to law enforcement was, "Has my dad sent you?" He told Idaho officers, "my fingerprints are all over the place" and he waived his rights to an attorney. County Attorney Jack Pinsoneault filed a first-degree murder charge against Tamietti.

David E. Tamietti was the son of Mineral County Sheriff Francis Tamietti. He was raised and attended schools in Superior. His Superior High School yearbook photo in 1961 shows a handsome, ordinary kid wearing a suit and tie; below his name was the quote: "All the world may not love a lover, but all the world watches him." He attended the University of Montana for five years and had been employed by Castles Empire Foods in Superior for six.

Tamietti's connection to McCallum was nebulous, though he could have first come in contact with the former boxer at the Maverick Bar. In the 1962-63 Grizzly Guide at Montana State University, Tamietti was registered in Pre-Forestry as a resident of Elrod Hall; the following year he was registered in Business Administration and living at Eddy Avenue.

"I was 19 years old when my dad was killed," says Anita Spooner. "I just called him the day before to let him know I had had a baby girl, and he didn't answer."

Spooner once lived at the Ryman Avenue house with her father, and she remembered visiting him a few months before he was killed and seeing Tamietti there. "Dave Tamietti was at my dad's house and I didn't know who he was at the time," says Spooner. "Dad was big on bringing in people who were bad to help them. He had a big heart. I was sitting on the couch and Dave Tamietti kept walking around the living room in circles, and he never said a word. Of course, I didn't stay very long. I didn't feel comfortable with him there. My dad seemed okay. He had David living with him."

Theft as Motive

James Roark testified that theft was Tamietti's motive for murder. Roark said that about one week before Spider was killed, Tamietti ran out of money and robbed a camera and transistor radio from the home of a woman who the men had done work for while employed by Spic and Span Cleaners. Tamietti, he said, had suggested a place on Ryman for more goods.

When he took the witness stand, Tamietti denied killing McCallum. Asked under direct examination by defense attorney Anthony F. Keast if he had caused McCallum's death, Tamietti replied slowly and deliberately: "No sir, I did not. "In addition, Tamietti denied "participating" or "conspiring" in the crime. Tamietti, who spent about an hour on the stand, testified that he was inside McCallum's residence February 20 and saw McCallum lying in bed.

Tamietti said that he had gone to the McCallum home after returning to Missoula from a trip from Wallace, Idaho. He said he noticed that no smoke was coming from the chimney and the door was padlocked. He said, "having lived there," that he knew he could open the lock by twisting it.

When he got inside, he said he took a container of beer from the refrigerator, lit a fire, and went to the bathroom. He said that he assumed Spider was in bed asleep because of a drunk bender. He said he approached the bed and "probably uttered an obscenity" to awaken McCallum. However, when McCallum did not respond, Tamietti said he pulled back the covers and "saw that he had been beaten to his head."

Tamietti said that he was "sick and disgusted" and that he rushed to the bathroom and vomited. Afterward, Tamietti testified that he met John McCallum, the dead man's son, and another man inside the house. He estimated that he had been in the McCallum residence "a half hour to an hour." He said that he didn't notify John that his father was murdered in the bedroom, but instead he "packed goods that I believed to be stolen and left the house." He said that he did not call police because to do so would have been to invite implication: "In my own mind, I believed that I would be blamed if I called the police—so I didn't."

The trial lasted 12 days. At its conclusion, Judge E. Gardner Brownlee turned over proceedings to jurors and instructed them to ignore Tamietti's previous criminal activities while rendering the verdict. Tamietti had committed other crimes, including forgery. "You are not to infer that if he is guilty of some other offense that he is guilty of murder."

County Attorney H.J. "Jack" Pinsoneault said: "There's one thing he doesn't want you to believe—that he didn't kill Spider. But he did. He killed Spider McCallum just as sure as I'm standing here." Deputy County Attorney Loren Gerdes contended that robbery was primary motive for McCallum's murder. In addition, he added, Tamietti "was afraid of the consequences if McCallum discovered he had been robbed." Pinsoneault at one point in his closing arguments turned to Sheriff Francis Tamietti, who sat beside his son throughout the trial, and said, "Sheriff Tamietti, David is guilty of this charge."

Tamietti's trial ended in a mistrial after the jury failed to reach a verdict, but Pinsoneault pressed hard for a second trial.

Second Trial of Tamietti; McCallum's Killer Sentenced

The second trial had been scheduled for November 30, 1970, but was vacated two days before it was to start when Tamietti pleaded guilty to a reduced charge of second-degree murder. Tamietti was sentenced to 20 years in prison. While Tamietti did not admit to killing McCallum, he admitted that he "knew of his death" and failed to contact authorities, and that he had robbed McCallum's house and forged checks in McCallum's name. He admitted removing "many articles" from McCallum's house, including his checkbook with the intent to forge checks.

In addition to approximately 638 days in the Missoula County jail, Tamietti served about four years of his sentence at the state prison in Deer Lodge. "My brother Patrick ended up in prison at the same time as Tamietti," said Anita Spooner. "He thought that Patrick was over there to kill him, and he had the guards lock him in his cell all of the time. Patrick was in trouble for getting a bunch of tickets and they sent him to Deer Lodge to shape him up. He wasn't there to kill David."

After his release from prison in the late-1970s, Tamietti returned to live with his family in Superior. Unable to cope with the reintegration of society, Tamietti died of a self-inflicted gunshot wound on June 5, 1981, at Fish Creek State Park Campground in Alberton, at age 37. His suicide note included instructions to "bury me at the Big Tree," a location that perhaps only Tamietti and those closest to him knew.

It wouldn't be last violent death associated the legacy of Spider McCallum. One of his sons, Patrick Oren McCallum, 25, died of a self-inflicted wound from a .22 in his Missoula home in 1974. In 1965, Patrick had enlisted in the Marines and served in the Vietnam War. He was discharged in 1972 and had worked as a roofer in the Missoula area.

Colorful in life and convoluted in death, McCallum was as hard as nails and as puzzling as a 10,000-piece jigsaw puzzle. "My dad was never around a lot," says Spooner. "There are a lot of things about him and his life that I myself am still learning about."

15

MONTANA LABOR LEADER ORDERS HIT ON HIS RIVAL

Pennsylvania, 1969
Victims: Joseph Albert "Jock" Yablonski,
Margeret and Charlotte Yablonski
Case Status: Solved

Montana-born "Tough Tony" Boyle ran the United Mine Workers of America union with a clenched fist. When his authority and status as the president of the UMWA was threatened by "Jock" Yablonski, Boyle ordered the murders of Yablonski and his family. The rise and despicable fall of Boyle was illustrated in the 1986 film *Act of Vengeance*, with Charles Bronson starring as the protagonist Yablonski.

Absolute power corrupted William Anthony "Tough Tony" Boyle absolutely. Boyle rose from the dirt and dust of the Montana mines through the ranks to become the president of United Mine Workers of America in 1963.

Born in 1902 in a gold and silver mining camp in Bald Butte, (about two miles southwest of Marysville, on the slope of the Continental Divide), to James and Catherine (Mallin) Boyle, Tony derived from a long line of Irish miners. His father began working in the mines in Scotland at age 9, and his maternal and paternal grandfathers and great grandfathers all worked in English mines. Tony attended public schools in Montana and Idaho and went to work in the mines alongside his father, who died shortly thereafter from tuberculosis. Boyle first became active in union affairs at the local level, joining the United Mine Workers of America (UMWA) soon after going to work in the mines.

Boyle studied law at LaSalle University while strengthening his union affiliations. In 1940he was appointed president of District 27, which covers Montana, and he served in that capacity until 1948. During World War II, Boyle served on several government wartime production boards, and he was the first labor representative on Montana's Advisory Council to the State Unemployment Compensation Commission. He married a schoolteacher, Ethel Williams, and they had a daughter, Antoinette.

In 1948, UMWA president John L. Lewis made Boyle his assistant. He served until 1960, acting as Lewis' chief trouble-shooter and the union's chief administrator. Lewis at the same time appointed him director of UMWA District 50 and regional director of the Congress of Industrial Organizations (CIO) for four western states. In 1963, Boyle succeeded the late Thomas Kennedy as president of the United Mine Workers of America.

"The 58-year-old Boyle has a fine set of red eyebrows and a gift for direct, plain and vigorous speech," said the *Roundup Record Tribune* at the time.

Boyle's leadership in the union was challenged in 1969 by Joseph Albert "Jock" Yablonski. Earlier that year, Yablonski had become the first United Mine Workers of America (UMWA) official in more than 40 years to challenge the union's entrenched leadership. Born in Pittsburgh in 1910, Yablonski was a veteran of the mines who moved up through the ranks to become president of

UMW District 5 in Southern Pennsylvania. Yablonski hammered Boyle and other UMWA leaders with charges of corruption and nepotism. He was going to push as hard as he needed to democratize the United Mine Workers of America. Violence and division marked the campaign.

Account to *Time* magazine, "Boyle was, by almost any appraisal, a bully and an autocrat, ruling over the UMWA with an iron fist and brooking no dissent." In this fashion, he removed Yablonski from the presidency of District 5 in 1965. But now Yablonski was finding his voice and aiming to remove Boyle.

In the December 1969 union election, Yablonski appeared to have lost to Boyle by a decisive margin, 33,000 votes. However, that election was later overturned by U.S. District Court Judge William B. Bryant on grounds of "massive vote fraud and financial manipulation."

Murder of Yablonski, Family

Unsuccessful in his first attempt to unseat Boyle, Yablonski was preparing for another run when gunmen murdered Yablonski and his family.

In the early morning hours of December 31, 1969, a blue 1966 Chevrolet with Ohio plates pulled up beside Yablonski's Clarksville, Pennsylvania, fieldstone farmhouse. Three men got out and entered the house.

The political assassination and murders that followed were described in the book *Act of Vengeance: The Yablonski murders and their solution:*

> First they found Yablonski's 25-year-old daughter, Charlotte. They shot her twice in the head. Then, they went to the bedroom where Yablonski and his wife, Margaret, slept. Jolted awake, Yablonski

> reached for an unloaded shotgun he kept by his bed, as his wife screamed, but it was too late. The intruders fired on the couple. Additional shots were fired at Yablonski after he crumbled to the floor to make sure he was dead.
>
> The bodies went undiscovered for six days. By the time Yablonski's son, Kenneth, found them on Jan. 5, 1970, untouched copies of *The Pittsburgh Press* and the *Brownsville Telegraph* were strewn on the back-porch steps and mail had accumulated in the mailbox.

At first, union officials said they doubted that Yablonski's murder had anything to do with the election. But evidence was uncovered of a larger, more comprehensive plot. Even though two UMWA officials were indicted and convicted for conspiracy to commit murder, and one local president had been brought to trial and convicted, somehow, Boyle eluded charges and continued to deny the insinuation that he ordered the Yablonski hit.

In 1972, the autocratic Boyle, age 70, desperately clung to his presidency of the United Mine Workers. One magazine covering the rebellion and bloodletting within the union's politics noted that Boyle's eyes "flash with anger and bitterness. "With his $50,000 salary and posh Washington offices, critics charged that Boyle had grown "more and more distant from the grimy realities of the mines." According to *Life* magazine, "he appoints men to jobs that his foes say should be elective, puts relatives on the payroll, grants coal operators what seem like "sweetheart" contracts and pushes hardly at all for mine safety and fringe benefits."

In the spring of 1972, Boyle was sentenced to five years in prison for misuse of union funds. As it turned out, Boyle's financial activities with the UMWA—and the overall accounting of UMWA itself—had been the subject of a lengthy federal investigation.

Though the FBI had successfully prosecuted its case, Boyle was allowed out of jail pending appeal and continued to campaign for the UMWA presidency.

On September 6, 1973, Anthony "Tough Tony" Boyle, a former Montana miner who had become of the most powerful labor leaders in America, was arrested and charged with the murder of Yablonski, his wife, and daughter. Along with Boyle, eight others confessed or were found guilty of participating in the murder plot. Boyle was sentenced to three consecutive life sentences for authorizing the contract hit.

The Pennsylvania Supreme Court overturned his conviction in 1977 and Boyle was tried again, but the result was the same. He died of a stroke in 1985 while serving his sentence.

16

KILLER WITH A LICENSE TO KILL

1972-1973
Victims: Eight
Case Status: Solved

AT THE AGE OF 10 Edmund Kemper was a tall, odd boy exhibiting weird traits. He enjoyed ripping the arms, legs, and heads off his younger sister's dolls. When he was 13, he shot a dog belonging to a neighbor boy. Kids either avoided or teased him and he had no close contact with anyone other than his mother. Shortly after killing the dog, Edmund chopped the head off a Siamese cat, the family pet, and buried it in his backyard.

Edmund Emil Kemper III was born on December 18, 1948, in Burbank, California. His father was a gigantic man, standing 6 ft, 8 inches, while his mother, Clarnell, eclipsed 6 feet. In 1957, the Klempers split up, and Clarnell moved to Helena, Montana, where she worked as a secretary to make a new life for her three children.

Edmund, according to published news accounts, was "miserable" and "longed for his father," and "visited him at every opportunity at his new home in Los Angeles."

By the time Edmund was 15 years old he was already 6-feet-4 and angry at the world. He had high intelligence—an IQ of 136—but was an emotionally disturbed schizophrenic.

In the summer of 1962, Edmund went to live with his father, who had remarried, in Los Angeles. At Christmas, he visited his grandparents on their farm at North Fork, California. His father left him on the farm and returned to Los Angeles.

In the summer of 1964, he was staying with his father's parents, Mr. and Mrs. E. E. Kemper in North Fork, a Sierra foothills community.

On August 27, 1964, Edmund called his mother in Helena and told her he had killed his grandparents. He then called the sheriff's office and said, "there's been some trouble up here." He greeted the officers in the front yard. Maude, 68, was found in a bedroom, shot in the head and stabbed in the back. The grandfather, 72, was slain in the garage, shot to death. The weapons were a .22 caliber rifle and a butcher knife.

Edmund later told investigators that he had spent the fatal morning staring off into space, sitting at the kitchen table. There was a rifle at his side that his grandfather had given to him to shoot gophers and rabbits. He raised it and took aim at the back of his grandmother's neck. He dragged her body into the elderly couple's bedroom and waited for his grandfather to arrive and then waylaid him.

The psychiatrists who examined Edmund Kemper declared him insane. On December 6, 1964, the doors of Atascadero State Hospital, a hospital which specialized in sex offenders, slammed behind him.

Giant With a License to Murder

After about five years at Atascadero State Hospital Edmund was released in 1969 and paroled to his mother who had remarried and was working at the University of California. The 6-foot-9 giant enrolled in a community college, where he earned straight A's. According to the *Los Angeles Times*, "Edmund had a plan. California law had a unique loophole."

"On his lawyer's advice he was examined by two different psychiatrists. Both doctors gave him glowing, positive reports. Their recommendations were interspersed with words such as "normal," "adjusted," and "no danger to society."

These two reports were placed under the nose of a Superior Court judge, who then decided that Edmund's violent juvenile record be sealed forever. From then on, he had the full rights and advantages of civilized society: he could vote, serve on a jury, and join the army. Now, he could even legally obtain guns. The man who had slaughtered his grandparents now had a clean slate, a veritable license to kill again.

In 1972, Kemper began a series of killings in California in which he would pick up female hitchhikers, kill them, and engage in necrophilia with their bodies. He also murdered his mother and her best friend in 1973 before confessing to the killings.

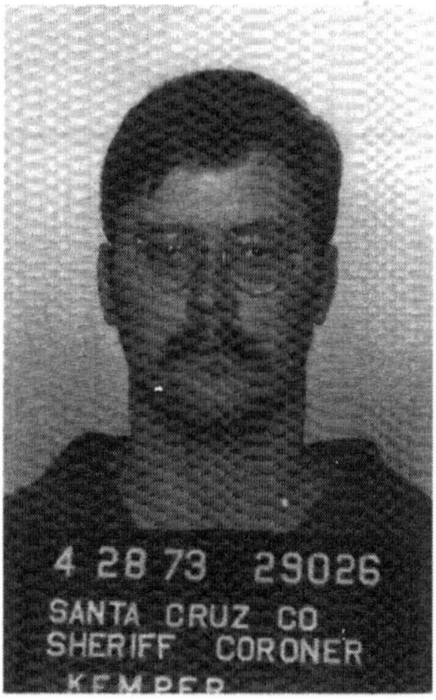

By the time he was 15, Edmund Kemper of Helena was already 6-feet-4 and angry at the world. In August 1963, Kemper called his mother in Helena and told her he had killed his grandparents in California. After being released from a mental hospital in 1969, he began picking up and killing female hitchhikers.

Twenty-five-years old at the time, Kemper pleaded innocent by reason of insanity. He admitted acting out homicidal, cannibalistic, and sexual fantasies in the killings. While being held pre-conviction, he tried to commit suicide four times. He said he thought he should be "tortured" as punishment.

Kemper could not be sent to the gas chamber because the slayings occurred between May 1972 and April 1973, before California reinstituted the death penalty. Instead, he was ordered to serve eight concurrent life sentences. The judge declared that Kemper should never be set free. Santa Cruz Superior Court Judge Harry Brauer told Kemper, "You will be sentenced to the penitentiary for the term of your natural life...I know that you should not be released from prison during your natural life."

District Attorney Peter Chang said at the time that while Kemper would be eligible for parole in seven years, "he'll never get out."

Kemper is currently serving his sentence in Vacaville, California.

17

A MURDERER COMES TO DINNER

Billings, 1973
Victims: Linda and Clifford Bernhardt
Case Status: Solved

Clifford and Linda Bernhardt of Billings were supposed to attend a family dinner on the evening of November 6, 1973, but at the last minute they turned down the invitation and stayed home. Their bodies were found there the next day. In 2019, new DNA analysis determined that their killer had been one of Linda's co-workers.

At one point there was a $100,000 reward for information leading to the conviction of whoever was responsible for the double murder of Linda and Clifford Bernhardt, both 24, in their Billings home on Monday, November 6, 1973.

Linda and Clifford had been sweethearts since junior high. The couple had saved for years to build a home and finally settled down on Dorothy Lane in the fall of 1973.

The Bernhardts were likeable and quiet people, according to their neighbors, and they kept a tidy house and a punctual schedule. They squirreled away funds for rainy days and looked at saving money as a requirement, not a lofty aspiration.

On the final night of their lives, Linda prepared hamburger casserole for her and Clifford, a construction worker who had served as an Army sergeant in the Vietnam War.

The Bernhardts were supposed to attend a family dinner that evening "but at the last minute turned down the invitation," according to the *Billings Gazette*. "They had an evening job cleaning an office building, and it was just easier to dine in," said the account.

And perhaps another person was supposed to have dined with them that final night, because three plates had been set at the table.

Discovery of the Bernhardts

The Bernhardts were found the following day by Linda's mother after her daughter failed to show up for work. She found her son-in-law face down in a pool of blood and her daughter dead in a separate bedroom. Her daughter had been sexually assaulted, her clothes torn away. Officials said that Clifford had been struck on the back of the skull; both were strangled.

The crime scene bore several other disturbing facts. The windows had been left open and the heat was turned down, which investigators suspected was intended to make it harder to determine the couple's time of death. The house had become so cold that a basin of ice found near Linda's body was still frozen. A suitcase, all of Linda's underwear, and some of her shoes were also missing. With no signs of forced entry—and the odd number of dinner-table settings—investigators speculated that their killer knew them.

For years, every lead was chased to oblivion, even the physical clues. The case file swelled to 3,600 pages. "More than 100 law enforcement officials were involved throughout various points over the years, 894 contacts were made, 21 law enforcement agencies around the country got involved, and 12 states provided forms of assistance," Billings officials said.

For four decades, the murders were unsolved. There had been no follow-up media coverage to speak of. The murders seemed to be remembered only within the Billings Police Department and by anyone who had ever met Linda and Clifford Bernhardt. Their flame was in danger of flickering out.

DNA Discovered

Technology finally solved what the combined efforts of multiple agencies could not. As it turned out, the killer had left behind one critical bit of evidence: DNA on Linda's purple pants.

In 2015 the Yellowstone County Sheriff's Office brought in Parabon NanoLabs, a company that could analyze DNA from small samples—a "genetic-genealogy report" Parabon calls it—and find possible familial links via public DNA databases. Parabon reverse-engineered the killer's family tree, and in January 2019, forty-five years after the murders, authorities had an answer.

DNA determined the suspects

Parabon NanoLabs found a likely match between the DNA found at the crime scene in the Bernhardts home and the DNA submitted to a public genealogy database by a man named Harold Caldwell. Harold Caldwell's DNA was further analyzed by the Montana State Crime Lab, which removed him as a suspect.

Apparently, Harold had submitted his DNA to a popular ancestry website in the aim of constructing a clearer composite of his family history; he had no connection to the crime. But that swab sample from his inner cheek led authorities to his brother,

Cecil. Upon further scrutiny, lab analysts were able to obtain an exact match—and, additionally, authorities could prove a direct relationship between the victims and the killer. Yet solving the cold case was more bitter than sweet: the killer was already dead.

According to published police and media accounts, Cecil Caldwell had worked at Ryan's Inc., where Linda Bernhardt also worked, for 10 years until 1976. Thus he knew Linda and probably her husband, which would explain the lack of forced entry at the crime scene—and perhaps the third plate for dinner. Officials believe Caldwell may have targeted Linda.

Born in Arkansas, Cecil and the Caldwell family had moved to Chester, Montana, in 1956, where he graduated from Chester High School in 1963. Shortly after graduation, he moved to Billings.

After working at Ryan's, Caldwell became a longtime employee of the Billings Sanitation Department. A father of two adopted children and two stepchildren, and who had no criminal history, Caldwell died in Billings at age 59 in 2003. According to his obituary, "He was loved by all and will be greatly missed."

18

WAYNE NANCE, SADISTIC SERIAL KILLER

Missoula, 1974-1986
Victims: Four, possibly more
Case Status: Solved

The first two bodies had been dumped on the eastern edge of Missoula, and the signature of the killer—his "modus operandi"—was there: the ropes, the knife, the sadistic, murderous rapes.

For more than twelve years, Missoula lived under a reign of terror because of a monstrous set of rape-murders that stumped the police. Beginning in the dead of winter in 1974 and ending in the early fall of 1986, life in the western Montana college town was unsettled.

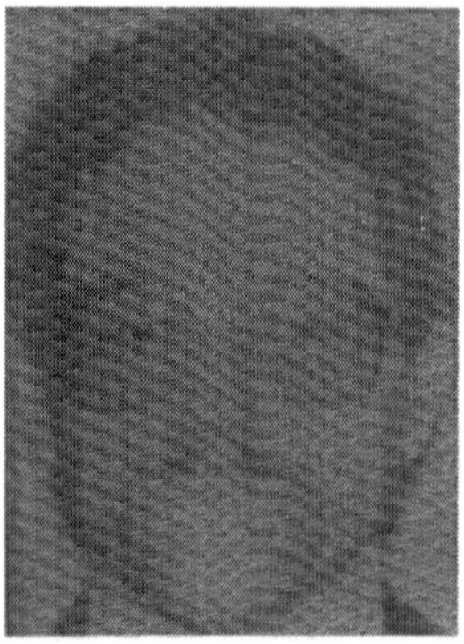

For more than twelve years, Missoula lived under a reign of terror because of a monstrous set of rape-murders that stumped the police. Wayne Nance, a local furniture deliveryman, was ultimately revealed as the perpetrator. Here is Nance's driver's license photo from 1985. Courtesy Missoula Historical Society.

Baby-faced, friendly Wayne Nance was "the veritable boy next door," a local furniture store deliveryman who remembered co-workers' birthdays and was a model worker. He was someone who could be counted on if a favor were needed. He was described as so "trustworthy" that some customers simply handed him the keys to their houses so he could deliver furniture if they weren't home. Women who knew him described him as the "kind of man one dreamed about marrying" and that he seemed like the nicest guy they had ever met.

No one knows precisely how many people Nance killed, though law enforcement in Missoula conclusively assigned him with four murders: Donna Pounds (April 11, 1974), a long unidentified girlfriend; "a late-summer fling" of his named Marcella "Marci" Cheri Bachmann (discovered December 24, 1984, and identified in 2006 through DNA profiling); and Mike and Teresa Shook (December 12, 1985).

Murder of Donna Pounds

Donna Pounds was a minister's wife and the mother of some of Nance's school friends. On April 11, 1974, she was found shot to death in the basement of her West Riverside home. She had been tortured and sexually assaulted and was found tied to a chair.

Two years after Pounds was murdered, Missoula County held its first grand jury hearing into the case. More than 100 witnesses were called, including the two possible suspects: Wayne Nance and Harvey Pounds. Donna's husband Harvey was considered a suspect based on criminal statistics—when a wife is found dead in her home, her husband is often the killer. Yet Harvey had an alibi and no known history of domestic violence, and, from the start, the police said they designated him as a victim, a man who suffered a hideous loss, not a perpetrator. No, this was the work of a reprobate who had some murky, less obvious linkage to Donna.

Harvey provided a lengthy list and a wide net of possible suspects, including Nance, an acquaintance of the Pounds' teenage son. When the police brought in Nance for questioning, he created the impression of someone who hid more than he told.

At the grand jury hearing, Missoula County Attorney Robert L. "Dusty" Deschamps III tried to rattle Nance, who was still a student at Sentinel High School. He thought Nance would be unnerved by the bloody crime-scene photographs, but Nance didn't flinch at any of it. Failing to meet the necessary legal requirements to indict Nance or anyone else, the grand jury ended without bringing criminal charges.

More Murders

After the hearing into the Pounds murder ended without charges, Nance enrolled in the United States Navy, serving from 1974 to 1977. In January 1980, the body of a 15-year-old girl, later identified as Devonna Nelson, was found east of Missoula, near Beavertail State Park. Little is known about Nelson other than that she ran away or "disappeared without a trace" from her Seattle home and was first reported missing in July 1978, according to author John Coston. While Nance is still strongly suspected to be involved in Nelson's death, he was never conclusively linked to the homicide.

The last time anyone saw the girl in this photo was on the night of September 28, 1984, when Wayne Nance (also in the photo) brought her to a party. Her nude body was found in a two-foot-deep grave in the woods above Bonner Dam. Photo courtesy Missoula Historical Society.

Then on Christmas Eve in 1984, a hiker in the Missoula area came upon a shallow grave and the decomposed, bullet-riddled body of "Marci" Bachmann, a runaway from Washington State with ties to Nance, who is considered the killer by law enforcement. On September 9, 1985, the skeleton of a woman, who, to this day, is only known as "Christy Crystal Creek," was found in Missoula with two bullets in the skull. Nance was never charged with this crime, but he remains the chief suspect.

On December 12, 1985, Mike and Teresa Shook were found murdered in their house in Ravalli County. The Shooks had been tied up and executed, and Teresa had been sexually assaulted and tortured. Then the house had been set on fire. Possessions stolen from the Shook household were later located in Nance's residence.

Crime author John Coston framed the terror gripping Missoula at that time in his book *To Kill and Kill Again*: "As word of this second murder spread, fed by rumor and exaggeration that further embellished the facts, Missoulians young and old were soon locked in a new, alien state of paranoia."

Law enforcement also claimed to be positive that Nance, at the height of his reign of terror, was the masked intruder who ambushed Janet Wicker in her apartment. Her assault had been interrupted when her husband arrived home. Alerted to his presence, Nance escaped the same way that he had arrived, sliding through the bedroom window.

Nobody knows who sexually abused and stabbed to death Siobhan McGuinness, a five-year-old Northside girl who disappeared only blocks from her home on the evening of February 5, 1974. Her body was found in a culvert near Turah. two days after she went missing. For decades law enforcement officials close to Nance's cases publicly stated that it was him, but in 2008 DNA evidence ruled out Nance as a suspect.

"A Killer is Killed"

After a revolving door of odd jobs in the mid-1980s, Nance landed a day job that he seemed to like at Conlin's Furniture in Missoula, where he made local deliveries and worked as a warehouseman. By 1986, though, he had developed a twisted obsession for Kris Wells, Conlin's manager, and had secretly put together an album of 35 photographs of her.

On Thursday, September 4, 1986, Kris and her husband, Doug Wells, were at home in bed. They had been up late watching television and reading when a meandering pair of bright headlights and the booming slam of a car door disrupted their quietude. There was a strange Ford pickup in the driveway of their west-side home, and Doug went to investigate. He spotted a man crouched down by the passenger-side window of the truck.

What followed was described in Costin's book:

> It was between midnight and 1 a.m. "Who's there?" [Doug] shouted. "Wayne from Conlin's Furniture," the man declared himself. Doug didn't question Nance, the trusted delivery man, who was standing in his front yard in the blackness. Nance entered the Wells's home under the pretense of needing a flashlight to find something he had lost in their yard. After entering the Wells' residence, Nance clubbed Doug in the back of the head and proceeded to the bedroom, where his wife, Kris, lay sleeping. He tied up both his victims, and stabbed Doug in the chest after dragging him to the basement. Doug was tied to a basement pillar.

According to published police and news accounts, while Nance tied Kris Wells to her bed upstairs, Doug managed to free himself and grab a .250 Savage rifle. He raced upstairs and cornered Nance in the bedroom. Doug shot Nance in the side with his only bullet. In the ensuing struggle, according to Sheriff Captain Larry Weatherman, Doug broke the rifle stock over Nance's head but Nance pulled out a .22 caliber pistol. Three shots were fired from the pistol: one hit Doug in the leg, another hit the ceiling, and the last struck Nance himself in the head, killing him. Kris and Doug Wells survived a harrowing nightmare. The terror of the Wayne Nance was over.

During the subsequent investigation, authorities found a box Nance had hidden in a corner of Conlin's warehouse. Inside the box were several photos of Kris Wells, along with other items. During a search of the East Missoula home that Nance shared with his father George, authorities found a ceramic bugling elk figurine and an elk-horn-handle Kelgin hunting knife that had been stolen from the home of Mike and Teresa Shook, linking Nance to their murders. The Shooks had visited Conlin's to buy furniture. It was later determined that Nance had used his job to carry out his sadistic sexual fantasies.

The city of Missoula exhaled a collective gasp of relief after learning that Nance was killed. Under the headline, "A Killer Is Killed—and a Fear Is Lifted," the *Missoulian* editors wrote: "Nance has been linked to the kinds of deliberate, meaningless, haunting crimes seldom seen in Montana…Horrible, tragic crimes now seem well on their way toward being solved, and western Montana may be a bit safer."

19

A CHILD WHO VANISHED

Clancy, 1983
Victim: Nyleen Kay Marshall
Case Status: Unsolved

On June 25, 1983, four-year-old Nyleen Kay Marshall disappeared while on a family outing in the Elkhorn Mountains near Helena. Barefoot, dressed only in a yellow T-shirt and shorts, Nyleen has never been seen since. COURTESY JEFFERSON COUNTY SHERIFF'S OFFICE.

ON JUNE 25, 1983, four-year-old Nyleen Kay Marshall went missing while on a family outing in the Elkhorn Mountains near her hometown of Alhambra, south of Helena. Daughter of Kim and Nancy Marshall, Nyleen was enjoying the day with relatives at a picnic. Barefoot, dressed only in a yellow T-shirt and shorts, Nyleen spent the afternoon chasing squirrels, trapping frogs, and jumping in the wet, spring mud.

One minute Nyleen was sitting alone near some beaver dams on Maupin Creek. When her friends turned around, Nyleen had vanished. She's never been seen since.

The other children told investigators they saw a strange man dressed in a jogging suit. The man stepped out from behind the trees. According to the statement of a six-year-old, that man told Nyleen to "follow the shadow," as if he were asking her to participate in a game.

No clues. No witnesses. No suspects. But what about the man in the jogging suit? Nyleen's family members denied the presence of such a person. The area was too open and too secluded for a stranger to go unnoticed at the picnic, they maintained. There was nothing solid that would lead investigators to believe that Nyleen's abduction was staged, or worse, that those who were responsible were those who were trusted to take care of her.

Nothing at first struck investigators as aberrant about Nyleen's parents, Nancy, a waitress at a restaurant, or her adoptive father, Kim, enrolled in electronics courses at Helena College UM. But investigators, incredulous that a stranger would be at the remote location of the abduction, wouldn't dismiss the possibility.

Nonetheless, an extensive search of the area turned up no indication of Nyleen's whereabouts. In addition to several police agencies, hundreds of volunteers searched the mountainous terrain. Search dogs from Great Falls, Billings, and Columbus were used extensively, and the Rocky Mountain Rescue Dog Team from Utah was flown in to assist. Airplanes and helicopters flew over the area and used infrared sensors to try to find the child through heat detection.

The organized search for the four-year-old was called off ten days later, the Fourth of July. She was barefoot, without a jacket, and there was snow on the ground. The little girl couldn't have survived, authorities concluded.

The Jefferson County Sheriff wrote in a prepared statement, "We have continued the search as long as there has been a reasonable chance that Nyleen would be found alive. After conferring with medical authorities throughout the nation, a decision was made to scale back the search effort. Heavy rains and low temperatures have made the youngster's survival virtually impossible according to the medical experts." Officials said that "any chances of foul play or kidnapping had been ruled out" because the area was "so isolated."

Despite the official statement, Nyleen is still strongly considered by many to be a possible abduction case. Suspicion of foul play was further supported by Nyleen's uncle, who believed that a composite sketch of a man and woman wanted for child abduction in another part of the country matched the profiles of a mysterious pair he spotted on the first day of the search for Nyleen. The uncle said that the suspicious couple who had participated in the search for Nyleen didn't seem like they were from the area. But other than a basic gut reaction, there wasn't much else to support his allegation, and police dropped his theory.

Letters, Phone Calls from Possible Abductor

Beginning six months after her disappearance, Nyleen's parents received three letters from someone claiming to be their daughter's abductor.

Two and a half years later, a typewritten letter, postmarked in Madison, Wisconsin, was mailed to investigators. The author claimed that he had been raising Nyleen under her middle name, Kay, and had taken her with him on his frequent travels. The man claimed that he and "Kay" lived off substantial investments and that the girl was well-traveled and home schooled. A person believed to be the same as the letter writer also phoned missing children networks to talk about the case, and made suggestions of activities that law enforcement officials described as probable sexual abuse.

All the letters and phone calls were believed to have originated in Wisconsin, and authorities believed that they had located the phone booth where the calls originated. However, some authorities were convinced that the correspondent wasn't Nyleen's abductor, but a despicable, sick prankster.

Subsequent claimed sightings of Nyleen, well-meaning yet most likely baseless, placed the girl in several different states. Amazingly, a tip from a viewer who saw the November 1990 episode of *Unsolved Mysteries* and believed one of his classmates was Nyleen Marshall led to another missing child being found. Monica Bonilla, who was abducted by her noncustodial father, Guillermo, was returned to her mother after being missing for nearly eight years.

Other than the occasional remembrance profile in the local newspapers, no activity was reported on the Nyleen Marshall case. Then, in 1991, a former Helena resident named Richard James Wilson, at the time age 42, turned himself into authorities in Livingston and confessed to killing Nyleen and at least one other woman. Officials said that they were skeptical of Wilson's claims, but authorities from three counties fully investigated his story. "We're not discounting what he has to say. We're looking into his statements," Jefferson County Sheriff Tom Dawson said.

Wilson, who had been on probation since a 1984 conviction in Lewis and Clark County for sexual assault against a minor, had his probation revoked. Officials, however, determined that there was no credence to either of Wilson's dark claims.

Using photographs of Nyleen, several age progression illustrations have been made throughout the decades. Still, no one has ever come forward with her whereabouts.

Nyleen's family has been questioned and re-questioned extensively about her disappearance. Her stepfather, Kim, according to the Jefferson County Sheriff's Office, was considered "a person of interest in her case" and has never been removed from that designation.

Nyleen's mother, Nancy, died in 1995; it was reported she was sexually assaulted and murdered in Mexico.

20

THE SUSPICIOUS DISAPPEARANCE OF A PRIEST

Ronan, 1984
Victim: John Patrick Kerrigan
Case Status: Unsolved

Shortly before 11 p.m. on July 20, 1984, Father John Patrick Kerrigan walked into a popular bakery in Ronan and visited with the late-night crowd. He was never seen again, except by his killer, who remains unknown. Kerrigan was later listed as a pedophile priest. COURTESY MONTANA HISTORICAL SOCIETY.

SHORTLY BEFORE 11 P.M. on July 20, 1984, Father John Patrick Kerrigan walked into Deneault's Bakery on 4th Avenue Southwest in Ronan. It was a Friday evening that flirted with freezing temperatures, the kind of chilly summer night well-known to people living in the Mission Mountains. The Ronan assignment was Kerrigan's 13th church since he started ministering 30 years earlier. The next day, he was scheduled to deliver his first sermon as the "permanent pastor" at Sacred Heart Parish, located across the street from the bakery.

Wearing red shorts, a white T-shirt, and tennis shoes, Kerrigan greeted the late-night gathering of locals at Deneault's. The 58-year-old priest made an impression on bakery owner and parish member Bob Deneault, who took notice of the man's "broad smile" and observed that at 6 feet, 200 pounds, Kerrigan appeared physically fit "but from his nature it appeared he couldn't harm anyone," according to a newspaper interview he later gave.

Several patrons chatted amiably with the priest, who told them that he was enjoying the brisk summer air and that there was no better way to get acquainted with Ronan than by taking an evening walk. He also informed them that he planned to attend a funeral and a wedding in Plains the following day. Saturday was going to be a full, exciting one. He then headed home to the red-brick Catholic rectory next to his new church.

The following day, members of Ronan's Sacred Heart Parish gathered for 5:30 p.m. Mass. More than 100 parishioners were there, eager to meet their new pastor. Sacred Heart Catholic Church had gone without its own priest since April, and though Kerrigan had transferred from Plains, only about an hour's drive away, most of the attendees knew little or near nothing about him.

Fifteen minutes elapsed, and impatience filled the church. How could he miss his first service? Most of the parishioners began clearing out, hopping into their vehicles and dispersing from Round Butte Road into the starry dusk, although several expressed concerned and called the rectory. No answer.

When Kerrigan also failed to show up for the Sunday morning Mass, the collective concern of parishioners deepened. "He would never miss his weekend liturgies — he just would never miss," Connie Erickson, at the time an administrative assistant to the chancellor in the Helena Diocese, later said on an episode of nationally televised *Unsolved Mysteries.*

Sunday night the first phone calls from parishioners trickled into the Lake County Sheriff's Department, and on Monday, July 23, Father Kerrigan was legally declared "missing." Then a woman setting up a roadside fruit stand in the area made a grisly discovery. As she unloaded crates of produce, she saw something red that might have been roadkill, perhaps a small animal carcass. But when she stepped closer, she saw it was a pile of bloody garments.

The small blood-soaked mound of clothes seemed to have been intentionally stacked alongside Montana Highway 35, five miles northeast of Polson. Placed at a turnout along on the east shore of Flathead Lake, the pile included a shirt, shoes, and a windbreaker. A $100 bill was stuffed in one shirt pocket, and "his wallet, containing about $200, was left with his clothes," according to published news reports. While not the same clothes that he had worn to the bakery, crime lab reports discovered that hair found on the items matched Kerrigan's. Near the abandoned clothes, authorities found a blood-splattered and "deformed" wire hanger, an object that might have been used to strangle or hold down the priest.

About one week after Kerrigan went missing, his Chevy Impala was found at the base of the radio towers off Skyline Drive, overlooking Polson several miles away from the rectory and just a few miles south of where his blood-stained clothes ad been stacked. The large, boxy-looking Impala had "been wiped clean of fingerprints," according to police and Associated Press reports. But there were copious amounts of blood on the car's interior and inside the trunk. Heavy smatterings of blood were in the front seat, on the passenger-side door, and spread across the passenger-side floorboard. In the trunk, police discovered a blood-drenched pillow, a bloodied shovel, and "Kerrigan's wallet, stuffed with more than $1,000 in cash." (Press accounts of Kerrigan's case are riddled with inconsistencies, including varying reports as to the location of Kerrigan's wallet and the amount it contained.) The keys to the car were said to be found in weeds about 30 yards away.

Hearsay and fear hovered over the Mission Valley like a glum inversion, and for good reason. The priest's presumed murder was just one of several frightening events to unfold in the area within a single week. On the same day that Kerrigan visited Deneault's Bakery, four inmates had fled in a state-owned vehicle from the minimum-security unit of the Montana State Prison at the Swan River Youth Camp, about 50 miles to the northeast. Two of the escapees kidnapped and raped a woman in Evaro. And in an unrelated incident, on July 22, 18-year-old Reed Nevins murdered a 41-year-old woman in her Polson home.

Moreover, rumors circulated that a serial killer of priests was on the hunt and that Kerrigan's fate was connected to the disappearance of an Episcopal priest in Townsend two years earlier. Reverend James Otis Anderson had been last seen driving east on Highway 12 towards White Sulphur Springs on the morning of June 13, 1982. He too failed to show up for services at his church. The two priests were said to be friends and had worked together in White Sulphur Springs at the same time. Now both were gone.

"Social Autopsy" of the Father

Despite red-hot speculation and an abundance of DNA evidence, the Kerrigan investigation chilled within months. Paul Choma, the chief investigator in the case, told the Associated Press that he had been surprised at the reluctance of many, including church officials, to provide critical information that he had to "learn from other sources."

"They are nowhere with the investigation, and it leaves people very sad and frustrated," Father Ernest Burns of Polson told the *Missoulian* in the fall of 1984. Deneault, the bakery owner, said for several months the priest's whereabouts were "the prime topic of conversation."

Police conducted what's now commonly referred to as a "social autopsy" or a "victimology" assessment, scouring the past life of the priest in search of clues into why he seemed to be targeted. The report was initially unspectacular. Born January 10, 1926,

John Patrick Kerrigan was a Butte native and attended St. Joseph Grade School and Central High School there before going to Seattle, where he attended St. Edward's Seminary. He was ordained in Butte and began work in the city's St. Patrick's Church in 1954.

"He loved rural parishes," Father James Gannon of Stevensville told the Associated Press in 1984. Gannon, who said Kerrigan assisted him for a couple of years in Dillon in the early 1960s, recalled Kerrigan as "outgoing" and said he "developed many friendships across the state."

But something about Kerrigan's transience, his shuttling from parish to parish, aroused the suspicions of detectives. After all, Ronan was Kerrigan's 13th parish assignment. After his first assignment in Butte, he was sent to Hamilton and then back to Butte, then Dillon, Butte again, and then to Browning, Bozeman, Drummond, White Sulphur Springs, Choteau, and eventually to St. James Parish in Plains from 1980 to 1984.

There was another curious stopping point on Kerrigan's trail: he had spent time in New Mexico at a rehabilitation center for wayward clergy. Why had he been sent to the Congregation of the Servants of the Paraclete in Jemez Springs? It troubled investigators to learn that the priests who were at Jemez Springs were there for alcoholism, depression, or sexual delinquency. Could the key to Kerrigan's death be extrapolated from the details of some clerical abuse or excess?

Indeed, investigators uncovered a dark side to the priest with the "broad smile," and they started to operate under a belief that perhaps it was the priest's own shadowy interior that sealed his fate.

Possible Connection to New Mexico Murder

Investigator Choma told the Associated Press that he contacted New Mexico authorities after he discovered that Kerrigan had been in the state nine months after the body of Father Renaldo

Riverawas found on a remote desert road outside of Santa Fe. On the night of August 7, 1982, according to church officials, Rivera answered a phone call from a man who was desperately seeking "the last rites" of a loved one. Three days later, Rivera's body was found, riddled with bullets. Rivera's sacrament bag, wallet, and glasses were never found. His car was located at a rest stop. The keys were missing.

There are several parallels between Father Rivera's murder and the evidence relating to Kerrigan's disappearance. Some are compelling: wire coat hangers were believed to have been used in both murders; robbery was excluded as a motive; both priests were members of the Order of Franciscans. Kerrigan was 58; Rivera was 57. Rivera's body was discovered near a road a few miles out of town, as was Kerrigan's bloody clothing. Both victims' cars were apparently driven away from the crime scene, then wiped clean of fingerprints and abandoned. There were also broader resemblances: both men died in the summer, one shortly before August 1, the other less than a week after. Both drove brown Chevrolets.

For several years, New Mexico authorities publicly sparred over the relevance of the Montana case to their investigation. Santa Fe Deputy Police Chief Gilbert Ulibarri told the Santa Fe *New Mexican* that he had "a gut feeling" the disappearance of the Montana priest and the killing of Father Rivera were tied to the same individual, perhaps even a serial killer. New Mexico State Police detective Eric Lucero rejected his counterpart's claim, telling the newspaper in 1994 that there was "no connection whatsoever." Ulibarri countered, "Whoever killed Kerrigan left his clothes in a neat pile right by the road. If he didn't want people to know (Kerrigan) had been killed, why would he leave the clothes there?"

When *Unsolved Mysteries* aired its segment on Father Rivera in 1988, the television program focused on similarities with the Montana case. During the segment, detective sergeant Bruce Phillips of the Lake County (Montana) Sheriff's Office once again eliminated robbery as a motive: "The money was not hidden, so we don't feel that robbery was a motive for this particular crime."

Several callers directed investigators' attention to other killings of priests or ministers. But after publicity from the show subsided, the tips dried up.

Possible Connection to Other Mysteries

In the summer of 1985, Lake County's new sheriff, Joe Geldrich, reported progress in solving the Kerrigan case. He wouldn't name the suspect but did say the man was "not in Montana."Geldrich said he was waiting "for the accumulation of additional evidence before taking action," and noted that "the chances of solving the case look very good." Yet, there was no follow-up report on that progress, and that was the last time such a rosy prognostication was made as to finding Kerrigan's killer.

While Kerrigan's name surfaced occasionally as a footnote in the larger context of the Father Rivera slaying, no direct connection between Father Rivera's murder in New Mexico and Father Kerrigan was ever established. Furthermore, there wasn't enough evidence to link the four escapees from the Montana youth camp (who were all apprehended within a week) to the Kerrigan's disappearance, and while Nevins, who murdered a Polson woman in her home, had been in Ronan the night that Kerrigan vanished, there was no evidence of his involvement.

Nor could police establish any criminal association between Kerrigan's case and the disappearance of Reverend Anderson in Townsend two years earlier. Anderson was reported to have been suffering from mental health problems and "may have been facing termination from his position in the church," according to a 1988 Lee Newspapers story. In October 1992, 10 years after his disappearance, Anderson's Volkswagen was found abandoned in the Big Belt Mountains northeast of Townsend. His body has never been located.

One other case tantalized investigators due to its proximity and time frame: Two days after Kerrigan was last seen, a 31-year-old schoolteacher named Curtis Holmen went missing from Missoula. Holmen, a math teacher at Target Range Elementary School, was last seen in Missoula on July 22, 1984. Twelve days later, his Toyota pickup truck was found abandoned on a logging road around Placid Lake. Authorities suspected Holmen had taken his own life, and he was later declared dead. But Holmen's brother fueled greater speculation when he told a reporter that the fate of his despondent sibling might have been linked to Father Kerrigan's.

Father Kerrigan Listed as a "Child Sexual Predator"

Conjecture over Kerrigan's death reemerged in April 2015 when the Roman Catholic Diocese of Helena settled a large civil suit alleging that several priests had been sexual abusers. The lawsuit charged that church leaders had been repeatedly reassigning those priests to new parishes, giving them no punishment but an admonition to quit molesting. Church hierarchy agreed to a financial settlement and disclosed the identities of 80 former employees, most of them priests and nuns, "who had allegedly sexually abused children in western Montana." Kerrigan was on the Roman Catholic Diocese of Helena's list of "child sexual predators."

Geldrich, the former Lake County sheriff who started working the case in 1985, told the *Missoulian* shortly after the church's report was released that even back then "authorities were aware" of allegations of child sexual abuse involving Kerrigan, but he dismissed the theory that a victim of Kerrigan's acted out of revenge. When contacted twice in 2020, Geldrich reiterated the same line of reasoning as he did in 2015, and emphasized that he didn't want "to reveal anything that might hurt the boys' chances of solving this thing."

21

"MOUNTAIN MEN" MAYHEM AND MURDER

Big Sky, 1984
Victim: Alan Goldstein
Case Status: Solved

On July 16, 1984, two self-styled mountain men, a father and son named Don and Dan Nichols, abducted world-class American biathlete Kari Swenson at gunpoint while she did a training run on a forest road near Big Sky. The kidnappers, who lived in the wilds, hunting, raising some food and stealing the rest, intended to found a "tribe" and planned some type of "mountain-man marriage" between Swenson and the son, 19-year-old Dan. They bound Swenson's hands and led her off into the timber, expecting that she, with a smidge of forceful persuasion, would become a willing bride.

Life of the "Mountain Men"

Maggie Engelmann had three children by Pat Nichols. The youngest of the three, Don Nichols, was born in either Kansas or Sterling, Montana, in 1931 (Don Nichols' manifesto alternates both places as his birth site). During the Depression, Pat Nichols moved his family to Montana, where they lived around the towns of Norris and Harrison. Pat and his brother found work at one of the gold mines near Norris, the Boaz Gold Mine, Don Nichols later recalled in a manifesto. Pat Nichols and his brother died one night when their car failed to handle a corner on their way back from a party in Ennis. Maggie Nichols took in laundry and did sewing for the miners. After a while, Maggie remarried another miner, Steve Engelmann, and sometime during WWII, the Engelmanns moved ten miles up the valley to the ranching community of Harrison.

After high school, Don Nichols joined the Navy for an eight-year detail, got married, and moved to West Virginia, where he worked as an assayer.

Ten years later, he returned to Montana, bought a cabin near Bozeman, and began raising hogs. He and his wife divorced in 1971 and his wife received custody of their two children, Barb and Dan, but Don could spend several weeks with his son Dan each summer. After the divorce, Don worked in various Wyoming and Montana towns, sometimes at machine shops or lumber mills. In 1980, Don was arrested and charged with "violating the terms of his visitation privileges" for failing to return Dan to his mother at the agreed time.

Dan was a troubled boy and a poor student in school. He dropped out of high school during his junior year and moved to Jackson, Wyoming, to live with his father.

When Dan was 18 years old, he and father moved into the Beartrap Mountains. They had several remote camps stocked with provisions and carefully concealed, and they had at least one underground hideout. Come the summer of 1984, the pair was living self-sufficiently, off-the-grid in the mountains, poaching game and growing hidden gardens at their various camps. Their contact with other humans was minimal. If encountered by hikers, hunters, or local ranchers, the men gave off the appearance of recluses preoccupied with enterprises they did not wish to divulge. Most people took the cue and left them alone.

Kari Swenson (right) of Bozeman was one of the top female biathletes in the world when she was kidnapped by so-called "mountain men" at Big Sky in 1984. In a rescue attempt by two of her friends, she was wounded and one of her friends was killed. COURTESY BOZEMAN HISTORICAL SOCIETY.

Kari Swenson

Kari was born in Philadelphia, Pennsylvania, where her father headed Temple University's physics department. When she was nine, her family moved to Bozeman, where she excelled in high school sports. When Kari was a junior, she picked up the sport of biathlon, a combination of cross-country skiing and rifle marksmanship, and quickly rose to become one of the top female biathletes in the world. In 1984, she finished fifth in the 10-kilometer race at the inaugural Women's Biathlon World Championships in Chamonix, France. She was also a member of the U.S. women's relay team, which won bronze in Chamonix.

Then came the summer and the Mountain Men.

Abduction of Swenson; Murder of Rescuer

On July 16, 1984, Kari Swenson was running the trails at the Lone Mountain Ranch. After she did not return home from her training run, her friends fanned out through the woods looking for her. They did not yet notify authorities. Assuming that at the very worst she sprained a knee or even broke an ankle, they expected to find their hobbled friend within hours. But what she had actually encountered was far more sinister, far more dangerous.

Swenson later wrote: "I endured being grabbed by both wrists, hit in the face, thrown to the ground, chained to Dan, threatened with knives and guns, marched through the woods, secured like an animal to trees and spent a terrifying night chained next to Dan. During the night we could hear searchers calling for me, and I was told repeatedly by Don and Dan that anyone coming into their camp would be shot and killed. This kept me quiet and hopeful that no one would find me."

The following morning two of the searchers, Alan Goldstein, 36, and Jim Schwalbe, 30, stumbled upon the Nichols campsite. Goldstein carried a pistol and pointed it at the Nichols but hesitated to pull the trigger. In that pause, Don Nichols, age 53, raised his rifle and shot Goldstein, killing him. Don Nichols later claimed self-defense and blamed Goldstein for his own death. He wrote that he "could see no alternative." He wrote that Goldstein had a pistol pointed at them, so he moved his rifle "over to where I thought it was pointed at the upper part of the middle of the chest and pulled the trigger and knew that one of us would be dead in the next second or two."

In the ensuing melee, 19-year-old Dan shot Swenson in the chest, apparently by accident. Schwalbe, the other searcher, escaped down the mountainside. Swenson later said the Nichols placed her in a sleeping bag and eventually "left her to die."

Bleeding from the chest wound, Swenson lay alone for hours with only Goldstein's body nearby. She did not know that Schwalbe had sounded the alarm and was leading rescuers, including law enforcement, back to the campsite. Weak but conscious, Swenson was evacuated to a hospital, and a search began for the Nicholses, who had disappeared into the Spanish Peaks Wilderness.

Goldstein, a native of the Midwest, was buried in Royal Oak, Michigan, his home state, leaving behind a wife and young daughter.

Capture of the Mountain Men

Madison County Sheriff Johnny France became the person chiefly responsible for directing the manhunt. At one point early on, he told an interviewer, "In my own way, I'm a mountain man too. It'll take one to catch one. I'll get them." France was once a champion bronco rider.

For four days following Swenson's rescue, the search used helicopters, police SWAT teams, and search dogs. Warnings describing the Nicholses as armed and dangerous were posted at trailheads leading into the mountains, next to the customary warnings about grizzly bears. Nothing was found.

According to France's account in the book he later wrote called *Incident at Big Sky*, France called off the large manhunt on July 20, limiting the search to himself and his deputies. Kidnapping charges were filed against both Nicholses, and Don Nichols was charged with murder and aggravated assault.

Roland Moore, who was married to Sheriff France's stepsister, ultimately provided Johnny with the Nichols' location, the pointer that led to the outlaws' capture. On December 13, 1984, Roland was out alone in the woods, "breaking ice on a stock tank," and he was certain that he saw a pair of men who must have been the Mountain Men hiking a ridgeline near his home at Bear Trap Canyon.

The capture plan called for a large, coordinated assault named Operation Barnstorm, but the helicopters for it weren't immediately available. France feared the Nichols would escape if too much time passed, so, as he later wrote in his account of the situation, he went after them alone.

Dressed in a white snow camouflage and carrying a .223 semi-automatic rifle as if he were a coyote hunter, France drove a snowmobile as close as he could to the location of the small, isolated structure described by Roland Moore. Then he went on foot. Snowshoeing several miles, France passed a large herd of mule deer.

He noticed boot prints crossing the snow on top of the fresh deer tracks and followed them.

Through a cluster of trees, he saw Dan and Don cooking venison in a skillet over a fire. France had stalked the pair for nearly five months. He approached them and said, "Any coyotes around here lately?" Don Nichols reached for his gun. France drew his rifle on him and said, "Don't do anything stupid. Don't make me kill you." The Nichols surrendered.

On May 14, 1985, Dan Nichols was convicted of kidnapping and misdemeanor assault but found innocent of murder. He was sentenced to 20 years in prison. On July 12, 1985, Don Nichols was convicted of murder, kidnapping, and aggravated assault. He was sentenced to 85 years in prison.

Dan Nichols Paroled

Less than six years after he was sent away, the younger Nichols was released from prison. In 1991, the state Board of Pardons Chairman Henry Burgess of Helena said Nichols, 26, had met all the requirements set by the board to qualify for parole.

Montana Attorney General Marc Racicot, who had prosecuted the original case as a county attorney, urged the board to deny Nichols' release. Nichols' attorney, Steve Ungar of Bozeman, said the board made the just decision because Nichols was "a different man" than he was in 1984. "Dan Nichols poses absolutely no threat to the Swensons or any other members of society," Ungar told the media. "His crime was highly situational, and he has changed over the past six years."

In the summer of 1996, Dan Nichols married a woman named Liz in a "pagan fundamentalist" ceremony in the mountains southeast of Great Falls. In 1996 Liz Nichols told Reuters news service that she never questioned Nichols about Swenson's kidnapping or about prison. "After all, it's not the kind of thing you can say, 'Oh, and by the way, honey,'" she said.

Parole Hearing of "Crazy Misfits"

In 2012, at a parole hearing for Don Nichols (his third attempt), Kari Swenson argued against the release of the self-styled mountain men who had abducted her. She wrote in a letter that Don and his son were "crazy misfits" and argued that the 81-year-old Nichols should not be paroled. Society did not benefit by releasing Nichols, she wrote.

In her letter, Swenson, who had long refused to discuss the incident publicly, rebuffed the "mountain man" label applied to Nichols, writing that the term implied they were "hardworking outdoorsmen" and legitimized their pursued of an unconventional life. "Ultimately they were caught without a fight because they were cold, hungry, and tired of living in the mountains. These are not mountain men," wrote Swenson.

Swenson wrote that Don Nichols' "crazy, mixed-up mind" is evident in the muddled journals he wrote where he blames others for the crime. Swenson said the pair deliberately "left her to die."

Swenson said she spent years in counseling dealing with post-traumatic stress disorder, and that the shrapnel in her chest still caused pain, a burning reminder of "that awful day."

"This is not justice," Swenson wrote. "I do not believe anyone could want him free and living in or around their communities. If he is released, I hope no one ever has to meet him on a street, in the mountains of Montana or anywhere."

Swenson noted that at the time of Don's parole hearing, federal agents had filed drug charges against Dan, who was on the run and considered "armed and dangerous" by the U.S. Marshal for Montana.

"Since [Dan's] release from prison he's been unable to assimilate back into society and become a productive citizen. Where is he? He could be anywhere," Swenson wrote to the parole board in 2012. "If the parole board lets Don out of prison, they might end up back in the mountains of Montana together and who will be their next victim?"

In the end, the board denied parole for Don Nichols in 2012.

More trouble for Dan Nichols

Around that time, Dan Nichols had already absconded from charges stemming from an apparent drug deal he was making during a rock concert in Three Forks. Nichols was spotted selling marijuana at Rockin' the Rivers and was arrested after a short struggle. Nichols failed to appear in court on multiple charges of drug possession and intent to distribute.

In May 2012, Nichols phoned the U.S. Marshals Service and told them he would be in the Wal-Mart parking lot in Butte between 2 p.m. and 3 p.m., according to Butte-Silver Bow Sheriff John Walsh. Nichols showed up as promised in a 1982 red Honda Prelude with Bozeman license plates and was arrested without incident.

In January 2013 Dan Nichols was sentenced to four years in prison after being arrested in 2011 during a federal sting of 26medical marijuana locations in Montana. He was a security guard at one of the locations. He was placed in the custody of the U.S. Bureau of Prisons for his guilty plea to conspiracy to maintain a drug-involved premises. According to court documents, Nichols provided security for a Helena greenhouse "where 950 plants along with processed marijuana and marijuana products were confiscated."

In January 2013, Dan Nichols, the son of "mountain man" Don Nichols, was sentenced to four years in federal prison for his role as a security guard at a medical marijuana operation. Courtesy Montana Department of Corrections.

Don Nichols' Manifesto, Parole in 2017

For many years, Don Nichols stewed in his prison cell, convinced that he and his son did nothing illegal or criminal. He claimed their abduction of Swenson was "distorted by the media" and his shooting of Goldstein was "self-defense."

In 1993, Don Nichols sent the Associated Press a 242-page manuscript about "the incident." Much of Nichols' manifesto centered on his view about life and his disdain for a justice system that he maintained treated him and his son wrongly. "I don't know how we'd have gotten Kari to come with us if she hadn't decided to cooperate. The main thing is that we didn't want to shake any girl up real bad," Nichols wrote in his "book." Nichols claimed that Swenson lied about him threatening to strike her, but despite that assertion, he recalled striking Swenson when she resisted. "I barely tapped her on the lips...I slapped her three times with my fingertips and said shut up three times. She shut up."

Eventually, Don Nichols served about 32 years for kidnapping Swenson and killing Goldstein. Parole board members weighed Nichols' long, clean record in prison and his completion of educational programs, including anger management and life skills. Nichols, 86 at the time of his parole in April 2017, lives in Great Falls and reports to a parole officer. His terms of parole stipulated that he wear a GPS monitoring device and register as a violent offender.

Aftermath

The attack on Kari Swenson drew widespread media coverage and became the subject of several films and books, including a widely panned, exploitative made-for-TV movie in 1987. John J. O'Connor of the *N.Y. Times News Service* called *The Abduction of Kari Swenson* a "fact-based but faintly silly" production, an interesting story about a harrowing experience that "keeps toppling over into unnecessary titillation or exaggeration:"

> In fact, this sort of story, and the use of the word "abduction" attracts considerable attention primarily for one reason. It immediately raises the more sensational question: Was the victim raped? And William Gray's teleplay, directed by Stephen Gyllenhaal, manages to keep the question simmering for three-quarters of the movie. Near the conclusion of the drama, Swenson is rushed to a hospital and the first thing she blurts out to assuage her distraught mother was that she wasn't raped.

Swenson, despite diminished lung capacity from the gunshot wound, went on to win a bronze medal in the world biathlon championships. She is currently a veterinarian in Bozeman. In an ESPN podcast in 2019, Swenson spoke candidly of her frightening kidnapping and shooting, as well as the difficulty of her recovery. "I wasn't going to let this define who I was," she said.

22

RANDOM ACTS OF VIOLENCE

Great Falls, 1985-1986
Victims: Morris Davis Jr.,
Suzette Pritchard
Case Status: Davis Jr. (Unsolved);
Pritchard (Solved)

On the night of April 5, 1985, Great Falls pizza delivery man Morris Davis Jr. was shot several times and killed when delivering an order to a house that turned out to be vacant. Was he set up, was it a robbery that went bad, or was it a kill for thrills? No arrests have been made. COURTESY CASCADE COUNTY SHERIFF'S OFFICE.

On the night of April 5, 1985, Great Falls pizza delivery man Morris Davis Jr. was shot and killed when he delivered an order to a vacant house.

Morris, 23, lived at home with his mother, Delnita, in Great Falls. His younger brother, Clifford Davis, became an EMT and enjoyed working on the ambulance core. The two brothers were close, and Morris, "big, shy, and quiet," loved to hunt and fish, and was described as outdoorsy.

"I never worried about him (Morris) when he went out because he was so big," recalled his mother Delnita.

Sometime after 8:30 p.m. on April 5, a phone order came into Howard's Pizza and Davis was the next driver in the delivery rotation. He was never seen alive again. Another delivery driver, who was sent to the house to look for Davis, found his body. Davis had been shot multiple times.

Meanwhile, Great Falls police and medical services had responded to the sounds of gunshots at 1015 6th Ave. NW. Soon after, two hours into his shift as a paramedic, Clifford Davis and his partner took a distress call for the same place. The frantic dispatcher stated that a man had been shot to death inside of a vacant house.

The paramedics and police found a grisly drama: blood in the entryway, a pizza box lying inside the door—unopened and undisturbed, a bullet shell casing sparkling off to the right. At the backdoor to the house, EMT technicians and police noted broken pieces of glass, apparently from a forced entry. The "For Sale" sign that had been in the front of the house had been moved inside.

No amount of training prepares first responders for what Clifford Davis encountered. "There were rainstorms that night," Clifford Davis later told the television program *Unsolved Mysteries.* "It was very wet outside. It was very dark that night. As you enter, you are trying to process what you are thinking. One of the officers had a flashlight in one of his hands and a weapon in the other. I could see the light beam hit the boots of the victim, and I noticed that those boots were the ones I bought for my brother for the Christmas just prior to that. At that point the world slowed down and stopped. I had no idea when I'd first arrived if he was alive or dead."

Morris Davis had no pulse or vital signs. He wasn't breathing. En route to the hospital, he died.

Sergeant John Cameron determined that Morris had been mercilessly ambushed at the front door. According to authorities, Morris was shot multiple times, ran out and fell on the front steps, and then was dragged back into the house by the killer, who put final shots into his head. All total, the assailant shot Davis nine times with a small caliber weapon.

Police initially suspected that Morris was intentionally targeted. The level of overkill couldn't have suggested otherwise. In fact, everything about the crime scene suggested an execution. They wondered if the shooting death of the 23-year-old deliveryman was an act of revenge, or a paid assassination.

But even with that theory in the mind, the details of the shooting weren't cohesive. Police were baffled by the cold-blooded randomness. How could someone have known that Morris would be the driver making the delivery? Why had the suspect broken into the house, set up an ambush, and fled the scene with Davis' printed receipts and paper pads, but not taken the cash inside of Morris's work-issued wallet?

Indicating that police at first leaned heavily on their assassination theory, one deputy said it would take "a real good tip" to solve the murder. He said the shooting appeared to be a set-up and was "a real slick operation."

Less than 24 hours after Morris had been shot to death, Great Falls police raced to another 9-1-1- call. There was a man with a rifle on the Southside, holed up in a house, firing rounds out the window. After an intense standoff, police convinced the shooter to surrender. They soon confirmed that the gunman had nothing to do with the Davis murder.

New clues suggested the murderer might have been a serial killer or a spree killer. Police determined that the phone used to order the pizza was most likely made from a location near the pizza joint. They even suggested that the killer was voyeuristically watching the restaurant.

Pizza employees recalled seeing three young men at the same phone booth at the time of the murder. They were identified as the Lewis brothers. According to published police reports, "the Lewis brothers were a troubled bunch of young adults who lived across from the crime scene." They became the number one suspects. They had been seen at the house earlier in the day. After police hauled them in, the men were uncooperative. One of the brothers said he was out burglarizing a house at the time of the murder, which was confirmed by the owner of the house. Police stated that, although they were "never able to get rock solid alibis on the other two, we let them go."

Police on Davis Murder: "It's going to be a tough one."

"My brother was extremely well-liked," said Clifford Davis. "Detectives could not think of anybody who would ever have a reason to kill him."

Reward money from Crimestoppers, the Cascade County Tavern Owners Association, Howard's Pizza, and public contributions soon totaled more than $7,000. The hope of finding information, however, grew dimmer each passing day.

Police detective Sgt. Bob Jones said months later that there was still some hope of solving the murder, though he conceded to the *Great Falls Tribune* that there had been "no solid leads for quite some time."

"It's going to be a tough one," Deputy Sheriff John Strandell told the *Great Falls Tribune* on the one-year anniversary of Morris's slaying, adding that a number of anonymous tips had been given through Crimestoppers, but none of them was solid. "The police department has been following hard on it, but they haven't been able to substantiate anything," Strandell said. "It's just dead-end information."

Strandell said there had been no Crimestoppers calls on the Morris homicide for almost a month. "We're still looking for anything we can get," he said. "It gets tougher as we go with the increased time period."

A break in the case seemed imminent three years after the murder when a receipt for a .22 caliber pistol sold to a Great Falls pawn shop was found on the driver of a stolen car more than 180 miles away from Great Falls. Authorities learned that the gun had been stolen from a man living in Oregon. Ballistics analysis linked the gun to the Davis homicide, although the soundness of those examinations has been called into question. According to published police accounts, "Both the man who stole the gun and the man it was stolen from have been cleared of any involvement in the murder."

As time frittered away, police considered the possibility that a 1986 murder of a Great Falls convenience store clerk could be connected to the Morris Davis case.

Suzette Pritchard Slaying

October 6, 1986. One year after the Morris Davis murder, and two miles away from where Morris had been gunned down, 18-year-old Suzette Pritchard started her night-shift job at Keith's Town Pump. It was the kind of neighborhood that didn't reflect well on the city—which is to say, it was slatternly, sour factory smelling, and cheap. Suzette, an identical triplet, was working her first shift alone. Before, she always had someone training her. A hard worker, Suzette was attending a Baptist college to become a religious schoolteacher.

Some of Suzette's friends came by to see her and remembered an "eerie man" standing by the microwave. He was described as a "creep" with a "distinct limp and a dirty beat-up red vehicle." Regrettably, there were no surveillance cameras inside or outside of the store to preserve the image of the man or his car.

After 1 a.m. Suzette's friends decided to head home for the night. At 1:21 another friend stopped by and didn't hear or see anything in the store. She looked behind the counter and Suzette was on the floor looking up, her eyes open, blood coming out of her mouth. The killer had stabbed her 24 times with a Buck knife. Less than $300 was missing from the register.

Quickly after the heinous discovery of Suzette, Great Falls police stationed squad cars on the city's exits and bridges. Sergeant Cameron pulled over a car similar to the one seen by Suzette's friends at the gas station. The two men in the car were "no strangers to authorities," according to Cameron, who later blogged about the case on his personal website." But neither man fit the description and they were released.

According to the available media and police reports, "One of Suzette's co-workers, Jay Green, who called in sick the night of the murder, bore an uncanny resemblance to the freshly circulated composite sketch." One picture jumped out at one of the witnesses: a photo of Green. He had a domestic abuse charge, which would fit the profile of someone who might have killed Suzette.

Green offered an alibi which couldn't be corroborated. But he didn't walk with a distinct limp and didn't at all match the physical description of the "creepy" man. Cameron chalked up the apprehension of Green as a case of mistaken identity.

Two Cold Cases

There was more to the crimes perpetrated on Suzette and Morris than simply robbing somebody: both crimes were vicious examples of excess.

"They were both overkills," said Morris's mother, Delnita Davis. "Morris was shot more times than he needed to be. She was stabbed more times than she needed to be. I thought that same person had probably done it."

Cameron told a local TV news station that there was no way that Suzette had been specifically selected. "She was outstanding, clean-cut, and a really good kid. This had nothing to do with Suzette and the family."

Eventually both murders became cold cases. Without a solid clue, investigators had little to work with. There were no good suspects.

"Being a cold case hurts," said Delnita Davis. "It makes you feel as if your child isn't worth something."

"I would say that we interviewed hundreds and hundreds of people and the case file itself is massive," says John Cameron, in 2020. "But it just never went anywhere."

In December 1990, a leadoff segment about Morris on the NBC television show *Unsolved Mysteries* prompted 176 telephone calls offering information on the case. The morning after the broadcast, the Great Falls Police Department received about a dozen calls "from all over," though detective Al Redenbaugh noted to the Associated Press that it was too early to evaluate their merit.

The airing of *Unsolved Mysteries* may have had unintended deadly consequences: within a week of the broadcast a young deliveryman working for Domino's Pizza in Billings was murdered. Detective Al Redenbaugh of the Great Falls Police Department commented on the eerie similarities of the cases but stopped short of calling the Billings case a copycat of the 1985 slaying or that the crime was carried out by the same person.

Likely Suspect Emerges

In 1996, police received a letter from one of the men who was stopped in the car by Sergeant Cameron the night of Suzette's murder. The letter writer said that it had always bothered him that a man named Donnie DuBray was in Great Falls at the time of the murder, and that DuBray, too, had a car similar to the killer's car. And on top of this, DuBray had gotten rid of the car shortly after the murder happened.

DuBray was from the Blackfeet Reservation, 100 miles north of Great Falls. He looked very similar to the police composite. A drifter, he rarely gestured and almost never laughed. At the time of the letter, he was in federal prison for rape. And there was another part of DuBray's physical makeup that was too distinct to be dismissed as coincidental: he was missing a kneecap on one of his legs, causing his gimp appearance. Police delved into their records and, according to published reports, "noticed that two parking tickets attached to DuBray's vehicle were written within blocks of where Davis was shot."

Within days of being alerted by the letter, police served a warrant to DuBray for the murder of Suzette Pritchard. Detectives suspected that DuBray killed both victims but struggled to tie him to the Davis case. In the end, they were unable to come up with evidence they could present to the jury to convict DuBray of killing Morris Davis. However, in 1999 DuBray was convicted of the Pritchard murder and sentenced to life imprisonment for robbery, felony theft, and murder.

For years after the Pritchard conviction, authorities pleaded with DuBray to draw the inside layout of the house where Davis was ambushed and explain the sequence of what happened that night. But DuBray died from diabetes in prison in 2016. Whatever despicable secrets he might have clung to as part of his "near-continuous record of law breaking," as one judge called it, went with him to the grave.

Though DuBray is strongly suspected of killing Morris Davis, he was never charged with the crime. Officially, that homicide remains unsolved.

23

MURDER AT THE BAD ROUTE REST AREA

Glendive, 1985
Victim: Dexter W. Stefonek
Case Status: Unsolved

In the winter of 1985, Dexter W. Stefonek, 67, embarked on a long road trip from his son's farm in the Portland, Oregon, area to Stefonek's home in Rhinelander, Wisconsin. It wasn't unusual for him to drive alone for 2,000 miles across five sparsely populated states. A few years earlier he had retired from a Wisconsin paper mill and only a year before, his wife, Vivian, died.

Stefonek was employed by the Rhinelander Paper Co. for more than 30 years before retiring to care for Vivian, who was ailing from severe arthritis. As the first anniversary of her death approached, he told his son that he felt a little melancholy and he wanted to go home to their home in the Oneida County town of Pine Lake.

Stefonek left his son's house in Oregon on November 18, 1985. He told his son that he planned to sleep at rest stops along the way. He drove a light brown 1984 Plymouth Horizon. He was last seen at the Bad Route Rest Stop on Interstate 94, approximately 20 miles west of Glendive, Montana.

Dave Stefonek on Father

A lifetime Wisconsinite, Dexter Stefonek's father died of tuberculosis when Dexter was a young kid. Mild-mannered, Dexter grew up in the bounty of the outdoors: trout fishing, duck hunting, ice fishing, and shell fishing. While he had a couple of odd jobs, including once driving a delivery truck for a local dairy operation, he spent many years of his life working at the paper mill in Rhinelander.

Dexter worked his up to a foreman position. But after a bout of pneumonia revealed a cancerous spot on his lungs, doctors recommended that he take off from work, at least temporarily. While recovering, Dexter leaned on public assistance for approximately four years. However, the inactivity gnawed at him and eventually he went back to work at the same paper mill. Having lost his former seniority, he had to start from scratch in the finish department, working the day shift.

Dexter Stefonek son's Dave described his father's circumstances around the time that he last saw him: "Mom had severe arthritis and dad and her came out for treatment here (in Oregon) for that. She died in the hospital on Christmas Day and dad took it hard. Next year, he was going to stay with us for the winter. When he was here, he got the meals ready for the kids when they got home from school.

"Dad had quickly become friends with a woman from his Adventist church in his hometown, and I discouraged the idea of him getting married again. He had a couple of things he was working through. She had a long illness and dad was lonely."

Bad Route Rest Area, Glendive

One day after leaving David, Dexter's car was found in flames in the late morning at the Bad Route Rest Area southwest of Glendive. The driver's seat had been pushed all the way back, and the fire had been deliberately set using gasoline as an accelerant. Stefonek was nowhere to be found.

"His habit would be to go to a rest stop until he got tired and then he'd go to sleep," said Dave Stefonek. "He left on a Monday.

That was his habit. He promised me he would stop at a motel. Next morning, I got a call from the sheriff in Rhinelander that his car had been found burning at Bad Route Rest Stop in Montana. I'm assuming he got to Montana and went to sleep."

The rest stop's custodian, Fred Siegle, and Clyde Mitchell, a Montana Highway Maintenance Supervisor, had both stopped at the rest stop shortly before the burning car was discovered. According to published police and news accounts, between 8 a.m. and 8:45 a.m., both men noticed "a white Chevrolet pickup, possibly a Blazer, with a blue stripe on the side. Clyde Mitchell noted that the pickup was four-wheel drive, had Arizona license plates, and a cow catcher on the front." Several witnesses described the vehicle as a three-quarter-ton cab with a white trailer.

Sixty-seven-year-old Dexter Stefonek (shown here on his driver's license) was driving home to Wisconsin from his son's home in Oregon when he was last seen at the Bad Route Rest Area on Interstate 94, approximately 20 miles west of Glendive. That's where his car (above) was found incinerated and close to the location where his body was later discovered. The Stefonek murder was featured on the television series *Unsolved Mysteries*, but it remains unsolved. Courtesy Stefonek Family.

At about 9:30 a.m., according to a pair of Montana Department of Transportation employees, Stefonek's car pulled into the Bad Route Rest Area. The driver, who did not match Stefonek's description, got out and retrieved from Stefonek's vehicle two plastic jugs or three one-gallon jugs apparently containing gasoline. He poured the contents into an unoccupied van already parked there in the parking lot. The man was described as about 6 feet tall, between 35 and 40 years old, clean-shaven with a light complexion. Video surveillance equipment was not installed at the rest stop at the time.

Finally, at 10 a.m., Dexter's car was observed in flames. The stranger who was spotted earlier with Dexter's vehicle was never seen again.

Body Discovered in Dump

Months later, on March 8, 1986, William and Cynthia Shaw were dumping garbage in a private landfill about seven miles west of Glendive and discovered Stefonek's wallet. The Shaws knew of the disappearance and they searched the dump for more clues. They discovered a shaving kit, a suitcase, and several pieces of men's clothing, including a boot. Under a discarded mattress, they found Stefonek's body, well preserved by the cold winter. There were marks on his hands and damage to his neck and throat area and the front part of his skull. He had been shot twice in the head.

Stefonek's suitcase was found in the landfill and still contained money. This led investigators to rule out robbery as a motive for the killing. Oddly, the suitcase and clothes appeared to have been placed there only days before they were found, while Dawson County Coroner Lance Silha concluded that the body had likely been in the dump since around the time of the murder.

"The things that we found that day were just not things that had not been here before," Cynthia Shaw told the Associated Press. "It disturbed me that the week before everything [at the dump] was normal and seven days later all of this stuff appeared."

One more clue investigators found before the case went cold was inside the men's restroom at the rest stop. According to the *Wisconsin State Journal,* "scrawled in pencil on the restroom wall was the message "HOT JOCK SHOT WAD FROM WISCONSIN 11/85 SATURDAY THE 3rd."

Dexter was hard of hearing, and it has been law enforcement's theory that Dexter's killer was already at the rest stop when Dexter arrived, probably at around 7 a.m. According to their theory, when Dexter arrived, the killer might have tried to get his attention but failed. Furious, the killer abducted Dexter and hid his body in the landfill. The killer, they suspect, returned to rest area in Dexter's car and doused the car to destroy evidence and to distract officials so that he would have time to escape.

The murder on Unsolved Mysteries

The airing of the murder on April 12, 1989, on *Unsolved Mysteries* kept the Dawson County sheriff's department busy sifting through 16 direct tips and leads and 132 calls to the show's hotline. "Most of the calls have been from other law enforcement officials who had similar incidents happen in their cities," said Dawson County Sheriff James George to the *Billings Gazette.* "We got it out across the nation, and that was our intention," he said. "It will give other agencies something to look for." For the segment, *Unsolved Mysteries* returned Dexter's charred vehicle to the rest stop and showed his burned Bibles played out in the back seat.

The Dawson County Sheriff's Office reopened the case in 2018, but Dexter's son, Dave, is pessimistic about the likelihood of any new information surfacing.

"My impression of [Sheriff] James George was that he could do well with stray dogs, but this was out of his league," said Dave Stefonek. "My suspicion was that I was his number one suspect. For the filming of *Unsolved Mysteries,* he didn't even look at us. I believe that the person who murdered my dad knew the area well.

He dumped the body in a rancher's field and covered it with a mattress. I've always suspected that someone was out there who knew more about it and didn't come forward."

A couple of times Dave Stefonek has driven past the rest stop where his father's car was found incinerated. The first time was going to and from Wisconsin to clean out his dad's house shortly after the crime. On the return, Dave said he stopped at the rest stop where his father met his violent end and called Sheriff George for an update on the case. Dave said George told him that the rest stop "was too far away" from police headquarters to go there and visit with him.

The other occasion was the filming of *Unsolved Mysteries* segment, where, Dave said, he learned more about the details of his father's murder than at any time before or since.

"The medical examiner said that perhaps dad had been shot twice in the back of the head with a large caliber weapon," Dave said. "The first one didn't kill him, the second one did. Being that it's an active case, we've never really gotten much information from the police.

"Dad may have just gotten his Social Security check, and the most likely way for him to carry it was to put it in the bottom of his shoes. We have no clue as to what's in the boxes that they have of dad's, and they still won't tell us about it."

24

A LIFE, AND A DISAPPEARANCE

Livingston, 1986
Missing: Amy Marie Johnson
Case Status: Unsolved

THERE IS A TENDENCY in crime reporting to get bogged down in a morass of distant language, of callused formulas, or even worse, a quagmire of apathy. Blanket explanations separate the general public from the murder victim and words are applied, albeit often unconsciously, that make the death just one of another non-relatable incidents.

Amy Marie Johnson reportedly ran with "a bad crowd," and "a rough crowd," and she was labeled as "troubled." But that's not much of a foundation or conclusion for any story.

While Amy Johnson's life may be observed in frosty statistics—24-year-old Native American female, black hair, brown eyes, last seen in downtown Livingston, disappeared May 16, 1986, told roommate she'd be back in a few hours—this cold data doesn't expand the understanding of the mother who never returned to her baby girl, or a daughter who left behind a grieving family. Perhaps what follows here provides a less impersonal launching spot to re-examine her life.

Amy Johnson was the fourth child out of the five adoptees of Cliff and Peg Johnson. Clifford was a native of Wheatland, Wyoming, and Peg was born and raised in New York. The Johnsons had met in Alameda County, California, during World War II at the once-bustling Naval Air Station. Cliff was a seaman second class, employed as a cook, and Peg, a fresh college graduate with a degree in food nutrition, worked as a food inspector.

At the conclusion of the war, Clifford and Peg were still smitten and jointly searching for the next step. Peg knew a couple of family members who were frequent summer vacationers at Livingston, Montana, and after their military discharge and marriage in Big Timber, it became the newlywed's home.

Peg was a devout Irish-Catholic, and she convinced Cliff to replace his Lutheran faith with a more dedicated variety of Catholicism. Unable to conceive biologically, they adopted five children. Four of the kids were Native American. Cliff, who was always mindful of his own adoption, saw adoption as a compassionate act, a vital part of the imperfect rotation of life. Setting aside historical grievances about the harsh realities of transracial adoption in the United States, the Johnsons' hearts seemed to be in the upright place.

Amy was born on the Flathead Reservation, most likely in St. Ignatius. Perhaps she was Salish or Kootenai. Little is known about

While Amy Johnson's life may be observed in frosty statistics—24-year-old Native American female, black hair, brown eyes, last seen in downtown Livingston--this cold data doesn't expand the understanding of the mother who never returned to her baby girl, or a daughter who left behind a grieving family. COURTESY JOHNSON FAMILY.

her biological parents. Born September 4, 1961, and adopted through a Catholic charity service, Amy attended Saint Mary's Catholic Church in Livingston and was baptized there along with her other siblings.

The love which the Johnsons bestowed their children appeared to transcend race—at least for them, at least inside the control of their own home, and at least in the fair manner that they reportedly conducted their own lives. Some others, however, were less benevolent in their judgment of blending Native children with white households.

"I am the only white boy in the entire bunch," said Amy's brother, Chris Johnson, born and adopted in 1952. "My family was so progressive at the time that they took in Native Americans. It wasn't a political thing where they wanted to just steal a kid from the reservation and bring them into white society. That was the philosophy in the 1950s, getting them off the reservation, get them into town, and break their traditions.

"Mom and Dad were not that way. They were accepting. Every one of my siblings is at least half-Indian, and that caused problems in Livingston. Livingston didn't like dark people. It was a very prejudiced town—and it still is."

Sweet and Shy Child with Parents Like Saints

Clifford Johnson carried mail through the chill of snow and the gloom of night in Livingston for 30 years. As one of the community's lifelines, he delivered not only cheery correspondences and telegrams but even death notices postmarked from Vietnam.

"Dad was a conscientious worker," recalled Amy Johnson's sister, Brigit Craig. "He must have gotten the most presents out of everyone who delivered the mail in Livingston. One of the things he used to do around Christmas time was that he would note which houses hadn't received a card, and he would leave a card in their mailbox, on a plate with a homemade cookie that was made by my mom. Dad would say that everyone deserved to get a card at Christmas."

Peg stayed at home with the kids, kneading bread and concocting meals. No Swanson's TV dinners were served in their household; Peg prided herself in the food that she made from scratch. The Johnsons were progressive, only using their Corvair van to go to church or transport groceries, electing to ride their bicycles or walk around town whenever possible. Cliff was proficient at a number of instruments, including the clarinet, piano, and organ, and he performed in a swing jazz band on the weekends at local dinner clubs. He also ran the Catholic choir.

Housekeeper Peg squeezed out enough time to organize the event schedule of the Catholic Daughters of the Americas. The Johnson children counted their blessings before each meal and enumerated their gratitude at bedtime. In fact, the kids were so embedded in their religion that, after eight years of instruction, they hadn't known many people from other faiths, a fact that changed soon after they started attending public school.

"My parents were like saints," explained Brigit. "They were really good people."

"They were not social people in the town," said Chris. "They didn't belong to the golf course or the doctors' or lawyers' club, but they were active in their church and they were respected, and they raised us to be good kids."

Chris Johnson said that his family paid little attention to the pronounced social split of Livingston society, though it was hard not to be aware of its existence. "Back then, Livingston wasn't the artsy-fartsy shit, the celebrities, and the candy-flavored alcohol and fruity beers. It was a town of farmers and rednecks. As a kid, the East Side kids were tough as nails, home to the railroaders, and the West Side kids were a bunch of pansies. The east side was the rundown houses and weed-filled yards and apple trees which hadn't been trimmed in a hundred years."

Nonetheless, recollections of Amy as a young girl are uniformly pleasant. Descriptions of her frequently included the words "reserved," "shy," "caring," and "artistic." She was said to be compassionate with all the younger kids in the neighborhood. Most of her friends lived within a few blocks of the Johnsons' family home on Fifth Street. She loved marching around the block, invariably finding a few minutes to stop to play with the neighbor's dog, irresistibly named Taffy. If you handed her a sheet of paper, she'd represent the world in patterns, lines, and shapes. Her adoption was no secret; her parents thought it would eventually become a source of strength.

"Our parents never hid the adoption from us," remembered Chris. "Mom and Dad had a suitcase stored that you never touched with all of the information about each one of our grandparents' info and info about the tribes and agencies we all came from."

There is a bleary picture which supports the depiction offered by Amy's siblings of her being painfully shy: she is in the foreground, her knees tucked to her chest, wearing an almost pained expression. She seems to be wanting to seek a corner and not be bothered.

Despite her timidity, Amy developed into a solid, kind, and likable girl, a healthy 5 ft. 3 inches. "I thought she was one of the most beautiful little girls I had ever seen. And she was so sweet and shy," recalled Agnes Schafer, the Johnson family's neighbor. "And, sad to say, I don't think I ever told her so."

Babe Thrown to the Wolves

School was hard fought, and when she wasn't feeling confident, Amy's grades suffered; she sacrificed sleep and stress blackened her mood. Amy's innocence rammed against her. As a teenager, she engaged with alcohol and drugs and a mostly idle collection of friends. Though she graduated from Park County High School, booze and hard drugs accelerated the difficulties of a young woman who for many years already had been struggling with her mental health.

Factors spiraled: gloomy bars compounded her depression; the inevitable stupor of drugs led to her being labeled by some others as undesirable; the scene was rife with accompanying predators who took pleasure in exploiting the vulnerabilities of a young person sorely lacking in self-confidence.

"She was a babe and she didn't know the ways of the world," recalled Chris. "They threw her to the wolves—and fed her alcohol. Amy made some bad choices, but I don't think she was mentally prepared to understand what she was choosing. She was led into a pack of fucking wolves. These people were pukes when I was in high school."

Amy had a baby with one man, then a second child with another man, and then delivered another child fathered by yet another man. Two of the fathers had criminal histories; one had committed crimes that were predicated on violence, including a conviction for felony assault. Amy permitted her children to be removed from her custody; one of her offspring was adopted through Lutheran Social Services in Missoula, an exchange that her older brother Chris enabled.

"My mom was such a devout Catholic," remembered Chris. "The Catholic Church said don't give your kids birth control—and she didn't."

In the spring of 1986, Amy's life was a tidal wave of bad choices: drugs, familial detachment, pregnancies with hard men, babies given up for adoptions. Alcohol remained the hellhound on her trail. When she drank, she was usually aggressive and mean-spirited, even slipping into an alternate mental pathology, sometimes calling herself JoJo.

Alcoholic Amy wasn't the same Amy that most people knew; it wasn't the soft-spoken nursing assistant who politely served meals and kept the sheets clean or the aloof Amy who frequently stopped by to eat dinner and chat with her parents. Clifford and Peggy always remained firm in their love for Amy. Love and consistency would pull her through, they thought. They prayed harder, and counterweighted Amy's insecurities with kindness and smiles.

There were encouraging signs that Amy, at age 24, had started to recalibrate her sense of happiness and self-worth. She was working hard as a Certified Nursing Assistant at Livingston HealthCare. Feeding, bathing, and dressing patients were rigorous acts, but she enjoyed the boost to her self-esteem that the paycheck provided. Furthermore, she now had a newborn baby at home, a child she was determined to keep and support this time around.

Amy's Final Night

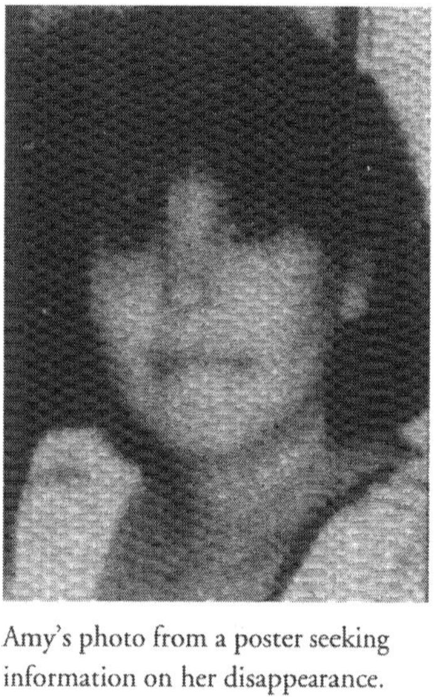

Amy's photo from a poster seeking information on her disappearance. Courtesy Johnson Family.

Amy's timeline on that fateful night of May 16, 1986, lacks structure or clarity, primarily recounted through the shifting recollection of her lone roommate. Mary Guana and Amy Johnson had been close friends since junior high school, rooming together on and off starting when they were teenagers.

"She was a good person who was full of laughter," explained Mary, who, she admits, has grappled herself with significant substance abuse and mental health problems. "She could make up a story just like that. We were not everyone's cup of tea. We would be considered what most people would call lower class people, but you know what, we didn't care. Amy was tribal and dark-skinned and I'm Mexican, and I guess that's why we fell into friendship with each other."

Amy and Mary had several pregnancies—overlapping only weeks apart on one occasion—but before either one had any children they traveled frequently as a tight tandem. Amy once lived with Mary in Idaho, but she was stricken with a dreadful bout of homesickness, and she and her friend returned to Montana.

"She was like my little sister," said Mary. "I got married on a bet, and Amy came to my wedding. One time we were both pregnant and we had a little black and white TV and were watching scary shows on the VCR. She was ready to go home, and we stepped outside and we saw the Northern Lights, and ran over to her dad's house and told him. We had our arguments, but she was always there for me, and I was always there for her. Except this one time."

May 16th was a Friday night. Amy was excited about her date. Mary, who had a male friend at the house, agreed that she would babysit for Amy if her friend promised to return no later than Saturday morning. Mary had made fun plans of her own for the weekend.

According to Mary, Amy agreed to the timeline before borrowing $20 from Mary's male friend. Mary, however, was worried about her friend, who, she said, left with a man she had never seen before. She remembered the horrible time that Amy was "beat up and left in the mud to die" about three years earlier when one of Amy's former boyfriends "hit her in the face with a shovel." Mary, already spread thin by the responsibilities of watching her own two children, agreed to watch Amy's infant too. Sure, there were times when Amy didn't come home for a day or two, or longer. But hopefully this wouldn't be one of them.

Amy Marie Johnson never returned

Amy was supposed to have dinner on Saturday night with her parents, but she didn't appear. According to police reports and news accounts, Livingston Police Captain Steve McCann affirmed that Amy was seen with former boyfriend, Ron Phillips (referred to as "a tribal member"), the evening of her disappearance.

When questioned, according to McCann, Phillips said that "he had dropped her off downtown that night after they had driven around awhile." A report came in that she was seen six days later in a bar at Gardiner, 50 miles to the south, but that information couldn't be verified.

The police inquiry fell short. Authorities suspected that she was murdered. Suspects were rounded up, but the absence of a body made the prospect of pressing charges unlikely. Rampant speculation dissolved into passive gossip. People close to Amy clammed up. The pendulum of the investigation swung fast from hot to cold. It stayed stuck mostly on the latter.

Honest Lead to Follow

In the late 1980s, people jotted down their grievances on sheets of paper, and back then, there were many more editors working at messy newspaper desks who would hear them out. Chris Johnson took to scribbling missives—it was, he said, a healthier alternative than drinking prodigious amounts of alcohol and pounding his fist full-force into furniture or occasionally even someone else's face. Dark and desperate, Amy's brother's written appeals embodied the cruelest aspects of what it's like to bear witness to the disappearance of one's own family member.

"What happened? Where is she? Why can't we get anyone to give an honest lead to follow?" Chris wrote. "I and my parents are hoping that there is someone who can shed a light on this problem and help put this painful and nagging question into focus for us." He always concluded his letters with a plea seeking the public's help to end his family's nightmare, along with the meekest of thanks.

The Johnsons eventually turned over Amy's fourth child to Child Protective Services, and the toddler, like her mother and her grandfather Clifford, was put up for adoption. (Today, she is a vibrant, successful person, who is said to look exactly like her mother.) Cliff and Peg coped with Amy's disappearance and possible murder the best way that they knew: through stronger prayer and the re-application of greater faith. Let the law do what it does; the rest must be turned over to God.

Despite their renewed reliance on their faith, Amy's parents never reconciled how such a shy, quiet, precious living thing could be torn from their home without forever rupturing it. There was no psalm that could lighten the truth that their daughter might never join them again at the dinner table. Even with the grace of God and one another, some days the house was all echoes and loneliness.

The Johnsons eventually moved out of Livingston, following Amy's siblings who were either gone from there before Amy disappeared or subsequently dispersed. Clifford died in 2006 of complications due to Alzheimer's; Peggy died a few years ago.

In the early 2000s, Livingston police were approached by a guilt-plagued man who took them to the craggy, high-mountain draw where he claimed Amy's remains had been buried, at least at one point. Police extensively questioned the individual. According to police records, he denied that he participated in Amy's murder but did admit to his "forced participation" in the disposal of her body. A team of cadaver-sniffing canines canvassed the area. They did not find anything. No charges were filed against the man.

More than thirty years later, Amy Johnson's family members remain convinced that Amy's body was moved several times. They firmly believe that some of the family members or friends of Amy's killer must possess information as to what evil befell her on that fateful night in May 1986.

Chris Johnson still seeks answers. "The Department of Justice in Helena is supposed to be the overseer and auditing all of these people," he said. "Why does Livingston have so many unsolved homicides and suspicious deaths, and most other places don't have any? Amy wasn't one of Livingston's model residents, but doesn't her family have the right to learn of her whereabouts?"

25

SHOTGUN SLAYINGS OF A TV STAR'S PARENTS

Boulder, 1986
Victims: Terrence and
Marie "Babe" Duffy
Case Status: Solved

"Dallas" star Patrick Duffy went into seclusion with relatives and friends. Stunned residents of Boulder, Montana, expressed outrage at the shotgun slayings of his parents.
—*The Los Angeles Times*

THE MURDERS of actor Patrick Duffy's parents reverberated from tiny Boulder, Montana, to the front pages of worldwide tabloids and star magazines. Everyone in the community of 1,500 people, halfway between Helena and Butte, knew of the Duffys, and not just because their son had found fame and success in television. Patrick played the part of Bobby Ewing on the hit CBS television series *Dallas*.

The Duffys owned The Lounge on the main street, the kind of place a local would want to go for a quiet drink or gossipy chitchat. A bottle of domestic beer in those halcyon days cost a dollar or less. The most familiar clientele had all drunk in the bar since they were kids. Still, the Duffys didn't tolerate rowdiness. They were calm people, who, according to patrons, "kept most of the riffraff out." If any trouble started, the troublemakers were pushed

Terrence and Marie "Babe" Duffy were killed by shotgun blasts during an apparent robbery at their tavern in Boulder, Montana, on November 18, 1986. At the time, their son, Patrick, played Bobby Ewing on the hit CBS television series *Dallas*. COURTESY BOULDER COMMUNITY LIBRARY.

out the door—at the point of a shotgun. In like fashion, Terrence and "Babe" took satisfaction in knowing that people felt at home at their dive bar.

In 1986, Patrick was an occasional visitor to Boulder and a tremendous source of pride to his parents. There was a wall of pictures of him in his parents' bar and they never missed one episode of *Dallas*. If work interfered, they always taped it. Usually his father, Terence, or "Terry," was tending bar during the program, so Marie, nicknamed "Babe," would cue the VCR so her husband could see it later.

Ordinarily, Terry and Babe—and even their tavern—led a peaceful existence. Their tranquility came to an abrupt, vicious end, riddled by shotgun blasts during an apparent robbery at their tavern on Tuesday night, November 18, 1986. Their bodies were found by a group of people who stopped for a drink after a shift change at the nearby Montana Development Center. The Duffys, both in their 60s, died from gunshot wounds to the chest.

"My father kicked these two young men out of the bar at some point in the evening," the 70-year-old Patrick Duffy told *Closer Weekly* in 2019. "So they went and drank elsewhere... and came back to the bar to kick his a—. When they stepped in the bar with their guns, they shot him. There was nobody else in the bar, so they shot both my mother and my father."

The shocked and disgusted reaction of the townsfolk was uniform. Everyone knew everybody else. No one could believe that the couple was executed. It hadn't sunk in yet—and perhaps it never would.

"Things like that just don't happen in Boulder," said Bud Smith to the Associated Press. Smith, an auto repair shop owner, said that he had been at the Duffys' bar "little more than an hour" before they were killed.

"Overcome with Grief"

Both Patrick Duffy and his sister, Lt. Joanne Hunt, who worked at the Seattle Police Department, arrived in Boulder the day after the homicides. Unsurprisingly, Patrick's celebrity garnered the case increased attention. At the time, Patrick had recently returned to the long-running series after a year's absence.

Likeable and handsome, Patrick was born in Townsend, on the other side of the Elkhorn Mountains from Boulder, and went to school in Boulder and later in Washington State. At the time of the murders, he was 37 years old and living in Los Angeles with his wife, Carlyn, and their sons, ages 10 and 6.

The show shut down production briefly "but resumed at Duffy's urging," according to *People Magazine.* Lorimar, the parent company of CBS, issued a statement in the *Los Angeles Times* expressing sympathy. Everyone is overcome with grief, it said.

Two Teenagers Charged

The day after the murders, two Helena men were arrested and charged with the double homicide after telling one of the men's girlfriend about the crime. Helena Police Capt. Ron Morley told *US Magazine* in 1986, "They mentioned a crime where some people had been shot and were dead. They left the girlfriend's house and she immediately called her mother, and she (the mother) called us."

Sean A. Wentz and Kenneth A. Miller, both 19, were charged with two counts each of deliberate homicide and held on $500,000 bond. The two teenagers, employed as janitors by Kleen King in Helena, were arrested following a brief auto chase.

Co-defendant Sean Wentz (shown here) named his friend Kenneth Miller as the one who fired the shots that killed the Duffys. Later, Wentz recanted his testimony and admitted he murdered the couple. Courtesy Boulder Community Library.

Unpleasant depictions emerged of the two young men. Wentz was an oddly skittish young man, awkward around people and hard to pin in a conversation. Miller was said to give off the appearance of a hustler. Blinking rapidly, he would turn his head and look downward or sideways, so that even close up it was hard to appraise the teenager. They were described as "sketchy" and "elusive."

Clearly, robbery was the motive. While Rex Davison, a bartender at the Duffys' bar, "estimated there was $750 to $775 in the bar when he left work at 6 p.m. Tuesday." Others who knew the couple doubted the Duffys would normally keep that much cash on hand and estimated the bar's till contained only a couple of hundred dollars. United Press International referred to the double-slaying as an event that transpired "during a $90 robbery."

No matter: in the mind of the people who knew the Duffy family, no amount of money could rationalize such a despicable end to the lives of such two beloved residents. "We don't have enough money in the whole town of Boulder to make it worth getting shot over," Phil Yanzick, owner of another bar in town, told the Associated Press.

Conviction and Punishment

During his nine-day trial in 1987, Sean Wentz said that Miller was the one who fired the shots that killed the Duffys. Robbery was the motive. The murders were a postscript. Wentz testified that it was Miller's decision to rob The Lounge and that Miller grabbed his shotgun and "blasted" Terrence Duffy in "cold blood."

Wentz, according to his testimony, walked into the bar with the shotgun but then handed it to Miller. As the two men began to ransack the place, Wentz handed him back the gun. Marie Duffy walked into the bar from a back room. Wentz said Miller reached over and pulled the trigger, dropping Marie. Seconds later, he then killed Babe Duffy too.

Miller denied shooting either person and named Wentz as the one who fired the shots that killed the Duffys. He testified he didn't see Terrence Duffy get shot, but he saw Babe Duffy walk into the bar. According to Miller, Wentz was the cold-blooded killer who remorselessly massacred the couple.

Miller testified that Babe Duffy said to Wentz, "'You're going to have to kill me, too.'" Then, Miller continued, "He just shot her. She just about fell on me."

Kenneth Miller was convicted on March 19, 1987, of deliberate homicide and sentenced to a 180-year prison term. Under Montana law, a person can be convicted of deliberate homicide if they are involved in a robbery in which someone is killed. Pre-sentencing, daughter Joanne Hunt said she preferred that Miller receive the death penalty; Patrick Duffy declined to comment of the proceedings.

Miller took the stand during his sentencing hearing and pleaded ignorance and forgiveness, "I'd like to tell everybody how really sorry I am about what happened that night, and I'm really sorry about what Patrick Duffy and Joanne Hunt have had to go through…If there was anything I could have done to stop what happened, I would have, but it appeared there was nothing I could have done."

Shortly after that, Sean Wentz was sentenced to 190 years in the Montana State Prison for the double homicide.

Release and Parole

Years later, Sean Wentz recanted his testimony and told prosecutors he was the one who murdered the couple. After Wentz confessed that he was the killer, Kenneth Miller was released on parole in 2007.

Wentz was eventually granted parole in 2015 when he was 50 years old. Shortly after that, the *Billings Gazette* highlighted Wentz as part of a feature about the Adullam House Ministries, a transitional housing program for men and women who have been incarcerated.

The article stated that Wentz lived independently for the first time, held a job, and was in a relationship. He credited Adullam for his success. "I basically grew up in prison," Wentz said to the *Billings Gazette* in 2017. "The Adullam house has helped me in so many ways that when I got out of prison I had an instant family that loved me right away."

26

THE MURDER OF "LIL MISS"

Billings, 1988
Victim: Lisa Marie Kimmell
Case Status: Solved

On March 25, 1988, Lisa Marie Kimmell, 18, left Denver in her Black Honda CRX Si with the license plate "LIL MISS" and headed north to see her parents in Billings. She never arrived. A massive manhunt could not find her. Later, her car was found deeply buried on a loner's isolated property in Wyoming. COURTESY KIMMELL FAMILY.

LISA MARIE KIMMELL was born in Tennessee, where her father was stationed in the U.S. Marine Corps, and she was raised in Billings. After graduating from high school in Billings in 1988, Lisa moved south to Colorado.

On March 25, 1988, Lisa Marie Kimmell left Denver in her Black Honda CRX Si with personalized license plates that read, "LIL MISS" and headed north to see her boyfriend, Ed Jaroch, in Cody, Wyoming. From there, Kimmell and Jaroch planned to make their way to her parents' home in Billings Heights. Kimmell, an 18-year-old restaurant manager, never arrived.

Four hours after Lisa had left Denver, however, she was right on schedule. On Interstate 25, sixty miles south of Casper, at 8:39 p.m., Wyoming Highway Patrol officer Al Lesco clocked Kimmell's 1988 Honda as traveling 88 mph in a 65-mph zone.

The trooper wrote Kimmell a citation and told her she would have to post a $120 bond, but Kimmell didn't have the cash. "I have $40 with me," she told Lesco. On the extant audio recording, Kimmell timidly asked if she could go to a cash machine.

At her request, Lesco followed her to a cash machine in Douglas, but she couldn't get any money. "It won't take my card," Kimmell said, her voice barely audible because of the background static on the tape. Instead of taking her to jail, Lesko decided to let Kimmell sign a promise to appear on her ticket and gave her directions back to I-25.

The teenage girl was never seen alive again.

Ground and Air Canvass

When the girl failed to arrive at her boyfriend's house, the missing teenager's mother, Sheila, and father, Ron, immediately feared the worse. The Kimmells had four children, and years earlier, their only son, Ricky, died at age three in a tragic accident.

Distraught, the Kimmells spent the following week flying over northern Wyoming and searched the area by car; Lisa's aunts and uncles searched the area by ground and plane. Ron exhausted every ounce of his strength in Casper and beyond, canvassing hotels and convenience stores.

The Kimmell family printed and disbursed posters with a photograph and description of Lisa and her car in Montana and Wyoming. Montana's Yellowstone County sheriff's office said teletypes with descriptions of Lisa and her car were sent to agencies in Montana, Wyoming, Colorado, and Nebraska.

In Billings, a friend of the Kimmell family started a fund to help defray the costs of searching for Lisa. "I was really overwhelmed," Sheila Kimmell said of the fund. The search was costly, but "I would sell my house, my car—anything to find my daughter."

Police tried to discern Kimmell's whereabouts by comparing the statements of nearly 1,000 people, including several law enforcement officers, who believed they had seen Lisa or her car. Many of the sightings reported an unknown male companion with Lisa. Three of these sightings that were believed to be among the most reliable were reported on March 26 and 27. One of them was in Cody, and the other two were in Buffalo, two hours' drive outside of Casper. In none of the three alleged sightings did Lisa appear to be beckoning for help.

Two hours after one sighting in Buffalo, a gas station attendant in the same town said he spotted Lisa. He was struck by the distinct "LIL MISS" Montana license plates and the nice-looking young lady at the wheel. However, in the car with her, he told investigators, was "a man, small, and a swarthy-complexion."

Kimmell Found Stabbed to Death, Possible Cult Connection

On Saturday April 2, a mechanic went fishing on the North Platte River flowing north of Highway 220, southwest of Casper. He stepped off the side of a bank and spotted a woman's naked body in the shallow water, floating with the spring runoff.

The body showed no obvious signs of decomposition. Apparently the cold water had slowed its breakdown. Police were called, and they identified the body as Kimmell.

The body was found near Government Bridge, an inaccessible and seldom used suspension bridge. This led authorities to believe that the killer was someone local. Indeed, residents reported seeing unexplained bright lights on the bridge in the early morning hours of March 26. Police theorized that an unknown assailant, operating under the cover of darkness, brought his 18-year-old victim to the bridge, stabbed her repeatedly with a dagger or hunting knife there and threw her body into the chilly waters of the North Platte River. According to authorities, the killer left a handwritten note at the crime scene, and although the contents were never made public, it was believed to be a "first-hand confession."

Authorities said that before she was killed, Kimmell had been sexually assaulted "in a manner that suggested some kind of bizarre torture." FBI agents brought in to assist the investigation said the unusual pattern of knife wounds—five cuts in a pentagram pattern on the chest and a sixth under the sternum—indicated a possible cult connection. Her stab wounds were so unique and methodical, the agents had the impression that someone took their time doing it.

During the subsequent investigation, authorities interviewed about 20 people in the Casper area who, it was reported, claimed they were members of some type of mysterious cult. It was reported that some wore robes with a symbol similar to the pattern of knife wounds found on Lisa's body.

According to the *Casper Star-Tribune*, "the cult members, including professionals and housewives, said they held meetings outside of town where unusual rock formations jutted up from the central Wyoming plains."

Sheriff Suspect, Suicide

Two years passed without breaks in the case. Then in March 1990, Natrona County Sheriff Ron Ketchum, whose jurisdiction covered the territory where Kimmell was discovered, was found in his home unconscious from a drug overdose. He returned to work three weeks later and told the newspapers he was being treated for depression. Unable to sufficiently govern his mental health issues, he resigned from the sheriff's office the next year.

The timing of Ketchum's apparent suicide attempt—the two-year anniversary of Kimmell's disappearance—along with the other information raised Montana authorities' interest in him. A detective from the Yellowstone County (Montana) sheriff's office asked Ketchum for a blood sample and "was met with a hostile rebuke." An indignant Ketchum threatened to file a libel lawsuit. The investigation became bogged down in a political squabble which ceased only after Ketchum submitted to a DNA test. Ketchum was cleared as a suspect after he left the sheriff's office.

In May 2000, Ketchum drove to a remote area outside of Casper and fatally shot himself in the chest.

DNA Profile of Dale Wayne Eaton Identified

In the summer of 2002, investigators from the Federal Bureau of Investigation researching cold cases came across Lisa Marie Kimmell's rape kit, stored among thousands of boxes of similar untested evidence in a regional crime lab. Now a DNA profile could be developed from the physical evidence. The Combined DNA Index System created by the FBI known as CODIS matched the DNA to Dale Wayne Eaton, 57, of Moneta, Wyoming, who, true to criminal habit, was serving time in federal prison in Colorado on a weapons charge. Eaton lived in a two-story clapboard house on a five-acre plot about an hour's drive from where Kimmell was last seen alive.

Eaton's DNA profile was placed in the CODIS database after he was arrested in 1997, charged with kidnapping a family at a rest stop at gunpoint in Wyoming. Eaton made off with the vehicle and left the family unhurt along the roadside. After his arrest, Eaton escaped, and at the time of his recapture, less than two months later, he possessed a weapon, which elevated his crime to the federal level.

Authorities now had forensic evidence and handwriting samples to compare with the note the killer left at the crime scene. Along with this, Lisa's car was found buried on Eaton's land.

Eaton's next-door neighbors later reported to investigators that they had seen him using an excavator to dig a large pit on his property. (Apparently, in their minds, digging an enormous hole wasn't behavior suspicious enough to suggest that he'd been involved with a murder or even to prompt a phone call to police.) The site was excavated in August 2002 and Kimmell's Honda CRX was unearthed, still bearing her distinctive "LIL MISS" license plates.

Eaton was charged with eight crimes connected to the Kimmell case, including first-degree premeditated murder. Foul details of the murder emerged at Eaton's trial. At a rest stop near Cody, Eaton somehow struck up a conversation with Kimmell. One of Eaton's fellow inmates testified that Eaton told him that he talked Kimmell into giving him a ride, during which he made blunt sexual advances toward her. Kimmel rebuffed his crude behavior and, alarmed, pulled over to the side of the road to let the hitchhiker out of her car. That's when the situation violently escalated to kidnapping, rape, and murder. Eaton, who did not take the stand in his defense, was found guilty of all charges, and on March 20, 2004, he was sentenced to death by lethal injection. The prosecution never established what the strange pattern of stab marks on Kimmell's body denoted, if anything, and didn't submit evidence linking Eaton to a cult. On the contrary, he was depicted as a volatile, anti-social individual who pursued his vile desires alone.

On Monday, July 18, 2005, on what would have been Lisa Marie Kimmell's 36th birthday, her family, friends, and a host of media watched the buildings that once belonged to her convicted murderer burn to the ground. The property had been awarded to Ron and Sheila Kimmell in a civil suit, and they lit the trailer and shed on fire. They stood next to where Lisa's car had been unearthed almost three years earlier.

Dr. James Thorpen, Natrona County's coroner, who had examined Kimmell, shook his head as the buildings smoldered. "To think back, 17 years ago, about what horrific things happened here," Thorpen said to the Associated Press.

Eaton appealed his conviction, lost, and was scheduled for execution in February 2010. He received a stay of execution in December 2009. That reprieve was overturned in 2014, and as of 2019, Eaton was the only inmate on Wyoming's death row.

27

THE DOUBLE HOMICIDE OF TOURISTS

Seeley Lake, 1991
Victims: Kenneth and Iva Larue Cheetham
Case Status: Unsolved

Kenneth and Iva Larue Cheetham left their home in Sumner, Washington, in late July 1991 to visit Glacier National Park, a place they loved. Their intended route would take them through the beautiful Swan Valley for the first time. The couple never made it to Glacier. COURTESY MISSOULA COUNTY SHERIFF'S OFFICE.

KENNETH AND IVA LARUE CHEETHAM had been missing for more than a month. Kenneth, 60, and his 55-year-old wife Larue had left their home in Sumner, Washington, in late

July 1991 to visit Glacier National Park. Kenneth was employed by the Sonoco Products Co., and she was a homemaker.

Their intended route cut a swath through some of the most beautiful terrain in the Pacific Northwest. After Glacier, they would circle back for a quiet visit with family members in Spokane.

The couple had visited Glacier several times but had never taken the route through Swan Valley. It was another new adventure for them. Unfortunately, their travel somehow intersected with a vicious killer.

When the couple did not stop in Spokane to visit relatives as planned, family members reported them missing. Authorities retraced their route, learning that they were sighted shopping in Missoula. Witnesses later recounted the couple and their vehicle passing through Clearwater Junction on July 30, heading north toward Seeley Lake. As days passed, hope diminished that the vacationing couple would be found alive.

Then the investigation took a devastating turn.

On August 5, the Cheetham's van was found on a newly cut logging road west of Lake Alva. A month later their bodies were found about two miles away. They had each been shot. Courtesy Missoula County Sheriff's Office.

On Aug. 5, 1991, the couple's van was found on a newly cut logging road west of Lake Alva. Larue Cheetham's purse had been dumped out inside the van, and a pair of shoes she bought in Missoula was found outside the vehicle. The van's key was found not far down the road.

Authorities deployed search parties by ground and air but with no success. By August 30, Missoula County Sheriff Lt. Ed Brannin said that best hope of finding the Cheethams rested with "early season hunters who may find the bodies dumped or buried in the woods."

But it was a man walking his dog who made the gruesome discovery. On September 11, the man's dog took off deep into the woods, returned, and alerted the man to the bodies. It was a humid fall day, and the sun was just beginning to burn off the morning haze. The decomposed bodies of the couple were found in an autumn swirl of leaves, about two miles south of the spot where their van had been discovered about one month earlier.

Each person had been killed with a single gunshot: Kenneth in the chest, his wife in the head.

At the time, Sheriff's Capt. Gerald Crego told reporters that 9-millimeter shell casings were found near the bodies, but the bodies were found in a popular shooting area, so the casings may have been fired before the killings. Police considered the idea that the perpetrator, like the victims, was from out of state and that somehow they'd all met inadvertently. Others weren't convinced, noting that the apparent familiarity that the killer had with remote logging roads could only indicate a local person. In the following months, authorities interviewed dozens of people but made no arrests.

The next year, Missoula detectives believed they had found a suspect. A Florida man, Lloyd Wayne "Buddy" Allen, had been convicted and sentenced to death for the November 13, 1991, murder of Florida woman Dortha Cribbs. Apparently, Cribbs had met Allen at a truck stop while driving to Florida from her home in Ohio. Cribbs had been stabbed to death, and her $8,000 diamond ring was missing from her Key West home, as well as $4,100 belonging to the woman.

Allen, according to published police reports, had been in the Missoula area in the months before the Florida slaying, possibly during the time the Cheethams were robbed and killed. But no evidence definitively tied Allen to the Montana crime.

Case Reopened in 2019

In April 2019, authorities announced they were reopening the unsolved murder case. Two retired federal investigators who were committed to solving Missoula County cold cases said they would reopen the probe into the 1991 homicides of the Washington couple.

The Sheriff's Office said that it hoped "new technology and assistance from the public will bring closure to the family," if not the person responsible to justice.

"We believe people who are familiar with the circumstances surrounding this case remain in our community," Missoula County Sheriff and Coroner TJ McDermott told the media in 2019.He stated that authorities had identified several persons of interest, and said that the passage of time would perhaps soften the resistance that someone might have to stepping forward and providing key information.

"It is sometimes the case that people who may have knowledge don't initially come forward because of their relationships to the people involved, concerns for their safety, or they may not realize information that they had is important," McDermott said. "We recognize that relationships change over time as do people and their perspectives...It is not too late to come forward."

McDermott also said that investigators would be reviewing evidence found on or near the bodies of Kenneth and LaRue, as well as evidence from the van.

Stolen Hitachi VM-5200A Video Camera

One piece of evidence relevant to the investigation had been found a week after the bodies were discovered, and a significant distance away: a video camera strap. According to authorities, a Hitachi VM-5200A video camera and case had been stolen from the victims' van either by the killer or killers or possibly by individuals who moved the van. The rubber strap was found on Highway 90 between Fort Benton and Geraldine. It had the name "Cheetham" written on it.

Emphasizing the value of the Hitachi camera as evidence, McDermott'spublic statement in April 2019 also said, "If you saw, acquired or know someone who acquired a Hitachi camcorder in the summer or fall of 1991, we are asking you to contact us. The camera may have been pawned or sold and the person who ultimately acquired the camera would have no knowledge about its origins."

Today, nearly 30 years after the murders, authorities and relatives are hoping that someone, somewhere, will remember something.

28

KILLED BY A "SHADOW" FOR NO REASON

Ferndale, 1993
Victims: John and Nancy Bosco
Case Status: Solved

On August 12, 1993, John and Nancy Bosco were murdered in their home in Ferndale, a rural community near Bigfork. They had been shot to death while they slept in what authorities characterized as an execution-type killing. COURTESY ANTOINETTE BOSCO.

ONE AUGUST AFTERNOON in 1993, Antoinette Bosco, executive editor of the *Litchfield County Times*, a weekly paper in Connecticut, said she received the kind of telephone call that "leaves a family with lives permanently shattered."

Bosco was at home when the call came from Montana's Lake County Sheriff Joe Geldrich. It was his job to tell her that her son and daughter-in-law, John and Nancy Bosco, had been found murdered in their Ferndale home. John, 41, and Nancy, 32, had been shot as they lay in bed.

"Can you tell me what happened? Geldrich had no other information at that point but would let her know as soon as he had something to report.

Antoinette and her two sons quickly jumped on a flight to Montana, and there, "the first thing my sons and I did was go up the stairs to the bedroom where our loved one had been murdered." The residence bore all the hallmarks of a crime scene: police caution tape was hanging in sections, chalk marks traced the configuration of the scene, and her son's bedroom was marked with dried blood.

The murders happened on August 12, 1993. John and Nancy Bosco had been sleeping in their home in Ferndale, a rural community near Bigfork. Each had been shot in the head with an 8mm semiautomatic pistol, in what authorities characterized as an execution-type killing.

Investigators said someone broke into their residence, cutting both the electrical and telephone service. The intruder entered the house through the window of a ground floor bathroom and then went to the second-floor bedroom where John and Nancy were sleeping.

The autopsy showed that John died of one gunshot wound to the head. The bullet went through his head and was found by the police on his pillow.

Apparently Nancy woke from the gunfire and grabbed for her glasses, knocking the telephone off the bedside table. The intruder fired at her three times. The autopsy report revealed that "one bullet entered her back, hit one of her ribs, her lung, and her shoulder blade before it left her shoulder, then went into her head below her jaw, hit bone and ricocheted out her eye, breaking the lens of her glasses. The autopsy inferred that for the bullet to have traveled on that trajectory Nancy most likely had been in a defensive crouch with her back to the gunman, a posture like a fetal position.

The bodies were found August 19, but officials said they were murdered a week or more before that, eventually settling on August 12 at approximately 2 a.m. Little was known about the couple, who had moved to the Flathead Valley from Boulder, Colorado, just last spring.

Investigators hoped that laboratory work and FBI assistance would shed light on the case. "We're still waiting to see what's coming back from lab reports on the victims and some other evidence," said Lake County Sheriff Joe Geldrich to the press a short time after the murders.

Some evidence has been sent to the FBI, he said, and "when we get the final lab reports back, we will send everything to their behavioral science department." From the evidence, he said, "they attempt to tell you who the suspect will be" in terms of age, race, and other traits.

Geldrich said authorities were looking into the couple's past to determine whether they had problems that could have contributed to their deaths. In Colorado John Bosco had been involved in a bitter custody fight over children from a previous relationship. Nancy, a model, a cum laude graduate of Dakota State College, appeared to live a squeaky-clean life.

Geldrich said that Colorado authorities had seized files on a criminal forgery case that had been filed against Bosco, alleging that he falsified lien-release records on a home he sold. Bosco's family members told the *Denver Post* "that there is evidence to show that he had settled the lien obligations at the sale closing." Bosco, however, had been due at a court hearing in Colorado the week he and his wife were slain. Their bodies were not discovered for a week because their Montana neighbors thought they were in Colorado.

Geldrich said the court records were seized "so nothing can be altered." But he said for now the murder investigation was continuing to focus on local angles rather than any Colorado aspect. "This may be something right here under our nose," he said. "We've got to determine that before we go running all over the country."

The police investigation turned up absolutely no leads.

Psychic Provides Clues

Two months after the murders, Antoinette Bosco contacted Dannion Brinkley, a man who claimed to have psychic abilities, in hopes of finding clues to solve the case. His response seemed to offer evidence of the man's supernatural ability.

Brinkley's experience as a medium began on a blustery night in Aiken, South Carolina, on September 17, 1975. Brinkley, 25-years-old at the time, was on the phone with his best friend when a lightning storm passed overhead and he was hit with 180,000 volts of electricity, a jolt so powerful it left his shoes welded to the floor.

Pronounced clinically dead, Brinkley later claimed he embarked on a classic near-death experience, traveling out of body, down a tunnel, and observing a panoramic view of his entire life. He was led into a glowing, magical cathedral.

In the hospital, Brinkley's lifeless body was covered with a sheet and wheeled into a dark room, where his friend noticed a movement under the sheet. Brinkley claimed that he was dead for 28 minutes.

Upon release from the hospital, Brinkley was partially paralyzed for seven months. It took him two years to re-learn to walk and feed himself. While recovering, he reportedly witnessed 117 future occurrences, including the election of U.S. President Ronald Reagan, the collapse of the Soviet Union, and the Gulf War in 1991. The lightning strike had, somehow, given him clairvoyance.

According to Antoinette, Brinkley immediately began to describe a suspect. The killer, he said, was "a young, male acquaintance of the Boscos who knew the layout of their home." The suspect was a student at a western college, and the suspect would be arrested in or around December 1993.

Antoinette recalled Brinkley's account of the perpetrator: "This is a kid. This is a slight-build kid with black hair. He's away at college. This is someone who knows John. He knew the layout of the house. In the very early part of December, this little kid will be caught, and he is in a college somewhere out West."

Antoinette later told that *Unsolved Mysteries* television program that her initial response to Brinkley's revelations was skeptical. She said that she couldn't make sense of what he was saying.

Yet, it turned out, Brinkley was correct on many counts.

Joseph Shadow Clark

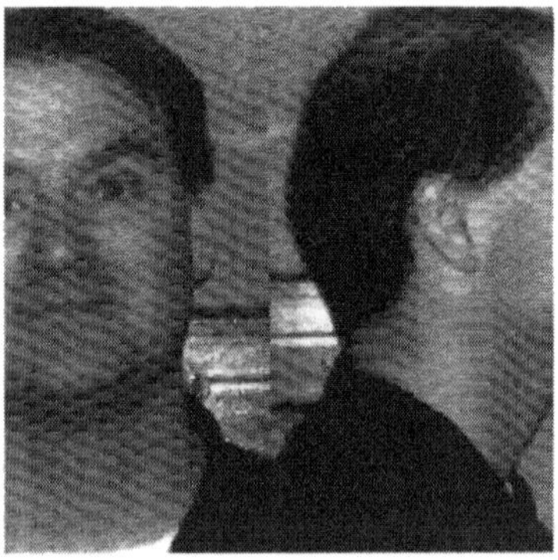

Joseph Shadow Clark, 18, a 1993 graduate of Bigfork High School, was arrested for the Bosco murders. Clark knew the Boscos and had formerly lived in the murder house. He said he had been having nightmares about killing them and one night simply woke up "and did it."

Many of Brinkley's predictions turned out to be true when Joseph Shadow Clark was arrested on December 7, 1993, at George Fox College, a Christian college in Newberg, Oregon. Incredibly, Clark did know the Boscos, and he knew the house. In fact, authorities soon learned that he had once lived in it. Too, Clark was living in a college town in the West. Among family and acquaintances, he was known to most by his middle name "Shadow"—a peculiarly fitting name for a person who carried out his double homicide at night, while his victims slept.

When asked about the Boscos, Clark quickly confessed to authorities, and he even agreed to return to Montana voluntarily. The 18-year-old college freshman, a 1993 graduate of Bigfork High School, was accompanied by his parents at his initial arraignment before Justice Chuck Whitson, where a public defender was appointed to represent him on murder charges.

It was established that the Boscos had bought their house and a nearby woodshop from Clark's parents. The Clarks, then, moved their rustic furniture business and residence to Somers.

Clark was an honor student, dubbed as "a nice, quiet boy" by many of his teachers, though some remembered him "for being hooked on crime and blood-and-gore stories." On top of this, a fellow college student recalled how "Shadow" had shown him a gun he kept under the front seat of the car and a macabre incident where the young man put a stick figure that had x's for eyes and the word "death" on it on the door of their dormitory.

Clark confessed at his double murder trial that he had stolen a handgun and ammunition from his father and used it against the unsuspecting couple, and that afterwards he placed the murder weapon in a music case under his bed. According to Antoinette, Deputy Attorney Bob Long told her that Sheriff Geldrich had searched the Bosco house and later the Clark family house but did not find the gun. The gun was turned in to the authorities by Shadow Clark's lawyer a few days later. Evidently, Joe Clark had found the gun under Joseph's bed and handed it over to a friend of his from the Assembly of God church in Kalispell, who then turned the gun over to Steve Nardi, Clark's court-appointed lawyer. Nardi, ostensibly hoping to shave some years off his client's presumed stiff sentence, cooperatively handed over the weapon to authorities.

Clark was sentenced to 220 years (later reduced to 150 years) for the murders. Attorneys said Clark likely would have received a lighter sentence if he had provided a motive, but the killer claimed that he didn't know why he did it.

Clark never made a public statement as to the reason he acted out with such violence. He simply told police that he left the room after the shootings, admitting that he put a pillow over Nancy's head and may have "touched her" after killing her.

Clark told the investigators that he held no grudges against the Boscos, but he told investigators that he had been having a recurring nightmare about breaking into John and Nancy's home. This nightmare continued every night for three weeks, and finally "... one night I woke up and did it."

Clark chillingly meandered on, "Well, you know, I realize that I have messed up. But I'm not a bad person, and anybody you talk to will tell you that. I think it's bad, but I don't think it's the end of the world for me, you know...I shouldn't be condemned, you know, for doing one little, one thing. I've done a lot of good things and sure they don't make up for doing that bad thing."

No motive was ever determined for the crime. Not even a team of psychologists who interviewed Clark could discern a hint of any motive. That's what made the Clark case doubly disturbing.

"As a society, we all like to think there is never a randomness to such a vicious act," said Nardi. "It scares the hell out of us. That could have been anybody's house. I lock my door these days."

Clark remains incarcerated at the Montana State Prison in Deer Lodge. He will first be eligible for parole when he is 60 years old.

Mother of Victims Refutes Death Penalty

Despite the horror of losing one of her sons to a senseless homicide, Antoinette Bosco said that she never considered the death penalty for the murderer. Boscohad long opposed the death penalty, having grown up knowing of a relative who died in the electric chair at Sing Prison in New York. Bosco wrote that putting a murderer to death doesn't provide closure or peace to the survivors: "It is only a delusion to believe that one's pain is ended by making someone else feel pain." Instead, Bosco argued that forgiveness was her only option.

Bosco said that the road to forgiveness was pocked with challenges, but that she ultimately arrived at a place where she was able to release the bitterness. Bosco wrote that she "cried and screamed at Shadow Clark before I was able to let him go." She ultimately realized that to hold on to that anger would mean being "bound to him in a destructive way" for the rest of her life.

29

THE UNSOLVED MURDER OF BARKEEPER

Montana City, 1994
Victim: Donna Meagher
Case Status: Open, unsolved

On the morning of January 12, 1994, the body of bartender Donna Meagher, 34, was discovered in a ditch outside Helena. The night before, Donna had been working alone at the Jackson Creek Saloon in Montana City. Two men were convicted of the crime but were ultimately released after DNA evidence implicated a serial killer. COURTESY MEAGHER FAMILY.

ON THE MORNING of January 12, 1994, the body of barkeep Donna Meagher, 34, was discovered in a ditch outside of Helena.

The night before, Donna was working alone at the Jackson Creek Saloon in Montana City. For the most part, the saloon was a local hangout, certainly not the sorriest dive in the area, just a drinking bar where the clientele felt at home among the most pedestrian characters. That night, the last payout for slot machine winnings was at 12:45 a.m. Soon, as was the schedule,

Donna locked up the family-owned casino—it was owned by her brother—and left for the night.

Shortly thereafter, according to available police and media accounts, Meagher was confronted by her assailants. They forced her to reopen the bar and robbed the cash register. They took poker machines and approximately $3,300 in cash. They moved Donna's truck from the bar's parking lot to another location behind a building across the street.

Police said that the perpetrators, not satisfied with the theft, abducted Meagher, taking her through Helena to Colorado Gulch, west of the city. The autopsy report declared that sometime between 12:45 a.m. and 1:36 a.m., Meagher was bludgeoned to death. She had been bound with a cord and struck in the head 10 to 12 times with the claw end of a hammer.

Meagher was found the following afternoon by a local resident who spotted the body in plain sight, close to the road.

Meagher's murder generated a substantial reward, and as a result, authorities were contacted by Dan Knipschield, who implicated Fred Lawrence, his 31-year-old son-in-law, and 39-year-old Paul Jenkins in the crime.

On August 31, 1994, law enforcement officers traveled to West Yellowstone to interrogate Lawrence, incarcerated in Park County on an unrelated charge, a traffic violation. Lawrence, according to his attorneys, "denied any involvement in the crime" but he implicated Jenkins and another man, Jimmy Lee Amos, as being responsible.

Based on the information obtained from Knipshield and Lawrence, law enforcement officers traveled from Montana to Oklahoma to interview Paul Jenkins, his wife Mary Jenkins, and Jimmy Lee Amos. Amos, described as "mentally challenged," and of "diminished mental capacity" was under the care of Jenkins and his wife.

Lawrence requested to be moved from Livingston to Jefferson County Jail in Boulder, in exchange for his cooperation. However, once he was transferred, he recanted his testimonial and said it was all a lie.

Mary Jenkins said that she was outside the bar the night Meagher was killed and that she saw Meagher "tied up" inside and Lawrence "playing with a toy car behind the bar." In the fall of 1994, Paul Jenkins and Fred Lawrence were arrested and charged with the robbery, kidnapping, and homicide. The defendants were tried simultaneously before separate juries, and both were convicted on all charges. The prosecution's case was tied tightly, if not exclusively, to the account of Mary Jenkins. Amos was declared "incompetent to testify" and he was never charged with a crime.

Exoneration

No DNA belonging to Jenkins or Lawrence was found at or near the crime scene. Principal witness Mary Jenkins was diagnosed with "organic brain damage" and died within five years of the trial of Alzheimer's disease. A state law passed in 2015 allowed Paul Jenkins and Fred Lawrence to petition for DNA testing on evidence related to the case. Tests on a cord found near the victim's body found Meagher's blood and DNA belonging to a convicted murderer named David Wayne Nelson. On top of this, the nephew and former sister-in-law of Nelson told investigators that Nelson told them he kidnapped and killed Meagher as she closed up the casino in Montana City in January 1994 and that he had "bragged about killing people in Florida, California, Nevada and Washington."

After serving more than 23 years in prison, Jenkins and Lawrence were exonerated of the murder. In the summer of 2019, the men instigated a civil lawsuit against three counties and several people who investigated the Meagher's killing.

Federal lawsuits filed by the two men allege that investigators acted on a tip from "a known liar, coerced a confession, coerced mentally unstable people to corroborate false evidence" and failed to follow up on crucial DNA evidence—the bloody cord that linked the case to Nelson.

An attorney for Lawrence told the *Missoulian* in 2019, the lawsuit "will prove the misconduct allowed the true perpetrator to kill again."

Nelson, a two-bit criminal and career thief, pleaded guilty to killing Bev Giannonatti, 79, and her son, Greg Giannonatti, 57, in Deer Lodge in October 2015. He is serving a life sentence for the double murder.

Notwithstanding the DNA link to Nelson, Meagher's killing remains under investigation and, as of 2020, Nelson has not been charged with the crime. Nelson denied making such statements or having any knowledge of Meagher's murder. Meagher's attorney told the *Spokesman-Review* in 2018 that the state of Montana was investigating Nelson as a suspect in the death of Donna Meagher.

30

STRANGE STORY IN PARADISE: LOOKS LIKE MURDER, AUTHORITIES SAY SUICIDE

Livingston, 1995
Victim: Nelson McNair
Case Status: Unsolved

IT HAS BEEN NEARLY 25 YEARS since the black-and-blue body of an 18-year-old Livingston youth was found on the banks of the Yellowstone River. According to witnesses who saw the body at the scene, the young man's hands were bound and there was a gaping hole in the back of his head, possibly from a gunshot. Yet to this day, local law enforcement officials claim the teenager most likely either committed suicide or accidentally drowned. "Open and indeterminate" is their succinct and oft-repeated description of the case, and no conclusive ruling has ever been rendered as to the cause of the young man's death.

Such ambiguity and inconsistency have sparked serious public allegations from the man's family and friends, who argue that Livingston authorities and the Park County Coroner are more invested in burying the truth than illuminating it.

***

On May 4, 1995, local fishermen discovered the body of 18-year-old Nelson McNair in the Yellowstone River near Livingston. Witnesses said his hands were bound and the back of his head had a gaping wound, possibly from a gunshot. At first, Livingston law enforcement said he had drowned; later they claimed he had committed suicide. No one knew or admitted why his body was quickly cremated, and weeks after his death a suspicious suicide note turned up. COURTESY ARLETA BERG.

Generations filter and pass, yet a cluster of Livingston residents vividly remember Nelson McNair's renegade teenage charisma. Charisma is a word that is difficult to bring to life on the page. When compared with the flesh experience it tries to capture, it falls short. But Nelson McNair had it and, according to friends, family, and law enforcement, someone may have purposely eliminated it by taking his life almost 25 years ago.

Two Sides of Livingston

Nelson's mother, Arleta Berg, opens a small plastic folder of newspaper clippings which cover the rudiments of her son's death. Scattered across the kitchen table, they are surprisingly few, and almost all of them are terse, providing a slight amount of copy and not very much insight. After all, how could they capture just how smart and athletic and funny her son was? Accompanying images preserve his edgy 1990s skateboarder persona, his blonde hair, parted in the middle, often tightly tied back. He was handsome with a distinct jaw line and eyes full of marvel, waywardness, and possibility.

As the physical pain and mental anguish washes over her, Arleta peels back the layers of her only son's life. Thomas Nelson McNair was born December 2, 1976, in Bozeman, the son of Clifford McNair and Arleta Berg. He was a "good baby" and "a happy camper," says Arleta. When Nelson was five years old, his parents separated.

Nelson was a product of the days before Livingston was a gentrified tourist town. It was rather "a rough railroad, sawmill, and mining town," as one resident described it. Indeed, the small town's anodyne watercolor paintings, Americano shops, and expensive restaurants are only half of the story. The other half, the so-called outskirts or fringes, continues to be characterized by a poorer landscape and a more parochial way of life that has remained basically unchanged for a half a century or more.

That other half—Nelson McNair's half—is a story of limitation and determination. It's the story of an artistically inclined, likable kid living with a single mom, who, not unlike many other children, lacked the advantages of guidance and direction. Here was a good boy who "wouldn't hurt a fly," raised in poverty by a hardworking mother who, proverbially speaking, did the best she could.

Beginning in his pre-teens, Nelson spent much of his free time at Chico Hot Springs, stretching out his calves by hiking in the Bridger Mountains, or zipping down the ski hill. He would celebrate the end of school with friends by fishing in the lagoon at Sacajawea Park, using worms or metal spinners, reeling in trout, some as big as 19 inches in length. One summer he worked in construction up the Mill Creek drainage. Another summer, he spent four days with a friend in the mountains of northwestern Wyoming, where he "survived on a bag of hamburger buns and a can of corn." Nelson liked classical music and poetry, and he was almost always drawing.

There were the typical rites of passage: shenanigans in the classroom, experimentation with pushing boundaries, occasional alcohol consumption, and the more frequent joint. Nelson wasn't confrontational, though he was no pushover.

Nelson's relationship with his dad, a logger who lived in Big Timber, was often strained. His mother Arleta's free-range parenting style was dictated as much by attitude as it was economics. It's hard to quantify latitude, but it's innocent to say that Nelson enjoyed a lot of it.

"Mom loved him a lot," says one of Nelson's longtime friends, "but she had her own issues and there was no structure for him to develop within, and he did what he wanted."

When he needed space, whether in sunshine or darkness, Nelson would wander the nearby woods, or squat under the I-90 bridge to get high, or sit alone at the river to scribble lines and images in one of his notebooks. Nights were passed with friends, fiddling with musical instruments and art supplies in between breaks of peanut butter and oatmeal concoctions.

Drugs eventually put him under a cloud, but just which ones he was using and how often are sources of contention. Friends said he frequently used marijuana and may have occasionally taken LSD.

The stigmatization of marijuana in the early to mid-1990s had a profound effect on the context of Nelson's life and death. On October 12, 1992, Park High School principal Robert Moore confronted Nelson about his drug-induced appearance and the youth provided him two baggies of marijuana. A third bag was found in a classroom where he had been sitting.

"Around Livingston, if you weren't a straight A student or athlete, you would never get a chance to be branded anything but a troublemaker," says his friend Candace Casey.

"Nelson was naturally cool," says Casey. "He was just a kid without a lot of structure. He wasn't a bully or a jerk. He was the guy who, if a girl was too drunk, he was part of the group who would get her home and would be dropping her off. He talked of the possibility of getting out of Livingston, joining the Job Corps, but he thought that he didn't have the means. He had brains and talent, and he could've turned his life around."

Sean Gadberry was one of Nelson's friends and one of the first people to get involved with trying to build the skatepark in Livingston that now bears Nelson's name.

"Nelson was a good person with a good heart," says Gadberry. "He loved his mom and he was a good athlete. I miss him always."

Generations filter and pass, yet a cluster of Livingston residents vividly remember Nelson McNair's renegade teenage charisma: his edgy 1990s skateboarder persona, lengthy blonde hair parted in the middle and often tied back, handsome face with a distinct jaw line and eyes full of marvel, waywardness, and possibility. Though his case is riddled with unsettling circumstances, authorities refuse to admit it was murder. Courtesy Arleta Berg.

"Broken Kids" Who Identified with Nirvana and Skateboarding

Another one of Nelson's friends, Jackson Welker, recalls their relationship as bonded around mountain biking, skateboard hopping, and at one point even matching Mohawks. They were kids with little supervision who grew up in challenging households, "half-country" kids with the mind-set of nonchalance. They were the lower socio-economic couriers of the pre-Pilates and Airbnb-everywhere Livingston.

"We were 1990s grunge kids running amok," says Welker, who now lives in the Seattle area. "We were the broken kids. I can remember the morning that we got Nirvana's *Nevermind* CD (1991). We all lived that life for sure."

Skateboarding both filled a void and created a chasm. While its popularity, participation, and acceptance has increased exponentially since the mid-1990s, at that time skateboarding was viewed by many as nothing more than a rebellious activity with a dark side. Indeed, it is a sport that has long been identified with defiance, and many skateboarders have sought the image of being rebels in an outlaw sport in which escaping security guards and the police comes with the territory.

"There were people in Livingston who hated us because we were skateboarders," says Welker. "There were families and adults who went out of their way to make us miserable."

Welker says that when he was around 15 years old, he was involved in a collision while on his skateboard with a Livingston police officer. One moment he was riding on the sidewalk, the next he was prostrate on the pavement.

"The officer drug me to the police car and left the skateboard in the street," Welker said. "You would've thought that I was the devil himself for riding a skateboard. To me, the saddest part was that not a single adult or business owner or anyone raised their voice."

Indeed, at the time Livingston police seemed to be at war with skateboarders. "I was a promoter of (skateboarding) and I'd shown them how to build ramps at the old school," says Sean Gadberry. "We'd set them up and the police would destroy the ramps and throw them over the fence. You would see them do it. There was a ridiculous hillbilly redneck prejudice against something new. You had to deal with it, and that was ridiculous because none of us were bad kids. But the police had a target on our backs. We couldn't ride in the streets or the parking lots, and wherever we went, the cops would push you out. They made you a criminal."

"Everyone harassed us back then," says Welker. "It was the social norm to fuck with the poor kids. All of the cops had a thing for us."

Nelson's junior and senior years of high school were marked by pangs of growth, remorse, and confusion. School was both uplifting and soul-crushing. There were plenty of fun times and smiles, yet there was also an undercurrent of incongruity: he would receive straight A's in shop but flunk gym. He wasn't proficient with numbers or math, yet he took the initiative to find an algebra tutor and address his weaknesses. He was smart as a whip, but he could be reckless with his actions. Such as the time, recalled by friends, when he "ruptured his spleen, exploded his pelvis, and suffered internal bleeding" after he took a nasty fall on the ice while allegedly under the influence.

In the spring of 1995, Nelson expressed frustration to several friends that he had "gone too far down the wrong path." One friend remembers a telephone call with Nelson in which the young man described his desire to "get his shit together" and "to do better than this." He alluded that he had been "too far into drug activity." The friend speculated that Nelson might have been "helping transport some stuff."

The Big Bust

Still, Nelson generally proved himself capable of handling life's challenges—until the big bust that may have set in motion a series of events which led to his death. Few who attended Park High School in 1995 would forget the raid, a February day when a full-blown sting operation at the school saw officers authoritatively march students into closed interrogation rooms.

Nelson was found to be in possession of a marijuana pipe. City Judge Neil Travis fined him $420 and sentenced him to ten days in jail, with the jail time deferred on the condition he perform 160 hours of community service, undergo drug counseling, not be cited for controlled substance violations, and "provide law enforcement officials with information or testimony on illegal drug use upon request."

The latter condition would have made Nelson a drug informant and, if known, could have put a target on his back. So it was shocking that in March 1995, one month after his arrest, Nelson and another person, Carisa Schneider, were named as drug informants on the front page of the local newspaper, the *Livingston Enterprise.* The reason for this dangerous public excoriation, who ordered it, who allowed it, and for what benefit, has never been adequately explained. (The publisher of the *Livingston Enterprise* at that time has repeatedly denied requests to comment.) Alarmed by the obvious risk of reprisals, Schneider's family left town. Nelson had nowhere to go.

Why Nelson was revealed as a drug informant "is still a good question," says Welker. "Why on planet earth would you do that to a teenager other than to simply mess with a kid who you thought was trouble?"

Disappearance

Nelson McNair disappeared on or about Wednesday, March 29, 1995, after ending what was a rather bland night. Nelson and his friends had almost no money and even less marijuana. After they took turns shooting at empty beer bottles at the town dump with a .22 pistol, Nelson dropped off Jon Romans and Joshua Kronske.

Nelson invited Romans to come over to McNair's mother's house east of Livingston (near the intersection of Highway 89 North and Interstate 90 near the Yellowstone River) the next day. Then Nelson dropped off the fourth kid, Eli Fisher, and headed home.

"I'll pick you up tomorrow for school," Nelson told Romans and Kronske. "'See you in the morning for jail,' were the exact words," says Romans. "That's how we referred to it [school]."

But Nelson didn't pick up his friends the next day. He didn't show up the following day either. Nelson had been working as a dishwasher at The Stockman's Bar and busing tables at a Mexican café, where he had plans to work that weekend. But no one had heard from him.

At first, his mother Arleta, who worked graveyard-shifts as a laundress at the convalescence center, had not been alarmed. Nothing of Nelson's belongings appeared out of place. His large collection of CDs, estimated to value $1,500, wasn't looted. Nelson's truck was parked in front of the house as usual. Wherever he had gone, he seemingly had gone willingly, perhaps on foot. But after three days without contact, on Saturday, April 1, Nelson's aunt, Peggy Berg, reported her nephew missing to the sheriff's office. On Friday, April 7, his father, Clifford McNair, filed a second missing person's report.

In drug-detection mode, police arrived at Nelson's house and ransacked his room. They confiscated a closet full of about ten marijuana plants. Later it was revealed that during the drug search, other evidence may have been compromised. A 9mm handgun that Nelson kept in his bedroom has never been found.

Discovery—and Doubts

On May 4, 1995, four fishermen in a boat discovered Nelson's body in the Yellowstone River near Ninth Street Island in Livingston. His body was face down on a sandbar. The fishermen noticed bindings around his wrists and that his sweatshirt seemed to have been pulled over his head, like in a hockey fight. The fishermen—all local residents—notified the police without disturbing the body.

An adjacent landowner also saw the body before the police arrived, and he later used his tractor to help police transport it across his property. The landowner, a highly respected member of the community, recently told the author that the back of Nelson's head appeared to have been blown off by a gunshot. He also told the author that he has been disturbed by the case for decades, especially because law enforcement at the time concluded there was no "foul play" involved.*

At first, according to media reports, Nelson seemed to be "the victim of an apparent drowning," but dirt or silt or unspecified sediment was found clogged in his lungs, perhaps indicating that he had been held face down in dirt or mud and had sucked in dirt in a desperate effort to breathe.

When Nelson's family pushed back against the hypothesis that Nelson had drowned, police put forward a new theory: suicide. *(Editor's note: In 2020, Livingston police again promoted suicide as the cause of death, despite several first-person interviews and evidence obtained by the author that appeared to refute this judgment.)*

Coroner Al Jenkins accompanied Nelson's body to the state crime lab in Missoula for the autopsy. Jenkins, who began working as the Park County Coroner in 1990, told the media in 2002 that there was nothing on the body to indicate that Nelson had been stabbed or shot, "but a body traveling in the water suffers all sorts of bruises and abrasions. It's also possible that *injury may have been inflicted before he went into the water* [emphasis added]." When interviewed for this book, Jenkins refused to elaborate on his 2002 statement.

Nelson's autopsy report provided to the author was highly redacted, but it did reference a gaping hole in the back of Nelson's head. The report, however, did not reference or acknowledge the likely wrist abrasions.

From the start, Coroner Jenkins has been laconic—a sentence here, a one-line declaration there. In a recent interview at the City-County Building in Livingston, Jenkins said time has not distorted his memory of the instant he arrived at the death scene. "*From the moment he was found,*" *Jenkins said,* "*I knew that it wasn't right, and it was proven out more and more that way as the hours went by* [emphasis added]." Jenkins declined to further explain this statement.

Possible Suicide Note Draws Disbelief

On May 15, 1995, a group of Beaverhead County high school students found a note under a rock near the Carter's Bridge Fishing Access Site about five miles south of Livingston, upstream from where Nelson's body was discovered.

The note read: "Dear God, All my life has been a big mistake. I can do no right. I have no one who cares. No matter how hard I try I am not a crazy person. I'm just damned to living hell. I can't take much more of it. I'm not living in self-pity either I've tried."

"[Park County Sheriff] Charlie Johnson showed the note to me—blue ink on white paper," says Nelson's mother, Arleta Berg. "I never believed it was Nelson. He was missing for 36 days and then [the note] showed up neatly under a rock? First of all, it was too religious. That wasn't Nelson."

"Nelson was an articulate kid who could write poetry, and this was a boilerplate suicide note," adds friend Jackson Welker.

Coroner Jenkins once publicly expressed his skepticism with the note's location and "its overall neatness," but he recently denied requests to elaborate on the note's characteristics.

Despite the despondency Nelson endured in the weeks before his death, not a single member of his family or friends believed that he committed suicide. "Nelson loved life too much," writes his friend Cody Redmon in a letter. "He appreciated its hardships and relished in its simple pleasures." Nelson's memorial pamphlet concluded with a one-page poem written by Clifford McNair: "Nels—I'll always have a hug for you in my heart, Dad."

Doubts and Questions

The timeline of Nelson's disappearance is nebulous, and certain ensuing activities have only intensified the family's suspicion of a plot to conceal or obscure the truth.

Indeed, one source of suspicion is the mysterious cremation of Nelson's body. On May 6, 1995, barely two days after its discovery, the body was cremated at the Missoula Crime Lab. Cremation took place immediately after the autopsy. But Nelson's mother, Arleta, insists she never ordered the cremation, and in a 2019 interview with the author, Coroner Jenkins affirmed that Arleta did not order it. Jenkins also added that he had nothing to do with ordering it. To date, it remains unknown who ordered Nelson's cremation, and why it took place so quickly.

To further complicate matters, one of Nelson's friends stated there was a phone call to the Berg residence in the early morning of March 30, and it was either fielded by or heard by Arleta and perhaps even transferred to Nelson. Arleta dismisses the allegation as false. Either way, something concrete—a phone call, a knock on the door—drew Nelson out of the house that fateful night.

No Statute of Limitations on Murder

Family and friends scattered Nelson McNair's ashes near Livingston Peak in late May of 1995. For Arleta Berg, now in her seventies, time stands still in a town of change. Decades of silence and unanswered questions have only amplified her feelings that Nelson's death will forever be associated with a fundamental absence of accountability.

Livingston is a rapidly changing town. It even has a skateboard park named after the charismatic boy who would now be a 42-year-old man. The skateboard park is a great introduction to Nelson McNair's indelible stamp on the town's character. Perhaps the resentment some Livingston police officers might have held toward skateboarders has diminished; perhaps skateboarding is now so normalized that an officer wouldn't even raise an eyebrow to some hormonal, shaggy-haired kid with a board and a bunch of brazen slogans on a T-shirt.

Coroner Jenkins says that Nelson McNair's death remains an open case, "an undetermined case which we are still looking for finality," as he recently put it. Park County Sheriff's Office Detective Brian Green reiterates Jenkins's opinion and points out there is no statute of limitations on murder.

Both the Livingston police and coroner Jenkins insist that they've been rigorous and inclusive in their truth-searching, but even today, the primary desire of Nelson's family and friends is to rekindle the investigation. In their defense, the police point to "inconsistent testimony and statements" among several of Nelson's associates, and they maintain they've done everything legally possible to deliver charges. If a break in the case is ever going to happen, they say, it's going to have to originate from within the soul of someone who knows the truth and is finally prepared to reveal it.

Many of Nelson's peers who were interviewed by law enforcement officials after his death allege that the same officials may have deliberately thwarted a possible murder investigation. The tension between the two groups during the 1990s is well documented in many statements from those familiar with the case, and it continues to be a bone of contention with Nelson's former associates.

"It feels like the officials and law enforcement of Livingston have always maintained some type of plausible deniability," says Welker. "We'd still like to know what the fuck happened. If someone drug him out there, we want to know. If so, someone deserves to pay for it. His mom deserves to know why her son never came home."

**The references to Nelson being bound and tied and possibly shot are based on my interviews with two of the people who discovered the body. The statements were preserved in both audio and written form. After extensive interviews with Coroner Al Jenkins and the Livingston Police Department for this book, I decided to present the peculiar and unresolved inconsistencies enveloping Nelson's death to Park County Attorney Kendra Lassiter. In 2020 Lassiter sought and prepared a referral to the Department of Criminal Investigation in Helena to request an independent investigation into the death of Nelson McNair. – Brian D'Ambrosio*

31

MONTANA'S BRILLIANT MADMAN: THE UNABOMBER

Lincoln, 1978-1995
Victims: Three
Case Status: Solved

MORE THAN 17 YEARS PASSED between the first Unabomber attack, in a parking lot at Northwestern University, and that cold afternoon in April 1996 in Lincoln, Montana, when FBI agents surrounded a ramshackle cabin and arrested Theodore J. Kaczynski.

Between 1978 and 1995, three people were killed and 23 injured during a frightening bombing campaign that extended from coast to coast. Most of the targets were academics or business professionals associated with transportation, travel, and technology industries.

Born in Chicago in 1942 to a working-class family of Polish ancestry, Theodore J. Kaczynski was a talented mathematician who went to Harvard on a scholarship at age 16. In 1967 he became the youngest ever assistant professor of mathematics at the University of California, Berkeley. But mathematics was of no great concern to him, he later said, and in 1969, Kaczynski abruptly walked away from academia and, in his mind, civilization.

"Ever since my early teens I had dreamed of escaping from civilization," he once told an interviewer. He built a small cabin in the woods near Lincoln, Montana, where he lived in survivalist mode. He eschewed electricity or indoor plumbing. He hunted deer, elk, and even smaller creatures such as squirrels and rabbits. He gardened parsnips, root vegetables, and berries. He didn't socialize or keep friends. He dressed in rags.

Between 1978 and 1995, three people were killed and 23 others injured during a frightening bombing campaign that extended from coast to coast. The murder spree ended in April 1996 when FBI agents surrounded this ramshackle cabin in Lincoln, Montana, and arrested Theodore J. Kaczynski, the nation's infamous Unabomber. Courtesy Montana Historical Society.

In 1978, something in the man's mind had snapped, and he began mailing parcel bombs to scientists, businessmen, and others whose work infuriated him.

Law enforcement dubbed him the "Unabomber" because his early targets were universities and airlines. Kaczynski's bombs were handmade, seemingly impossible to trace, and became more sophisticated with time.

Percy Wood, the president of United Airlines, was one of his earliest victims. He suffered extensive burns and cuts over much of his body. Janet Smith, a secretary at Vanderbilt University, sustained shrapnel wounds and burns to her face. Hugh Scrutton, a computer store owner in Sacramento, California, was the first target to die. On December 11, 1985, Scrutton was in the parking lot of his computer store when he bent over to pick up something that looked like trash. There was an explosion, and he was killed.

On December 10, 1994, while opening his mail at his home in North Caldwell, New Jersey, Thomas Mosser, an advertising executive, was killed by a bomb blast.

On April 24, 1995, Gilbert Murray, a timber industry lobbyist and Vietnam veteran, was killed in Sacramento. David Gelernter, a computer science professor at Yale, lost the use of his right hand, suffered severe burns and shrapnel wounds, and had his right eye damaged.

Initially, the FBI did not consider the Unabomber a terrorist: Beginning in 1978, he was a bomber. With the killings in 1985, 1994 and 1995, he became a serial killer. Finally, with his manifesto in 1995 attacking technology, law enforcement started seeing him as a terrorist.

In 1993, Kaczynski began writing to newspapers, mocking his victims, and threatening new objects of disdain. He wrote in the name of "an anarchist group calling ourselves FC." He railed against technology and how it was destroying both man and nature. Astonishingly, using an offer to "desist from terrorism," he convinced the *Washington Post* and the *New York Times* to publish, in 1995, a 35,000-word harangue called "Industrial Society and Its Future."

"The Industrial Revolution and its consequences have been a disaster for the human race," it began. The "manifesto," as it became forever termed, was a chillingly sane treatise, in 232 numbered paragraphs, on the evil role of technology in modern society. Part Henry David Thoreau, part violent abolitionist John Brown, part utopian fantasy, part dystopian nightmare, the manifesto wobbled from left-wing propaganda to scholarly text to unhinged, schizophrenic rant.

The manifesto said human freedom and autonomy were being eliminated by centralized systems of domination. Society had run amok and the only thing that could restore it to normalcy, he sermonized, was the separation of man from all of these controlling systems. These schemes needed to be destroyed and "wild nature" restored. The Freedom Club (FC) targeted "the technophiles [who] are taking us all on an utterly reckless ride into the unknown."

The author said that the group would continue to target those that they felt were contributing to the advance of modern technology and its dehumanizing effects.

Cabin in the Woods

Kaczynski constructed his one-room cabin alone in 1970 or 1971, according to different sources. The cabin measured 10 by 12 feet and had a root cellar but no electricity or plumbing. He chopped wood for natural warmth and preyed on deer for food. From time to time neighbors would see him "dressed in overalls and a straw hat" and traversing on a bike. He did not appear to have any regular means of employment, and local residents later told the *Washington Post* they "assumed that he lived off some family money."

Lincoln was where Kaczynski began concocting bombs as an expression of his antipathy to modernity, but the Montana connection wasn't revealed until authorities arrested Ted Kaczynski in April 1996. Sixteen bomb attacks, killing three people and injuring 23, were ultimately attributed to him. He was sentenced to eight life terms without the possibility of parole and is currently incarcerated at a federal prison near Florence, Colorado. All total, the chase for the Unabomber cost taxpayers more than $50 million.

The negative attention associated with The Unabomber put Montana in the national headlines for years. That negative spotlight has shown no signs of burning out or even ever shifting away from the state's most infamous resident.

For many years, the Unabomber cabin remained at steady draw at the Newseum in Washington, D.C. "Everyone who comes here remembers the Unabomber cabin, and we have a lot of people coming in wanting to see it," once said Maeve Scott, the director of collections at the Newseum, to the *Washington Post.*

The Newseum closed at the end of 2019. Earlier that year, the Montana Historical Society announced that it had inquired about bringing the madman's hut to the society's museum in Helena. "It tells an important story of Montana," said Montana Historical Society director Bruce Whittenberg to KXLH News in December 2019. "And it's not a story we're necessarily proud of, or that we like to relive. But it was a big story in Montana, big story nationally and internationally. And that's an artifact that represents that story and so part of our role here is to make sure those things are preserved for future generations."

32

CANNIBAL KILLER: NATHANIEL BAR-JONAH

Great Falls, 1996
Victim: Zach Ramsay
Case Status: Solved

MONTANA AUTHORITIES were convinced that Nathaniel Bar Jonah, a former Massachusetts sex offender, killed and cannibalized a boy in Montana in 1996.

In 2000, Montana authorities finally charged Bar-Jonah with murder in the 1996 disappearance of 10-year-old Zach Ramsay. They said they had evidence suggesting Bar-Jonah had butchered Ramsay's remains and disposed of them in meals served to unsuspecting neighbors.

According to court documents, at the time of Bar Jonah's arrest, "investigators found several pictures of young boys, two yearbooks from a local elementary school, stun guns, knives, batons, blue police-style coat, police badges and patches and a toy chrome pistol in Bar-Jonah's home. They found a list of names, including Ramsay, young relatives and children of friends."

The arrest of the Great Falls cannibal made national headlines, and ABC News spared no gruesome detail, including the fact that, in two separate writings seized at the time of his arrest, "Bar-Jonah makes references to 'Little Boy Stew,' 'Little Kid Desert,' 'Little Boy Pot Pies,' and anal sex and masturbation."

Incredibly, charges against Bar-Jonah for murdering and kidnapping Zach Ramsay were dropped in 2002. Even though her son was missing and a convicted sex offender and neighbor who kept detailed journals about him and other local boys was brought up on charges, Ramsey's mother said she was prepared to testify that she believed her son was still alive. Apparently, that was enough potential doubt to force prosecutors to drop charges. Zachary has never been found.

Freed to Murder in Montana

Some people are just born evil, and Bar-Jonah was one such person. His troubles started early, allegedly choked a schoolmate in 1963 when he was 6 years old. In 1974 he violently assaulted another boy.

Decades later, Bar-Jonah pled guilty in Massachusetts to charges of kidnapping, attempted murder, and impersonation of a police officer. He had been convicted of abducting and trying to murder two young boys while posing as a police officer. He spent less than two years in prison before being transferred to Bridgewater State Hospital, a state facility housing the criminally insane, in Massachusetts, where he spent 11 years.

In 1991, a judge released Bar-Jonah from the hospital despite a doctor's evaluation that he was an extremely dangerous man with an unlimited capacity for violent, deranged fantasy. A short time later he was arrested in Oxford, Massachusetts, where he had assaulted a boy sitting in a car outside a post office.

Hoping to keep Bar-Jonah locked up, Massachusetts authorities spent countless hours reviewing a list of names once found among Bar-Jonah's possessions, looking for links to the cases of several missing or murdered people. Despite these labors, authorities found none.

Under a plea agreement that became notorious as particulars of the despicable deviant's crimes in Montana materialized, Bar-Jonah received a suspended jail sentence on the condition that he gather his belongings and resettle in Montana with his mother. He was freed to kill and maim and prey upon defenseless children again, now in faraway Montana.

Notwithstanding the seemingly terrible injustice of the Zach Ramsay case, the habitual 300-pound sex offender and most vile transplant was convicted and sentenced in 2002 of kidnapping and assault involving a 15-year-old boy and his 12-year-old cousin, both of Great Falls, in 1998 and 1999.

In the end, Bar-Jonah, 51, was found dead in his cell at Montana State Prison in 2008, of complications from "poor health."

33

MONTANA MAN KILLS AT THE NATION'S CAPITOL

Washington, D.C., 1998
Victims: Two Police Officers
Case Status: Solved

THE UNABOMBER wasn't the only unhinged person to attract negative attention to the state of Montana in the 1990s. His lesser known counterpart, Russell Weston, shared several similarities with the notorious mad bomber. Most prominently, both were diagnosed paranoid schizophrenics. Similarly, both men ended up in Montana to escape the modern trappings of society, and both discontented transplants brought the state into pathetic disrepute through their violent actions.

Indeed, with the Unabomber's apprehension in 1996 still streaked across the front pages of newspapers nationwide and the lingering hoopla of the anti-government Montana Freemen militia and their 81-day standoff with FBI agents outside the town of Jordan still present, Weston's Montana connection became another focus of unwanted media attention.

After graduating from Valmeyer High School in Washington in 1974, Russell Weston moved to Montana and lived in an isolated cabin at Rimini, a tiny mining town in the mountains northwest of Helena. For many years, Weston split his time between the cabin and a small house in rural Illinois. To others he appeared to be a troubled recluse who aimlessly drifted back and forth between his two homes. His personal life was a mystery, his emotional one ostensibly marked by chaos and irrationality. It was later disclosed that Weston's extensive treatment history of paranoid schizophrenia included a 53-day involuntary commitment to the Montana State Hospital at Warm Springs.

On top of this, Weston was arrested in Helena on suspicion of selling drugs on August 7, 1991, but no formal charges were filed in that case. However, throughout the years, Weston seemed to have demonstrated several ticking-time-bomb symptoms stewed in anti-government zealotry. Twenty miles south of Helena, near Clancy, Weston had a brush with authorities in the mid-1980s, during which he exhibited a foreboding sense of menace.

Tim Campbell, undersheriff of Jefferson County, recalled the incident to the *Washington Post.* Weston threatened the undersheriff and several other county officials. "He confronted me and said something along the lines of 'you better watch your back,'" Campbell said to the Washington Post. "But he never made it intimidation. He knew where to stop."

Lone Gunman at U.S. Capitol

Later, he clearly didn't know where to stop. Certainly not on July 24, 1998, when he pulled out a gun as he entered the United States Capitol in Washington, D.C.

Scanning the environment unemotionally, Weston opened fire and killed a Capitol police officer. Another officer responded to the gunfire and critically wounded Weston before collapsing from his own fatal wounds. A tourist was also wounded in the crossfire.

Later, Weston told a court-appointed psychiatrist that he stormed the U.S. Capitol and killed two police officers, "to prevent the United States from being annihilated by disease and legions of cannibals," according to Reuters News Service. Weston main-

On July 24, 1998, Russell Eugene Weston Jr. entered the United States Capitol in Washington, D.C., pulled out a gun, and opened fire, killing a Capitol police officer. On the heels of the Unabomber arrest and the Freeman Standoff, Montana's reputation took a further hit after it was revealed that Weston had a cabin at Rimini, a tiny mining town near Helena. COURTESY MONTANA HISTORICAL SOCIETY.

tained that "he has valiantly battled enemies thousands, if not millions, of times."

At the time of the killings, Weston believed government agents were marking him for execution, that a computer chip in one of his teeth allowed him to communicate with Russia's ambassador, and that he had the ability to undo time, the Associated Press reported.

Weston has instigated several lawsuits while in prison, and all which have been dismissed as groundless or decided against him. In 2002, a federal judge ruled the government could continue "forcibly medicating" Weston. A federal judge ruled in 2005 that Weston suffers from "a mental disease" and should not be released from custody because his release "would create a substantial risk of bodily injury to another person," according to court records.

As far as determining some rationale or coherent motive for Weston's actions, his life was a volatile cocktail of mental illness, anti-government hatred, imagined slights, and frightening paranoia.

"He had something against" President Clinton personally and the government, said Jerry Swihart, an employee of the Montana State Hospital at Warm Springs, to the *Washington Post.* "He was possessed by it. He went on and on."

34

VIOLENCE AT THE VIDEO STORE

Laurel, 1998
Victim: Miranda Fenner
Case Status: Solved

Miranda Fenner arrived in Laurel, Montana, with her family in the spring of 1990. The Fenners wanted a change of pace from the rapid growth of Sacramento. Laurel didn't feel too large, too dangerous, too polluted. "We wanted to get away from the crime in California and come to a nice, quiet town," said Mike Fenner.

Miranda, 10, and her younger brother Tim quickly made friends in their new place. Miranda embraced a fresh start as a fourth grader. Later recollections of Miranda during her high-school days are exceedingly joyful: she enjoyed drawing and writing and made friends easily. She shared whatever she had—her time, her energy, her smile, and her spirit. In the spring of 1998, she suffered a broken neck in a car crash and still a great deal of pain when she received her high school diploma. Miranda was an "opinionated, sometimes feisty student," according to one of her teachers. She was described as "joyful" and "full of fun" by former classmates.

She spent most of the summer of 1998recovering at home. But come August, her strength had returned, and she was eager to be mobile once again. She was ecstatic when she was hired as a clerk at the Movie Store, a video shop at 419 W. Main Street.

Miranda, 18, wasn't fearful of working alone at the Movie Store, a video shop at 419 W. Main Street. The Fenner family residence was only a few blocks away. The Lohof Motel, owned by her grandparents, sat directly across the street.

Miranda often worked the night shift, which unsettled her father more than it did her. Mike Fenner would often drive by the store as he was coming home from work or running errands. Miranda agreed to call at least once a night to check in and say hello. She would close the store at 10 p.m., and then, ordinarily, hop into her father's truck and head home.

Earlier that year, Miranda had talked with her mother, Sherry, about heading to college. She had a few applications that she was planning to fill out and mail. Her future was undecided, perhaps she would work with children or maybe she would pursue a degree in the arts. She had plenty of ideas, and each idea provided a distinct set of possibilities.

An end "unbelievably violent, really vicious"

At around 8:15 p.m. on Sunday night, November 15, 1998, a passing motorist noticed a young woman trying to crawl out the doorstep of the video store. The motorist stopped and called 911.

Barely alive, Miranda Fenner was found lying in front of the store. Her throat had been cut from ear to ear, and she had been repeatedly stabbed. In the words of law enforcement, the attack was "unbelievably violent, really vicious." Miranda had been working alone.

Somehow Fenner had dragged herself through the store and crawled outside to seek help. She was still alive when a helicopter flew her to Billings, but she died at about 10 p.m. at St. Vincent Hospital.

A sheriff's deputy was patrolling the area that night, on the lookout for suspects in a recent string of burglaries. Only minutes before the passersby found Fenner, the deputy saw a dark sedan idling behind the video shop, but the sedan didn't match the description of the car he was looking for, and he moved on.

Trail Grows Cold

In murder investigations, motive creates direction. Find one and you've got something to work with: a potential pool of suspects, a pattern of behavior that's likely been acted out before. Officers in Laurel were in high gear, desperate to pinpoint the motive. But the killer's trail grew cold. "The longer it drags on, things get colder and colder and colder," Laurel Chief of Police Rick Musson said to the *Billings Gazette* less than a week after the murder. "Things start to wind down."

Even though Laurel officers and Yellowstone County sheriff's detectives interviewed nearly 300 people in the subsequent two months, police were frustrated by the lack of the leads. Investigators collected fingerprints from the store and hair fibers from the carpet and Fenner's body. However, Musson noted to the media, the hair fibers and fingerprints weren't enough to find a suspect.

The public can get exasperated as well, Musson said, because they see crimes solved and prosecuted on TV shows in one hour. "The problem is that citizens think we're stupid, but the amount of work is tremendous," said Musson. Even though Laurel officer Mark Guy and two Yellowstone County detectives had interviewed hundreds of people, "it's not narrowed down," Musson said.

Have information?

Police are still looking for any information in the slaying of Miranda Fenner. Laurel police are asking that anyone who was in the area of The Movie Store at 419 Main St. in Laurel between 7:40 p.m. and 8:20 p.m. Sunday, or who may have seen anything suspicious in that area, call the Laurel authorities at 628-8737.

Late one night in 1998, the body of Laurel teenager Miranda Fenner, 18, was found just outside the video rental store where she worked. In 2017, Zachary David O'Neill walked into the Yellowstone County Sheriff's office and confessed to killing her. Courtesy Author's Collection.

In one instance, officers were given a vague description of a man who had been in the video store. Laboriously, the detectives tracked down that person. Countless hours exhausted, it turned out to be a man who had rented a video just prior to Fenner's killing.

In many cases, police tracked tips to the source, sometimes through five or six people. "Then we get to the first person, and they have either no clue what we're talking about or have a good alibi," Musson said to the *Montana Standard.* It was a gritty, heart-wrenching case that police believed would most likely be cracked if people kept their eyes open and then their mouths, too. "A lot of these crimes are solved by someone who knows something. Somebody will come, for example, and say her boyfriend came home bloody and said he'd kill me if I tell," Musson said.

Judy Hatten Case

Musson knew what it was like to have a murder investigation turn indifferent. There was the bludgeoning of Judy Hatten, in which the killer entered her house quietly and then beat her to death. The body of the 48-year-old Laurel woman was discovered by her boyfriend on March 11, 1995. The victim's pickup truck was found later that day in Laurel, and investigators believe the killer drove the truck away from the scene. Police were never able to determine the instrument used to kill her. Burglary didn't appear to be a motive. And the stolen truck was abandoned barely a quarter mile from her home.

Musson was the lead investigator in that case. "It was one of the most frustrating cases. No one has called and said, 'I'm tired of living this lie,'" he said. "We haven't given up hope. These things don't ever stop. Homicide cases don't close."

While Fenner's case was not near closure, with each passing day it appeared more likely that her killer would remain unpunished. "Someone out there knows, and they will come forward. Somebody will walk in who will say, 'I've got information and I want money out of it, and protection,' and that will bust the case wide open," Musson said.

Police: "The Killer Could Be Anywhere"

Six months later, Musson remained confident of an arrest and told the media that the more posters announcing the $21,500 reward were distributed, the better chance it created to catch Miranda's killer. Laurel Crimestoppers distributed more than 25,000 posters nationally, with 6,000 of them scattered in Billings alone. The yellow poster featured a photo of Miranda, smiling and leaning her elbow against a tree trunk. Miranda's mother and father displayed the reward posters in their car windows.

"The killer could be anywhere," Musson told the *Billings Gazette* in February 1999. "We don't know if the person was a transient, a traveler going through, or a local. We're going to keep trying until this case is solved."

2001: A Killer in the Midst?

Three years after their daughter was slain, Miranda's parents, Mike and Sherry, said they were terrified by the prospect that their daughter's killer could still be in their midst. The idea that a local person killed their daughter was bloodcurdling.

"I'll never trust again, not a stranger," Mike Fenner said to the Associated Press. "There's always that second thought, you don't know what they are going to do or what they are thinking." That fear had permeated the town of Laurel, especially among Miranda's peers and schoolmates. "We still don't feel safe, deep down," said Dorel Hoglund, Miranda's art teacher for three years. "Everything wanes in town, but you definitely feel the fear."

Hoglund told the *Billings Gazette* that she believed that whoever killed her former student was not a stranger to Laurel. She said she was "angry with local law enforcement" for not pushing the case hard enough. "There are some people in our community that should be researched," Hoglund said. "And we don't know if they have been."

Musson said that law enforcement and the community shared the same goal: to identify and incarcerate the sick human being who murdered Fenner. Musson chided the media for its lack of understanding and patience, and added that murders in real life aren't always neatly and summarily solved as the ones on the TV. "They and we expect that it will be solved," Musson said. "But what does that mean? Today or 20 years from now?"

In 2006, Sherry Fenner was featured on *The Montel Williams Show,* part of her attempt to keep Miranda's name in the public arena and hope that someone would come forward with leads. She admitted that she was skeptical of the powers of the psychic Sylvia Browne, who Montel Williams added to the program's panel. What was most important, Fenner emphasized, was putting Miranda's story before a national audience.

Empty and numb. Redundant and futile. That's probably what it felt like to the hard-working officers who wouldn't let the memory of Miranda fade. Invariably, however, the tips would lead officers back to the "same people, over and over and over again," once said Musson. There was always the fatuous hope that the killer would walk in and confess, but "at this late date, that's probably not going to happen."

Miranda's Killer Confesses

In 2017, detectives escorted Zachary David O'Neill, 37, to a conference room inside the Yellowstone County Sheriff's office, and it was apparent that he had been crying. Detective Fritz asked O'Neill about his watery, red eyes, and O'Neill replied that he had seen the pictures of Miranda Fenner in the lobby. (Miranda's reward posters were in its lobby.)

O'Neill, a native of Laurel, was no stranger to law enforcement.

A hardened drug addict and petty criminal, he had spent most of his adult life in prison or in psychiatric hospitals. He was prone to violence. He had no known work history and no friends. His family members, who later suggested that he was involved in several other violent crimes, kept their distance from him.

O'Neill had trouble in his mind: he had come to admit to the two-decade-old murder. O'Neill immediately confessed that he had killed Miranda – and it wasn't his first declaration of guilt. He said that his stepbrother's death in an April 2013 arson fire led to his initial attempts to confess, according to court records. There was a crooked grin on his face, which, though subtle, was a virtually permanent feature—a smirk that curled with creepiness and seemed to suggest he knew something sinister that he would tell.

The Yellowstone County Sheriff's Office had received its share of bogus tips and leads. Detectives were skeptical. Confused, upset, and nervous, O'Neill did not appear well to investigators. Though visibly agitated, the man was polite and cooperative, and he wanted to know what would happen next, even before describing the particulars of the crime.

While authorities described O'Neill's information as "consistent," the confessor was not taken into custody.

Even though O'Neill was credible as the girl's killer, "Montana law doesn't allow us authorities to arrest in that circumstance, for the confession must be buttressed with strong factual evidence," said Yellowstone County Sheriff Mike Linder.

During his confession, a DNA swab was taken from O'Neill which eventually linked him to the rape and attempted murder of a Billings woman identified only as "JL," which also transpired in 1998.O'Neill's story about "JL" matched available DNA evidence and that led authorities to believe O'Neill's confession concerning Fenner was true.

Almost two years after he initially confessed, O'Neill formally admitted to the murder in a courtroom. He said that he "had smoked meth before renting several movies" that night of the murder. One of the movies was a porn flick, and after his mother discovered the X-rated video, she demanded that he return it to the video store. While he was there, O'Neill said that he impulsively decided to rob the store "to support his drug use" and murdered Fenner so she could not identify him.

In August 2019, O'Neill, 39, was handed three concurrent life sentences for both the murder of Miranda Fenner, and the rape and attempted murder of "JL." In the courtroom there were heavy sighs of exhaustion and hallelujahs. Family members of Miranda's pumped fists, hugged, and cried.

Without the declaration of guilt by the perpetrator himself, chances are that an arrest and conviction for Miranda's murder would never have taken place.

"He wasn't anywhere near our suspect list. It was a bitter pill to swallow," said one investigator close to the case to the *Billings Gazette*. "I know that Mr. O'Neill's actions have destroyed lives and hurt this community. No matter what happens here today, we are very sorry for that."

Despite a common perception that a conviction creates closure, Miranda's mother rejected such a concept. In her mind, there exists nothing that even comes close to closure. "It just never goes away," said Sherry Fenner. "Every once in a while, I'll think of something that reminds me of Miranda, something funny that she did. But then I think about why she isn't here. It always comes back to that."

35

THE LIFE AND ABDUCTION OF SHANNON LABAU

Helena, 1999
Victim: Shannon LaBau
Case Status: Unsolved

POSITIONED IN A HULKING 6'3, 240-pound frame, Shannon Clair LaBau's outward appearance often intimidated. He was large, even imposing, and now and again he was liable to embellish these aspects of his outer shell.

To those who knew him, on the other hand, the twenty-three-year old resonated more as an oversized child than as a brawny bull of a man. At his core, Shannon was a mischievous jokester, his size and strength much belying the insecurities of an amiable, fun-loving kid with a perennial "goofy grin," as one family member described him.

Family connections meant a good deal to Shannon. Indeed, before he would venture out to the store to pick up a gallon of milk or run some other simple errand, he'd phone a relative soliciting their company. He loved being around his mother, Sally LaBau. When he opened his first bank account in his late teens, he insisted that she oversee the transaction. In like fashion, Shannon's best woodworking project was a flower bed holder that he gave Sally one time as a present.

Indeed, he loved and trusted those nearest and dearest to him. According to law enforcement and available police records, such confidence in others might have led to his ruin.

Life of Shannon LaBau

Shannon LaBau was born on October 31, 1975, in Miller, South Dakota. His mother, Sally LaBau, was a California native who had married a man named Jerold Frederick Andersen and consummated five children. On June 7, 1966, Jerold was killed in a construction accident, struck by a piece of heavy equipment. He was 30. Sally, widowed at 28 and responsible for five children, who ranged in ages from six months old to age 8, packed up and resettled on a friend's farm in South Dakota. A new place would provide a new start, a chance to heal, a time to replace old memories with new ones.

There, Sally met Val Clair LaBau, a letter carrier, and she had two more children, Shannon in 1975 and then Josh in 1977. Val, nicknamed "Blondie," possessed a Jekyll and Hyde personality, with alcohol the principle cause of such marked duality. Affable when sober, mean when drunk, Val, a tall, gangly Vietnam veteran, suffered hallucinations and flashbacks, heightened in their intensity when he consumed alcohol, which was frequently.

Eventually, Sally, a sorter and dock worker at the United States Postal Service, transferred from South Dakota to another post office in Thousand Oaks, California. Her father was dying of cancer and she wanted to be nearby to take care of him. Now divorced from Blondie, the trip provided her with much needed personal space. It would be Sally, Shannon, and Josh who would experience California. The rest of Sally's brood would remain in South Dakota. Sally worked the night shift, and on special occasions, she would take her two boys on day trips to the beach, or the zoo, or perhaps whale-watching under blood-orange sunsets. This period cemented an attachment that would be central to Shannon's life.

"Shannon was extremely close with our mother," says Shannon's half-sister Kari Weber. "Mom was probably one of his best friends—and they did things together. He was always at her house, helping her out, or talking with her. He'd bring his car over there to work on it. They were very close."

Sally soon once again filed transfer requests, this time with several post offices in the Pacific Northwest. The first job response came from Helena, Montana. Sally embraced life there. Before long she bought a small house in the Ten Mile Creek Estates, hoping to provide the foundation of a good quality of life for her two sons.

Yet, Shannon longed for a bond with his father, and once he even convinced Sally to allow him and his brother Josh to live with their father in South Dakota. Invariably, Blondie's sharp tongue was employed against those closest to him, and Shannon, a sophomore in high school, resented such cussedness and meanness.

"It was a bad time for Shannon," says Pat Andersen, Shannon's half-sister. "Shannon was stubborn and he stayed with dad longer than he wanted. Blondie drank hard, and he tried to run Shannon over. Blondie was an abusive alcoholic. He was a hard man, who when he was sober was okay, but when he was drinking, he was hard on the boys."

"Good, Sweet Dude" Who Lacked Confidence

Unbowed, Shannon returned to Helena with his brother Josh, and, despite his feelings of dispossession, he did his best to re-adjust to Helena High School. Friendly but not extroverted, Shannon didn't crave a whole bunch of friends, leaning on his family for support.

"Unlike a lot of young people, Shannon always came to the family gatherings," says Weber. "He was at every single event."

"Shannon didn't like to go places alone," says Shannon's nephew Jon Andersen. "He was always asking me to go to the store to get milk, because he didn't want to go by himself. He was a mama's boy, always standing up for her, and always wanting to protect her. He was a good, sweet dude, yet people were afraid of him. He accepted the role…Shannon was only two years older than I was. Shannon, Josh, and I were almost like brothers because we were all so close in age. But Shannon wanted to be that big brother and that father figure to me."

One of his most memorable traits, Shannon loved to rib people, especially his mother, who was vegetarian. "He told vegetarian jokes to her," says Weber. "He liked to be funny and to make people laugh. He used to watch *Willy Wonka and the Chocolate Factory*, and he teased the little kids. He loved being taller than everyone else, and he'd swing the little kids around, and they loved all of that."

Despite this, Shannon sorely lacked self-confidence, and he found Helena harder to acclimate than to the small-town life in South Dakota or even life on the West Coast. In truth, he was a bit klutzy and uncoordinated, still acclimating to his large form and long limbs. Shooting hoops outside his mother's house was about the extent of his sporting life. Like most teenage kids, he tried to find a peer group, a pack of friends where it all jibed. He loved heavy metal and hard rock music—indeed, Guns N' Roses were the emperors of his airwaves—and he grew his thick, blonde locks disobediently.

Ultimately, Shannon found physical and, perhaps even more importantly to him at that time, psychological, validation through lifting weights and bulking up. "Shannon wanted to appear tall and strong and look like a big, tough guy," says Weber. "As big and imposing as he was, he didn't have any confidence. If you were to be tough with him, he was a bit of a softy on the inside, especially if someone really tough came along."

Shannon Meets Steve Rummel

Shannon LaBau and Steve Rummel met while they were students at Helena High School. They both desired to be buff alpha males, spotting each other at the Broadwater, the Helena athletic and health club where they bonded around bench presses, back squats, and very muscular necks.

Steve, according to investigative reports obtained under the Freedom of Information Act, "had a reputation as a bully and angry individual." "Abusive, aggressive, and deceitful," is how one witness later described Steve to investigators.

"Something about being the tough guy appealed to Shannon too," says Shannon's nephew Jon Andersen. "It might have been Shannon wanting to fit in and to have that connection of a friend. I never remember Shannon lifting his hand toward anybody. I don't know how he got so close to someone so different than him. "

From the onset, the six-foot eight-inch Steve Rummel was in complete control of the relationship. Shannon followed.

Fatherhood and Jaden

Shannon graduated from high school in 1994. One night a couple of years later, he met a girl named Leslie. Fatherhood arrived unexpectedly. On August 20, 1997, 10-pound Jayden Marie Pulliam-LaBau entered Shannon's world.

Although Leslie was "the only real girlfriend" that Shannon's family ever knew of, he and Leslie never married. The pair fought frequently, and, at times, their arguments were volatile. For starters, Leslie didn't like Shannon's choice of friends, particularly his association with Rummel. Shannon and Steve would drink at dingy bars, and at times an argument would develop between the two, especially if Shannon's generosity came to a halt and he refused to buy Steve additional drinks.

Leslie told Shannon that he needed to grow up, take on more responsibility, to be more serious about accepting the role of father.

"One time when they were fighting, Shannon ran over her foot," says Pat Andersen. "He grew up with that with mom and Blondie. After they divorced, she opened up, and she told us what was going on when they were married."

Around that time, Shannon and his father became further estranged. When Blondie came to visit his newborn granddaughter, the visit ended as caustically as Shannon's failed attempt to live with his father years earlier.

"When Jaden was born, she was dark-skinned and had black hair," says Pat Andersen. "Blondie ripped into him, told him that he was stupid because it wasn't Shannon's baby. Clearly, Jaden looks a lot like Shannon, mainly their blue eyes and their big, thick, blonde hair. But I don't know if they ever talked again before Shannon went missing."

Shannon then looked to other male members of the family for guidance. He liked to talk about muscle cars, or anything car-related, with his half-sister Kari's husband, Ron Weber. Shannon frequented Ron's garage, parking his Chevy Nova inside and talking with him about automotives. It was healthy outlet for Shannon: plenty of sparks, crossed wires, late nights, and elbow grease. Such time imbued him with a sense of purpose and accomplishment—precisely the kind of self-worth that was so hard to attain in the young man's life.

Working as a chef at Woodpecker's, a busy sports bar in Helena, Shannon learned several job skills. Despite his chronic tardiness, once he started with the skillet, underdog pride suffused his work, and he rarely declined an extra shift. When one of the staff would pop behind the line to let him know there was a table of his relatives outside, he would take a few minutes to go out and goof around with them, and then he would retreat in his lumbering gait back to the kitchen.

When the weather was nice, he went hiking, taking his dog, Harley, a stray from the Humane Society, on long walks. The two made for an almost comic pair. Big Shannon, and little Harley, a German shepherd mix with a lousy hip, strange walk, and exceedingly long tongue.

At 23, Shannon's life was a relatively ordinary mixture of straightening out and sowing oats. Smoking pot wasn't his pleasure. In fact, he disavowed drugs, and "he hated the fact that we were even pot smokers," according to one friend. His beer drinking wasn't fussy; the cheapest hooch satisfied him.

He enjoyed weightlifting and partying, and he lived alone in a property he had purchased close to Woodpecker's. He made efforts at becoming a better adult and man than his own father was. During this, Shannon's ex-girlfriend Leslie had indicated that she was considering returning to Helena with their daughter Jaden after a period of estrangement.

No doubt he would've grown and matured through the pleasure and punch of experience, learned from his mistakes, touched more lives with that "goofy grin."

February 23, 1999

Shannon Clair LaBau was seen for the final time between 9 a.m. and 11 a.m. in the vicinity of the 900 block of Kessler Avenue, in downtown Helena. Security cameras recorded Shannon at a downtown Helena bank about 9 a.m., where he withdrew about $3,000 in cash from the sale of an old black, Chevy Nova.

According to Steve Rummel's initial statement to police, he and Shannon were together on the Walking Mall at about 11 a.m. According to the April 28, 1999, edition of the *Helena Independent Record*, Rummel had told Sally LaBau that after Rummel and Shannon returned from Townsend, he dropped Shannon off in downtown Helena about 11 a.m.

Rummel also told Sally, according to the same article, that Shannon relayed a message to his mother through him: "She should go lock up his mobile home and pick up his checks from work."

According to investigative reports, Rummel told Shannon there was an old farmer who owned a muscle car somewhere close to Townsend which would interest Shannon. Rummel picked up Shannon, and according to Rummel's statement, they left to scope out the vehicle and, on the way, "shoot a couple cows."

According to multiple deposed witnesses, Shannon was "very excited" about buying the vehicle. But according to witness depositions, Rummel told several people that the seller of the automobile had raised his price "so Shannon had not bought the vehicle."

According to investigative reports, Rummel told one group of people that he dropped Shannon off at the Placer Building in downtown Helena. He told another group that he let Shannon off at the Atlas Building, and another that he had taken Shannon to the bus station in Butte "because Shannon was afraid of someone" that he owed drug money. Another witness stated that Rummel said he drove "clear to Billings and dumped his friend off there."

It was later revealed that two days before Shannon's disappearance, Rummel had asked a friend whether they had a pistol that he could borrow, "as he needed to help a rancher kill a cow."

A very dark pattern emerges while examining the life of Steve Rummel. His first felony conviction, a theft charge, dated back to 1994. By the time of Shannon's disappearance in 1999, he had already tallied a prolific criminal history, including arrests for Obstructing A Police Officer, Unlawful Transaction with a Minor, Domestic Abuse, Tampering with or Fabricating Evidence, Concealed weapons violations, and numerous probation violations.

According to investigative police reports obtained under the Freedom of Information Act, Steve often made fun of Shannon and his hair, "called him a girl," and Steve "used Shannon's friendship for his own benefit."

More troubling still, Rummel, according to police reports, threatened a woman with death and had stated his older brother was a "high priest of Satan worshippers" who had previously disposed of bodies. Rummel stated that if he were to kill someone that he would "ground teeth" to avoid the body's identification.

According to witness depositions, "immediately following Shannon's disappearance, Rummel was at Woodpecker's on a daily basis inquiring about the investigation and he "had a new tattoo right after the disappearance of Shannon."

From the beginning, Shannon's disappearance had been treated as a homicide. Shannon left behind a baby girl. His money remained untouched in his bank account, and paychecks were waiting for him at Woodpecker's. His ATM card was never used again. Brutally nearsighted, he couldn't have made it far without his contacts.

When Shannon missed a day at work, his mother, Sally LaBau, was overcome with unspeakable dread. From that point forward, his life would be a mystery to the people who loved him.

"He was the guy I looked up to the most and who I want to be like," says Jon Andersen. "He was smart and tough. When I heard that he was gone, it changed my life completely. Here was the strongest person I knew and he was gone, and it had everything to do with who he thought was probably his best friend. He was becoming the person he wanted to be—and that was all taken from him."

Shortly after Shannon's disappearance, on March 1, 1999, Steve Rummel purchased "a fairly expensive ring" for a girlfriend, "a 10K channel diamond band, ½ K diamond that cost $339.00, with an additional $69.00 for a warranty."

An ex-law enforcement official identified only as "OIC-16" detailed Rummel's "antagonistic" demeanor towards the police investigation, "almost bragging" that he had concealed facts and evidence from the police.

On June 8, 1999, Rummel showed up at a used car lot in Helena and traded in the vehicle that he owned at the time of Shannon's disappearance: an orange 1976 Chevrolet K-1500 pickup truck, valued at $3,200. But before the Helena police confiscated it for crime lab analysis, according to investigative reports, the truck "was cleaned and detailed."

Two days after the police returned the vehicle to the car dealer's lot, it was stolen. There was no broken glass in the lot, according to documents, and "it is assumed that the person who stole the vehicle had an extra set of vehicle keys." It has never been seen since. The VIN number of the stolen vehicle is CK446F479080.

Helena authorities have tracked down several tips as to Shannon's whereabouts. Searches have been conducted by foot, with packs of cadaver dogs, and through overhead aerials. Authorities searched streams and ditches, mine shafts and dark holes, even the cement plant that once employed Rummel's father.

Shortly after Shannon's disappearance, Steve Rummel was detained on a rape charge for a crime committed in Boulder, violating his probation for 1997 felony thefts by possessing a firearm in February 1999. In a subsequent federal court appearance, Rummel was remanded to custody of the marshals after a detention hearing in which Helena police officer Mike Saindon testified that the only real lead in Shannon's case led him straight to Rummel. Saindon, an amateur pilot, told the judge that for some time he frequently flew above Helena and several other surrounding counties searching for any sign of an obvious geographical disturbance that would lead to discovering Shannon.

Rummel served his time on the rape charge in Jefferson County, and as a habitual violent offender he must register his whereabouts with the state of Montana. According to the Montana Department of Corrections violent and sexual offender database, Rummel lives in East Helena.

Declared Legally Dead

In 2007, Sally LaBau faced the indignity and pain of declaring her son, Shannon Clair LaBau, legally dead.

"She didn't want to do it," says Pat Andersen. "She knew he

Shannon Clair LaBau was seen for the final time on February 23, 1999, in downtown Helena when he withdrew $3,000 from his bank account. Shannon's disappearance has been treated from the beginning as a homicide. It remains unsolved. COURTESY LABAU FAMILY.

was dead, even though she always held out that (tiny) hope that he wasn't. Mom declared him dead for Jaden and Leslie so Jaden could collect Social Security. It was one of the hardest days of my life to see that. It was so traumatic and awful for her."

Most murder victims are soon forgotten outside a small circle of family and friends. Even notorious cases fade in time. There are many in Helena far too young to remember Shannon's story as news. Indeed, since Sally LaBau died in 2007, Shannon's family members have struggled to keep his memory aflame.

Who would Shannon LaBau be today? Would he have furthered his interest in computers? Or perhaps own his own mechanic's shop? Perhaps culinary school followed by a career of cooking those prime rib dishes he loved to marinate and serve?

One thing he would undoubtedly be today is a grandfather. In 2019, his daughter Jaden welcomed her son into the world. Earlier that same year, at Jaden's wedding celebration in Idaho, an empty chair was placed at one of the head tables for her father.

"Shannon wasn't perfect, but he was a good person," says Weber. "He really had a good heart. He really would have grown into something good, a chef, a mechanic. I think about how he would be now, imagining him as a grandpa."

In the minds of Shannon's loved ones, there exists the hope that someone will feel obligated enough to answer for his life.

"All these people (who might be holding information) are in their forties and have kids the same age as Shannon was when he disappeared," says Pat Andersen. "If that was your child, would you want people to come forward with the information that would bring your child home? All we want is to bring Shannon home. He never had a memorial. He never had a funeral. He deserves so much more."

36

ALMOST HOME: ANOTHER UNSOLVED CASE IN LIVINGSTON

Livingston, 2000
Victim: Sheila Fallang Jordan
Case Status: Unsolved

"GLITTERING" IS THE WORD one person used to describe Sheila Fallang Jordan's smile. Another remarked that the gesture was "bright." Still another said it was "joyful."

Sheila's smile fueled her family and friends, and cheered up strangers. She owned it as a teenager, bopping along to "Stayin' Alive," her performance replete with hand gestures and embellished carpet glides. As a young lady, she carried it well during the holidays, a notoriously cozy but chaotic time, when this mother of two anchored large family dinners.

Her expression greeted customers at County Market, the grocery in Livingston where the curly-haired 29-year-old worked as a clerk in 2000. Her checkout line at the market was often extended; she wasn't slow, the regulars just liked to swarm her row to enjoy her good nature.

That same reliable expression could be observed in one of the final photos of Sheila taken in August 2000: hazel eyes, pretty without effort, hiking boots planted in a riverbed, a small rock smooth in her fingers, enviously abundant curly hair, sitting in the sun with her smile glittering.

A popular person in Livingston, her hallmark reliable smile and enviously abundant curly hair could be observed in one of the final photos of Sheila Fallang Jordan taken in August 2000. COURTESY FALLANG FAMILY.

THE LIFE OF A "VERY GOOD, SWEET YOUNG LADY"

Sheila Marie Fallang entered the world on May 4, 1971 in Bozeman, the youngest of William and Mary Fallang's three children. Sister Sherie had arrived first in 1965, brother Bill a few years later in 1969.

"She was two years old, happy and stubborn. I still see her quirks," says Sheila's second cousin Elaine Fallang. "Silly things like how she'd suck on her middle two fingers, and not her thumb, tapping on her cheek with her pointer finger as she did so, usually putting herself to sleep. To me, whoever killed her also killed that tiny girl."

Nursery school. First grade. Decorated handlebars of tricycles. Bath times followed by the firm "no" of bedtimes, the inducement of eating vegetables, the warnings to not chase balls into the street, the Fallangs navigated the decades of childrearing and nurtured three bright, healthy children.

"She was a very happy child," says Mary Fallang, Sheila's mother. "We thoroughly enjoyed her. She had a good family life. She had a gorgeous head of hair."

"She was so beautiful," recalls Sheila's older sister, Sherie Fallang. "Her hair was naturally curly, and she would blot it dry after she washed it; that was her secret to her curls. She could've gone to California and become an actress or a beautiful model, and made her fortune."

The Fallang family moved from Bozeman to the small rural town of Clyde Park before Sheila started the third grade. The move for her was not a problem; she made friends easily and retained them effortlessly.

"She seemed so worldly to us small-town girls at the time," says lifelong Clyde Park friend Chris Broell. "She was an advanced student and ahead in math and reading, and much more mature physically. She had a great home life and family, and her older sister had a large old record player in the living room. Sheila introduced me to Meatloaf, and we'd crank that up and dance. We were classic rock girls."

The less self-assured days of high school arrived. Tall and skinny, Sheila embodied the cutting-edge fashion and pop culture of the MTV-infused 1980s: acid wash jeans, sea-green tube tops, and her perennial favorite, a tank top and a T-shirt with the sleeves cut off. "She loved Mötley Crüe, Def Leppard, and she had a huge crush on Brett Michaels of Poison," recalls her friend Chris Broell.

"'Sweet Child O' Mine' from Guns N' Roses was one of her favorite songs, and every time I hear that song, I think about her in a lot of different ways," Broell says.

Karie Webb first met Sheila in elementary school at Clyde Park. Karie says she remembers the new girl as "lovely-looking, with big glasses and a tumbling mass of hair." The pair kept close through all the many transitions in their lives that followed.

Livingston authorities quickly asserted that Sheila Fallang Jordan knew the person who killed her on August 13, 2000. Witnesses said that right before the attack, Sheila was seen speaking with a man whom she appeared to have recognized. The case remains unsolved. COURTESY FALLANG FAMILY.

"We lived for MTV," Webb remembers. "She was the best air guitarist you will ever know."

After Sheila graduated from Clyde Park High School in 1990—the final year before the Clyde Park Blackbirds consolidated with the Wilsall school district and became the Rebels—she went right to work in Livingston, clerking and cashiering at Western Drug, the retail store Pamida, and County Market supermarket.

Sheila's older sister Sherie had married and moved away from Montana, switching addresses often as mandated by life as the wife of a Navy officer. The sisters closed the distance in 1990 when Sherie returned to Livingston. With Sherie's husband deployed in the Middle East, Sheila was the one who held her sister's hand and whispered words of encouragement in her ear as she gave birth to her third child.

The delivery of Sherie's third child was bumpier than the previous two, "but she was my outlet and she was there for me the whole time," says Sherie.

One year later, Sheila was pregnant with her first child. The father, Kevin Jordan, was a few years older than Sheila, and he had been divorced.

Jordan owned a couple of properties in Livingston, and Sheila met him while she was searching the market for a rental. It's not hard to envision why Kevin developed a crush on his bride-to-be;

her coquettish smile surely had been a catalyst. "Sheila was quite a catch," says Elaine Fallang of her cousin.

The Glue of the Family

Sheila Jordan's life became a version of the American Dream. The wedding of Sheila Fallang and Kevin Jordan took place in downtown Livingston in July 1993. The nuptials were "a happy, wonderful event," according to Sheila's family members. At the wedding her close friend Chris Broell sang a version of Rod Stewart's "Have I Told You Lately?"

Though she was a homebody and feared flying, Sheila visited sister Sherie and her family in several different locations, including California and Idaho. After the Jordans' second child was born, the expanded family ventured on family trips to places such as Seattle.

"They used to come to visit, and we'd do all kinds of things together," remembers sister Sherie. "We always had a good time, and they'd spend a couple of days together as a family—the Underground City, Pike's Market—and they seemed happy."

Cathy Fallang met Sheila's older brother Bill in 1996 and married him in 2003. She says she had several reasons to be grateful. After all, not only was she marrying her love-at-first-sight sweetheart, but she now had the ideal set of in-laws, including a sister-in-law in Sheila whom Cathy straight away adored.

Cathy envisioned a future of shared school performances, birthday parties, graduations, and many other milestones. "The plan was that we were going to raise our kids together," she recalls.

If the family was the structure, Sheila was considered by her relatives to be the nucleus, the central part about which all the daily rigmarole revolved.

"She was the glue to the family," says Cathy Fallang. "Sheila organized everything, and she worked hard, and she was an amazing mom. She took care of everything. She didn't go out. She did everything for her kids."

In the late-1990s, Sheila and Cathy were both employed as cashiers at County Market. Sheila's brother Bill worked in the meat department, and their father, Bill Fallang Sr., was one of the store managers.

"Everybody in the community loved her at County Market and it was a fun place to be," remembers Cathy. "People loved her—and they went to her line. She was always nice and cheerful and smiling. It's like she never had a bad day."

As time went on, cracks appeared in the Jordan marriage. Family members saw glimpses of these cracks and worried that their relationship was possibly unhealthy. Though she alluded to difficulties, Sheila kept the details of her marriage private. Despite that ambiguity, things took a turn for the worse. In the summer of 2000, Sheila and her two children, a 3-year-old girl and 8-year-old boy, moved out and told her family and friends that she planned to stay gone.

The pace at which things imploded surprised those who knew her, but not the swiftness of her actions. "Sheila didn't dilly-dally when she made up her mind," recalls Chris Broell.

In July 2000, Sheila's sister Sherie returned to Livingston with her husband to attend his high-school class reunion. Around the same time, Sheila informed her sister that she and Kevin had separated. "She was excited and optimistic about the new stage," says Sherie Fallang.

Sheila resolved her domestic discord in the same linear fashion many others did. She first stayed with relatives as she emotionally regrouped; she consulted a divorce lawyer; and then she relocated, kids in tow, to her own separate space. She reminded her loved ones that confrontation didn't suit her. She would return to the family house only to collect a few photo albums and some of her kids' favorite toys.

"She had gotten her own place pretty quickly," says Cathy Fallang. "When she first filed for divorce, she walked away pretty much with nothing." Despite the abruptness of the split, she reassured her family and friends that a girl of 29 didn't have to start over; she had not yet even to begin.

August 13, 2000

"The weekend that Sheila was murdered, I was trying to call her on Friday night," says sister Sherie." Her line was busy. Then I got the call Sunday night from my dad."

Sheila's sister-in-law Cathy Fallang was no longer working with Sheila at County Market, having started a different job about a year earlier. Her father Bill had moved on, too, by that time. Her brother Bill was still employed in the meat department, and he was working that night.

Something about the late shift unnerved Sheila and she voiced her concerns. Even though she lived just one block south of the market, the walk left her feeling vulnerable, shaky. So she asked for and got reassigned to the day shift. This Sunday would be her final late shift, her very last time working late-night at the store. She knew her boyfriend who lived next door was fixing a late-night dinner for her.

Still, Sheila was feeling weird. One of the crew—a night stocker—agreed to accompany her to the edge of the parking lot. Perhaps it was reassuring to her that she could see the fluorescent light of the entrance to her apartment at 1203 West Geyser gleaming in the short distance. The stocker said goodbye and turned around. At approximately 11:15 p.m., Sheila stepped into the shadows. She did not make it home.

A terrifying set of images come to mind, images that would make anyone shudder: an attack with a knife or a tool or a handheld weapon, sudden and atrocious. The blows brought her to the ground at 306 South 12th Street, in the center of the street only a few feet from her apartment door. "Mutilated and bloody," she didn't even have a hand to hold when she lost consciousness. Although she was discovered by a passerby soon after the attack, she died a few hours later at the Livingston hospital.

Sheila's family and friends allowed themselves to weep hard at her funeral. There were no words to make their grief more manageable or their horrific experience more comprehendible. No one could understand what made such a monster do what he or she did, and no one wanted to believe such a person existed.

She had been a woman so many Livingston people loved that their gifts and flowers and letters multiplied over every surface of the funeral room.

"What have you gained? We don't understand why you did this," Sheila's mother, Mary Fallang, wrote in a letter she submitted to the *Livingston Enterprise*. She wrote the heart-wrenching note because she assumed that whoever killed her daughter must be capable of remorse, of possessing emotions that resembled her own. Perhaps she was wrong.

Police: Sheila Knew Her Killer

Livingston authorities quickly asserted that Sheila knew the person who killed her. Witnesses said that right before the attack, Sheila was seen standing virtually in the very spot where she was slain, speaking face-to-face with a man whom, it looked to them, she had recognized. "It is not believed that this was a random attack by a stranger or that other members of the community are in danger," said a written statement from Livingston Police Department Chief Steve McCann, dated August 14, 2000. Sheila was murdered by someone whom she knew, asserted the statement.

Her boyfriend, John Payne, was cleared as a suspect and promptly left town. Her estranged husband Kevin Jordan came under an immediate suspicion.

"She had decided that she wasn't going to leave the divorce with nothing. That's when things changed and things got ugly," recalls Cathy Fallang. "There was a Fourth of July family gathering in 2000 and Sheila told every single person that she was scared for her safety and feared for her life. A little over a month later, it was over. She was afraid of Kevin, and she made that perfectly clear."

Kevin Jordan told investigators that he was home with their children the night of Sheila's homicide. He grew tired of being treated as "a prime suspect," he told the *Bozeman Chronicle* in December 2000. "I tried everything I could do to get our relationship back together," he told the newspaper.

Jordan, who now resides in Eaton, Ohio, has declined multiple requests to be interviewed for this book.

Another suspect, an acquaintance of Jordan's named Darren Hiller, was detained in the investigation, according to available police reports, and later released; he also declined to be interviewed for this book. According to the Montana Department of Corrections, Hiller had a history of criminal convictions; he was released from a prison facility in Helena in October 2018.

Out of Sight, Out of Mind

Weeks and months passed without any news of an arrest. In Livingston, family and friends stood at intersections handing out flyers printed with Sheila's picture over the word "REWARD." Her photo was hung in County Market.

In homicide investigations, time is often synonymous with dreaded inefficacy. Time changed slowly but surely, right before everyone's eyes. There were no clue-providing witnesses. The $20,000 reward for information remained uncollected.

The Livingston authorities have said they grabbed at every proverbial straw without success. Some years ago, acknowledging their frustrating lack of progress, they requested assistance from the state Department of Criminal Investigation (DCI). An agent is currently assigned to Sheila's homicide.

Sheila's Legacy

Today there are memorials preserving the memory of Sheila Jordan: a plaque next to the County Market where she worked, and another one with a loving inscription adjacent to a tree in Clyde Park. And there are two even more obvious testaments to Sheila: her two children, a boy and a girl now in their twenties.

The violence committed to Sheila's two children by their mother's death is something they carry. Homicide grief may be a kind of living bereavement. Survivors slog on, diminished by loss. Yet, her children have succeeded and advanced in a spirit that inspires the family members who have served as their protective surrogates. After the murder, the children resided in the full custody of their father, but then later moved in with Sheila's family.

"Even after all they've been through, [they] are such amazing human beings," says Cathy Fallang. "They've suffered the most in this, and they've excelled, and they are just amazing people. They are their mother's children through and through."

Sheila's family and friends retell her life in small bits and pieces, like the pieces of a jigsaw puzzle. They have lovingly archived their thoughts of her, polished and placed them carefully in their heads, but as time goes by, the retrieval mechanism, alas, is slower. When the memories do emerge, they invariably engender sadness.

"It is really hard for me to believe that she is gone," says her brother Bill Fallang. "Even after all these years, I can still hear her voice and her laughter. I can't believe that someone was such a lowlife coward that they couldn't live in this world with my sister."

Sheila's mother, Mary Fallang, says she is unable to clean out a closet or plant a flower bulb or open the oven to check the Thanksgiving turkey without thinking about her daughter.

While Sheila's killer has left her mother with the cruelest of scars, Mary says she has learned that she, not the one who injured her daughter, is the person who would suffer the most if she were to withhold her forgiveness. But the qualifier would be the distinction she draws between pity and punishment.

She wants justice; her forgiveness shouldn't suggest otherwise. That justice, she says, is holistic, relational, and framed in the broader societal context of a "resort town" wrestling with the unshakeable truth of its evil spirits.

Livingston's Unsolved Legacies

Two decades have now passed since Sheila Jordan was murdered, and a pall still hangs over Livingston. The crime now belongs to everyone in town. Unlike several other unsolved murders in Park County, many of which are crimes that involved impoverished and undereducated victims on the edges of society, Sheila's case was entirely different. She was a mainstream member of the community, a small-town sweetheart, the next-door neighbor whose friendly face lit up the grocery store.

It may be easier for people in Livingston to disassociate from victims of violent crime who skirt the edge of society, people like Angela Brown, 32, who was discovered in the Yellowstone River near Springdale in February 1998. Brown didn't present a happy face to the world, and the Park County Coroner Al Jenkins once called Brown's a "counterculture" life.

The same thing might have been said a few years earlier, when 18-year-old Nelson McNair was found in the Yellowstone River on May 4, 1995. Or earlier still, when 24-year-old single mother Amy Johnson disappeared after heading out on a date one Friday night in 1986.

Beyond the violent end to these Park County lives, all share one similarity: no arrests were made in any of these cases.

"What's been so devastating to us has also been devastating to many other mothers and fathers in Livingston," says Mary Fallang. "Suicides. Murders. Murders passed off as suicides. When people are interested in finding answers to the things that have happened in this town, they are cut off."

37

THE BEAUTY PARLOR MASSACRE

Florence, 2001
Victims: Brenda Patch,
Cynthia Paulus,
and Dorothy Harris
Case Status: Unsolved

EVEN BEYOND THE METHOD—a large, sharp blade across the skin folds of the throats—the killings were appallingly audacious.

The beauty shop was the former Florence Post Office. It was in the middle of town, bunched up with several other businesses a stone's throw from the loud and busy Highway 93. Indeed, The Hair Gallery, owned by Dorothy Harris, was about as obvious as Pinocchio's nose, which is the main reason she had selected the building for her business. You couldn't miss it.

Yet somehow, three women were secretly murdered there in the middle of a business day, in the middle of a small town, in a storefront building graced with several windows, in a place prominently observable by pedestrians and vehicles. Murder most conspicuous had come to the Bitterroot Valley.

Late in the morning of November 6, 2001, three women were found with their throats cut at this hair salon situated along a busy stretch of highway in Florence, Montana. COURTESY AUTHOR'S COLLECTION.

NOVEMBER MORNING MASSACRE

Late Tuesday morning, November 6, 2001, Brenda Patch, 44, of Stevensville, Cynthia Paulus, 71, of Florence, and Dorothy Harris, 62, of Florence, were found in the salon with their throats cut.

According to available police and news accounts, the morning at the salon started off similarly to any other one: the floors were swept; the utensils were sterilized; the coffee was percolated; and the television set was tuned to breezy ABC network fodder. Chit-chat and gossip permeated the business.

Paulus was getting her nails done by Patch. A second appointment was only minutes away. Somehow, someone took control of the three women, ordered two or all three of them into a small utility room, and killed them.

"Gruesome and violent," was how Ravalli County Sheriff's Perry Johnson described the crime scene.

Theory of an "Oddly Dressed Man"

According to the *Missoulian's* coverage of the bloody aftermath, "Investigators are roughly split into two theoretical camps about the murders. One camp, which includes the sheriff, believes the killings were committed by someone who knew at least one of the women. The second camp sees a randomness to the crime, a sort of drive-by stabbing."

Witnesses reported a strange man in the vicinity of the beauty shop that morning. In the media he became known as the "oddly dressed man" or "the top hat man," as shown in this police sketch. Two men were charged in the triple slaying, but the charges were later dropped. Courtesy Ravalli County Sheriff's Office.

According to police reports, a strange man was seen in and around the beauty parlor around the time of the murders, and, at last, walking away from the salon in a manner that appeared unhurried. Nothing about his demeanor suggested he was rushed or pressured or stressed. The reports said, "He walked north through the dirt parking lot of the Wild River, a bar and restaurant just south of the Hair Gallery."

No matter if the man knew one of the women, was a paid assassin, or whether he picked the seemingly bucolic setting to act out some type of inexplicably sociopathic fantasy, he and his odd apparel caught the attention of nearly a dozen people. In suitably macabre style, his presence was ghostly and undefined.

Witnesses said the man wore a dark suit, perhaps a duster, with a black hat, a short top hat, perhaps, or a fedora. His hat was said to be "faded." One witness described the hat as "pinched" near the front on both sides. His eyes were said to be "wide" and "transfixed" as if in the throes of a terrible emptiness. "Thin-lipped grin" is how one witness described the man's mouth. Some people thought he might have been carrying something, a rope, a cord, an umbrella, or even an attaché case. He was young, pale, even pasty, in his 20s or 30s, with fine, tapered features that led some to speculate the person might not have been a man. In his fashion, androgynous is the way one witness described him. "Pretty" said another.

At first, no one called the mysterious man the killer. But there was something disconcerting, perhaps too coincidental, about his presence. He became, after repeated media stories, the "oddly dressed man" or "the top hat man."

"There may be triple homicides and there may be cases that look and sound like this, but there are no cases like this," Sheriff Johnson said to the *Ravalli Republic* shortly after the murders. "The dynamic just doesn't exist anywhere around. We haven't found a sister case, a twin case, any kind of case that comes right back to us and says you guys should be looking in this direction."

Time pressed on. The "oddly dressed man," though indelibly etched in the minds of local residents, had vanished like water, or darkness, or nothing that could ever be apprehended.

Suspects Charged

Finally, news of a pair of arrests splashed across the front pages of local newspapers. In 2008, approximately 6 1/2 years after the crime, federal prosecutors in a packed courtroom in the Russell Smith Courthouse in Missoula accused two convicted drug dealers of killing the three women at the Florence beauty salon.

The men were Brian Walter Weber, 31, who bore a strong resemblance to "the top hat man," and Lincoln Christopher Benavides, 33. The men appeared before U.S. District Judge Jeremiah Lynch, where they were each charged with three counts of murder while engaged in drug trafficking, conspiracy to distribute methamphetamine, distribution of methamphetamine, and violent crimes in aid of racketeering.

About 70 family members and friends of the three victims listened as the charges were summarized. There were whoops and grunts. Weber, looking into the teeth of the law once again, was unfazed. Benavides also accepted the charges stoically unemotional.

Prosecutors tried to tie Weber circumstantially to the Bitterroot Valley and The Hair Gallery, where, they claimed, Weber "used to go to pick up his family's mail."

Federal investigators said Weber was in the Bitterroot Valley on November 6, 2001, at the behest of Benavides, who court records described as "the leader of a drug distribution ring that sold methamphetamine in Idaho and western Montana." Weber, records stated, was "a lower-tier distributor" and a henchman for Benavides, intimidating or roughing up other dealers who didn't pay the boss on time.

Court records revealed that Weber had been a person of interest from the onset and was questioned early in the case. Weber's whereabouts were transitory, but he reportedly lived in Nampa, Idaho, at the time of the killings. Weber had a long criminal history, and according to authorities, Weber was first interviewed about the triple slaying around Thanksgiving 2001. It appears that something in his exchange with investigators put him—and kept him—on the short list of suspects in the case.

Prosecutors alleged that the killings were "related to a drug debt" owed by someone affiliated with the victims. The indictment lacked specificity as to which of the women may have had a relative or family member linked to the drug ring.

Both Weber and Benavides pleaded not guilty.

Charges Dropped

In 2010, US Magistrate Judge Jeremiah C. Lynch of the Missoula Division of the District of Montana dismissed the homicide charges against Brian Weber after a legal motion filed by Assistant U.S. Attorney Joseph Thaggard claimed that the prosecution's case had been foiled and compromised, citing the death of a crucial witness and another witness's "lack of credibility."

Weber, in a November 2010 interview with the *Missoulian* from jail where he was serving a 25-year federal sentence for distributing methamphetamine and drug trafficking conspiracy, vehemently denied committing the murders and stated "he wasn't in Montana when the crime was committed."

Not hesitant to speak his mind to the media, Weber told the *Missoulian* that he was in fact questioned directly after the murders. But he claimed that his targeting as a suspect was misconceived and misdirected. He said that the police investigation of him revealed nothing that could be used against him to cement a criminal conviction.

In the years that followed the murders, Weber conceded that he had become a more concrete target in the investigation because of "incriminating statements" he allegedly made to others. Those utterances eventually made their way to authorities, who began to cobble together a case against Weber.

"They can't charge me with a whole bunch of hearsay from fellow prisoners," Weber told the *Missoulian.*

In October 2010, Benavides pleaded guilty to charges that he operated an extensive methamphetamine distribution ring in Idaho and Montana, but the charges levied against him in the 2001 killings were dropped too. Benavides is currently incarcerated.

Weber Back to Prison in 2018

In September 2018, a US District judge in Great Falls sentenced Brian Weber, then 42, to 15 years in prison, followed by 10 years of supervised release, for selling heroin and methamphetamine over a three-year span. At the sentencing hearing, prosecutors detailed Weber's extensive criminal history of prior felony violent crimes and a federal drug conviction, including brutality against family members, girlfriends, and members within his drug network.

Despite the 25-year sentence, Weber was back on the streets after a few years, distributing heroin and methamphetamine in Great Falls from 2014 through early 2017, according to prosecutors.

"Brian Weber is a dangerous criminal with a substantial criminal history. Because of that, we asked for an enhanced sentence provided by statute to make sure Weber is removed from our communities for a long time," said U.S. Attorney Kurt Alme.

Despite Brian Weber's identification as the prime suspect in the murders of the three women in Florence, the case of the Florence triple homicides is considered unsolved.

38

HOMETOWN SUCCESS MURDERED IN TEXAS

Columbia Falls, 2002
Victim: Jennifer Servo
Case Status: Unsolved

Is she sleeping? I don't think so
Is she breathing? Yes, very low
Whatcha doing, Jennifer, my love?

THE LYRICS FROM THE 1968 SONG "Jennifer Juniper" by Donovan inspired her namesake.

Daughter of Norm Olson and Sherry Servo of Columbia Falls, Jennifer Lynn Olson was kind, artistic, loving, and studious. Born September 23, 1979, Jennifer was named after a fanciful love song, and she brought love into the lives of those around her.

She grew up in a quiet, even idyllic, neighborhood. Like many other children, she adored Dr. Seuss and she liked the rhyme and banter of the author Theodore Geisel's wordplay. While her childhood friends built snowmen in their front yards, Jennifer crafted snow mice or some other non-traditional sculpture. In the summertime, she dressed up like a clown and went for a bike ride, or climbed a tree while singing "Yellow Submarine" with impish glee.

"We never let her cry herself to sleep," says Jennifer's father Norman Olson. "I'd walk down the hallway, open the door, and those big blue eyes would be staring back at me."

There were several family vacations, including one trip to the Las Vegas Natural History Museum, where Jennifer was fascinated by the T-Rex replica, as long as her school bus. Her father, Norm Olson, recalled how Jennifer could always bring a smile to his face, no matter how tense the situation. One example he likes to share is the family vacation in Honolulu, when he and Jennifer had to ride a transit bus to a far-off terminal for a flight to another island.

"The bus driver, who barked orders like a drill sergeant, was obviously irritated from the unscheduled overtime due to our late arriving flight. And Jennifer was not feeling well from airsickness of the long flight from Los Angeles. As we sat where the gruff driver directed us, I thought Jennifer was going to get sick as her mouth drew tight and her face tilted down. Then, in a low, rough voice, she mimicked the driver... "Get to the back of the bus! Get to the back of the bus!"

From an early age, Jennifer was singled out for her leadership qualities, her enthusiasm, and her motivation to learn and improve. She was nominated by Dan Fairbank, a teacher at Columbia Falls High School, to receive the United States Achievement Academy's national award winner in history and government. It wasn't all serious business for Jennifer. She liked video games, especially Super Mario Brothers, pumping her fist when she had the chance to select the princess.

Though it's hard to quantify, she might have been the biggest fan of The Simpsons in the whole Flathead Valley, and perhaps even laughed the hardest. Identifying with brainy, adorable Lisa, she too snickered and laughed at the antics of Bart. At one point, the musically inclined girl she juggled instruments before establishing comfort with the baritone sax, same way Lisa Simpson did. Even more profoundly, there was the episode that Lisa realized her dream of becoming a news anchor. The teenager now too wanted to be a broadcaster and a journalist.

Throughout high school, Jennifer worked at the Columbia Falls waterslides and Gary and Leo's Grocery Store. When she turned

17, Jennifer decided to join the Army Reserves, "against her mother's wishes," according to her family. She told her parents it would help pay for her college, and she would be able to travel to far-flung places she would not have seen otherwise, like Kuwait. Grudgingly, mother Sherry signed the enlistment papers, and, in the summer of 1997, she attended basic training.

Jennifer's monthly training sessions was in Missoula, where she was a specialist in the 347th Quartermaster for almost six years. During IT training, Jennifer, 22, was made the squad leader in her barracks.

Servo started dating 34-year-old former Army ranger Ralph Sepulveda, "a bad-looking man, with tattoos all over his arms," stated one of Jennifer's friend. Sepulveda represented something different from Jennifer's recent long-term college boyfriend—and not in a good way. They hoped that Ralph was a phase that would be over fast.

While the Army instilled in greater levels of discipline and self-respect, it was only a springboard to other things. Her life goal was to become a nationally respected TV news anchorwoman, to follow the footsteps of Katie Couric.

Jennifer enrolled in communications classes at University of Montana, working at Marina Cay in Bigfork during the summers. She became one of the "most well-liked students," in UM's radio-television department and cut her teeth reporting for both Montana Public Radio station KUFM and Missoula's KECI-TV.

"She stood out among the other students because of the seriousness she had about her work," said Sally Mauk, her boss at KUFM and UM professor.

Jennifer graduated from UM in 2002, and it didn't take her long to find work as a full-time reporter. There was a TV station in Abilene, Texas that would give Jennifer the experience she desired

Sherry Servo helped her daughter settle into her new apartment in the Hunters Ridge Apartments in the 5500 block of Texas Avenue. To her mother's dismay, she wasn't living alone: even though

Columbia Falls native Jennifer Servo graduated from the University of Montana in 2002 and quickly landed her first job as a television reporter at a station in Abilene, Texas. On September 18, less than a week before her 23rd birthday, she was found murdered. Despite a mountain of physical evidence, and suspicion about her ex-boyfriend, no arrests were ever made. Courtesy Servo-Olson Family.

she'd only known Ralph Sepulveda for a few weeks, he decided to leave his life in Montana to follow Servo to Texas.

Though ambitious, Jennifer expressed satisfaction, telling Sherry, "Life is good. I have my own apartment with a swimming pool, a new job reporting, my cat and cable TV."

At 22, she now had her first full-time reporting job, at the local NBC affiliate in a mid-sized market. She would adapt to the flatland and the at times oppressive heat and the buzz of the cityscape.

"She said, 'Don't worry,'" remembered her former professor at UM Bill Knowles. "I'll remember my Montana home. And I'll be fine."

Slain in Her Apartment

After work on September 15, 2002, Servo and Brian Travers, a weatherman at KRBC picked up a coffee table from a friend's apartment and then stopped at Wal-Mart to shop. According to available published reports, Travers reported that Servo told him "she thought he was being followed."

Perhaps it was Ralph Sepulveda, she feared. While in Abilene, Servo discovered that when she had first met the much older man in Missoula, he had a fiancée, who he failed to mention that he discarded after knowing Jennifer only for a couple of days. Too, he had a child who he never saw or even acknowledged. Distrusting, Servo broke it off with Sepulveda. On top of this, he had a violent fetish that Jennifer didn't like: he choked her during sex. Perhaps she even learned that, before he moved to Missoula, Sepulveda once had two criminal charges of child molestation filed against him in Phoenix, one of them alleged that he was having sex with his 15-year-old niece.

Travers said that he told Jennifer "she was just imagining things." In Travers' narrative, he asked Jennifer he could walk her to her car, she said no, but he insisted.

According to the Fort-Worth Tribune, Servo phoned ex-boyfriend Dave Warren, then a weatherman in Montana. Warren stated that they discussed possible plans to meet in Dallas in December, and that Jennifer did not reference any suspicions about anyone following her home.

It was Jennifer Servo's last phone conversation.

For several days, no one heard from Jennifer. Phone calls were not answered. Coworkers contacted the staff at the Hunters Ridge Apartments and on September 18, less than a week before her 23rd birthday, she was found murdered.

An autopsy report speculated that Servo had been dead for at least two days. She suffered various blows to the head, bruising around her neck consistent with strangulation and bruising consistent with sexual assault.

Detectives told the Fort-Worth Tribune that they did not believe at the time that Servo had been raped because she was "found fully clothed" and there were "no signs of a struggle." Her door was never forced open, part of the reason authorities believed someone she knew killed her.

Routine procedures followed: evidence was collected, including DNA, blood, hair, and other trace evidence, made especially difficult because of Jennifer's cat, Mr. Binx, whose hair was mixed in with any probable human hair in the apartment.

Several odd items were determined to be stolen from her apartment; one report notes that a Guess-brand purse, a cell phone, keys, and two DVDs ('Saving Private Ryan' and 'Sex and the City') were missing.

"Jennifer's mother called that night her was body found on September 18," says Norman Olson. "I screamed, and I couldn't understand. I paced back and forth and around. How could you get a grip on it?"

Her body was returned to the Flathead Valley of Montana for funeral services. In a tribute to Jennifer, the Reverend Dan Heskett read a letter prepared by her father. The lobby of the Kalispell church was adorned with photographs of Jennifer throughout her brief life—baby pictures, graduating senior shots, college, at work. Hanging on the rack in the vestibule were her blue high school letter jacket and her green Army Reserves jacket. The mood was distinctly somber. "Jessica was murdered," Rev. Heskett said. "That weighs heavy on us. A person filled with sickness or evil took her life... When someone this young dies a violent death, it's just unspeakable."

After Jennifer's funeral, Norman took in Mr. Binx, Jennifer's sage tabby, at first, the cat slept often in the girl's bedroom, but soon the animal and the father were in near constant contact.

"We shared the mournful days and nights, months and years together. I played the word games of decades ago with him that only Jennifer and I understood and laughed so hard at."

Suspects

Despite a mountain of physical evidence, no arrests were ever made in connection with Jennifer's murder. Over the years, several people in law enforcement in Texas have publicly voiced their resentment that Ralph Sepulveda wasn't charged. "All the times that we interviewed him he really never said anything that made us think this wasn't our guy," Jeff Bell, a detective for the Abilene Police Department, said in 2013.

After Jennifer's death, her mother Sherry Servo started blogging about "the narcissistic" Ralph Sepulveda, including a possible link between him and her daughter's missing purse from the crime scene and certain library books that had been checked out after Jennifer's death using her college library card.

Books were checked out from the Mansfield Library at the University of Montana on the account of Jennifer Servo on November 6, 2003, more than one year after she had died.

Barry Brown, the access services coordinator at the Mansfield Library, told the Fort Worth Tribune that, plausible as it might be that the transaction could've have been a clue to a crime, it was just as likely a clerical error could be blamed.

"We might have accidently brought up the wrong record and checked them out," Brown said Monday, "but we don't know for sure."

Detective Jeff Bell stated to the Associated Press that her account was used "to check out four books, which were mainly about philosophy, on Nov. 6."

That was about the last new evidence or lead in the case.

For Norman and Sherry, the daily reminders of their daughter's life in their hometown are visibly ubiquitous. To Norm, the Columbia Falls high school and its embedded memories of Jennifer inside of its swimming pools, lapping, competing, strikes him hardest. And there are the tributaries of the Flathead River, places where he and his daughter would cross the river, walk up a bank, or hold hands on the shallow ice. "The best days of my whole life," says Olson.

Justice is an odd concept to Olson, more like an abstraction, that, though tantalizing, offers little to alleviate the day-to-day reality of his everlasting survivor's remorse.

"I've never had any interest in life since 2002," says Norm Olson. "I laid in bed for five years. I'm just now starting to sleep again. I use audio books at night to control my mind, and to not let it get too dark. The negative emotions, the grief, the rage, they are still like an electrical storm and lightning between by ears."

39

MONTANA'S MOST FAMOUS EXONERATED MAN

Poplar, 1979-2015
Victim: Kim Nees
Case Status: Unsolved

Barry Beach was convicted of killing 17-year-old Kim Nees in Poplar in the summer of 1979. Nees, school valedictorian, national honors graduate, was celebrating a new beginning. She was finally about to escape the remote northeast corner of Montana for college.

Instead, Nees was found beaten to death, and one of her former high-school classmates, Barry Beach, was eventually charged with the sickening crime.

While many people believed Beach was fairly and equitably held accountable for a crime that he assuredly perpetrated, Beach became a symbol of a wronged man, a poster boy of a faulty system, and a rallying point of both rectification and change, among some influential state and national advocates who claimed his murder confession was coerced.

Beach was arrested on January 4, 1983, in Monroe, Louisiana for contributing to the delinquency of a minor. While he was in custody, detectives grilled Beach about the deaths of three young women in Monroe and learned of the unsolved murder of Nees in

Beach's hometown. Though he was later cleared as a suspect in the Monroe slaying, Beach eventually confessed to Nees' murder. The 20-year-old man allegedly telling Louisiana police, as reported in newspapers on January 23, that he beat Nees to death near Poplar in 1979 because she "resisted his sexual advances." On February, 24, 1984, Beach filed a motion to suppress his confession; a judge denied the motion.

In April 1984, Beach was found guilty of deliberate homicide and on May 12, 1984, he was sentenced to 100 years in the State Prison without the possibility of parole. Years of demands for his release – he was denied the claim that his confession was false in separate hearings in 1997 and 2005 – culminated in 2011 with a judge's mandate that released Beach and paved the foundation for a new trial, with testimony expected from witnesses who allege Nees was killed in a violent fight among girls on the Fort Peck Reservation.

After more than 27 years in prison for the killing, Beach saw the world for the first time outside of razor wires, turrets, and tall walls. Beach settled into a new life in Billings, starting his own handyman business, and later obtained a job doing maintenance at a hotel. He was quiet and mannerly and, for the most part, didn't cause any trouble. He started attending church service regularly. With the reality of the brutal reversal of fortune weighing heavily in his mind, Beach, according to one news source, "went water skiing, bowling, camping, fishing and attended local school sporting events." In sum, he lived as if each day were his last one of freedom.

Seventeen months later, the state Supreme Court reversed the 2011 order and put Beach back in prison. A majority of court justices ruled that Beach's lengthy 1983 confession prevailed over "hearsay witnesses" who told the district court judge in 2011 that Nees might have been killed by a mob of resentful girls or that they heard girls fighting.

The Beach case involved an endless string of peculiar details that seemed to weigh in Beach's favor. For starters, there was missing

DNA evidence, "a bloody palm print at the crime scene that didn't belong to either Beach or Nees," according to court documents. Plus, Beach's confession was repeatedly inconsistent with crucial physical evidence found at the scene of the murder and uncovered during the autopsy of the murder victim.

There were also the grumblings over the years that a group of women was secretly taking credit for the crime. On top of this, allegations persisted that a relative to one of the women who allegedly murdered Nees was "on the local police force" and unlawfully entered the evidence room prior to the trial and planted or tampered with evidence.

Barry Beach confessed to killing 17-year-old school valedictorian Kim Nees in Poplar in the summer of 1979 and spent 27 years in prison. Following much legal wrangling and despite the protestations of some of Nees' family, Beach was granted clemency and released in November 2015. Courtesy Jim DeMuth.

Eventually Governor Steve Bullock granted Beach clemency, and he was released from prison in November 2015. Bullock's letter supporting parole, told the Board of Pardons "it should focus not on whether Beach is guilty or innocent, but whether he's a good candidate for parole." In 2017, prosecutors for the state of Montana dropped their murder case against him, days after his case in Billings Municipal Court for sexually propositioning a minor was also dismissed. (In the summer of 2016, Beach was accused of sexually propositioned a 12-year-old girl, though he was not charged with a crime.)

Despite this, many people still side with the victims' immediate family and a number of authorities in fixed certainty that Beach murdered Nees. Among them, former Governor Marc Racicot, who challenged advocates for Beach in 2007, saying that his defenders were dishonestly cherry-picking testimony with the support of "conspiracy buffs or those that want to ignore the facts."

Beach resides in Billings, where he is self-employed as a handyman.

40

A FOREIGN AFFAIR: SUICIDE OR MURDER COVER-UP?

Singapore, 2012
Victim: Shane Todd
Case Status: Disputed

SHANE TODD, the son of an American Airlines captain and an evangelical pastor, was raised in a tight-knit family who lived in California and Florida before settling in Marion, Montana, near Glacier National Park. After earning electrical engineering degrees at the University of Florida and completing his doctoral studies at the University of California, he accepted a job offer to work in Singapore. He started at the Institute of Micro Electronics (IME) in 2010, and two years later, Todd's body was found in his Singapore apartment on June 24, 2012. Contrary to evidence provided by his family, police have maintained he killed himself.

Todd's parents, Rick and Mary Todd, owners of Cabin Creek Landing Bed & Breakfast in Marion, have said repeatedly that they believe the Ph.D. may have been murdered over his research in the U.S. into material used to make semiconductors, a technology with both civilian and military purposes.

The couple visited Singapore after Shane's death to try to puzzle together what happened. They soon discovered disquieting contradictions between the scene at Shane's apartment and the official accounts by Singapore police. As they were leaving, they discovered the backup hard drive for one of the laptops that Singapore police had accessed and presumably duplicated.

The Todds say that the hard drive contained thousands of documents he had backed up from his work computer. Several files included technical requirements for a joint research project between the Singapore government-backed research lab Todd worked for, the Institute of Micro Electronics, and Huawei Technologies, a China-based electronics and telecom giant. The project was geared toward making gallium nitride power amplifier chips. (In 2019, a report by the U.S. House Select Committee on Intelligence proclaimed Huawei to be a threat to U.S. national security).

Even though Shane was inclined to depression and at times he required anti-depressant medications, the sheer thought of Shane committing suicide is preposterous, say Shane's parents. Friends of Shane recall his wide mood swings and that there were long stretches where he had never been happy in their presence. The Todds, however, contend that Shane's alleged suicide note contained false, inaccurate information, referenced events that never happened, and had to have been written by someone other than Shane.

"This suicide note even thanked IME," says Mary.

When questioned by US government lawyers why police had not ordered an additional investigation of the apartment, Singapore police responded that "a preliminary assessment" pointed to suicide and concluded there were "no signs of foul play."

Singapore counsel presented evidence of links to suicide websites on Shane's laptop and suicide letters written to family members and loved ones. The Todds believe that those searches were conducted after Shane died and that the suicide letters were bogus.

The Todds have claimed their 31-year-old son expressed reservations about his safety before he died. "He started calling us and saying that his life was being threatened," says Mary, "And he said that he felt he was being asked to compromise U.S. security...He

Marion resident Shane Truman Todd's body was found in his Singapore apartment on June 24, 2012. Singapore police claimed he had committed suicide. His parents believe the Ph.D. was murdered, possibly because of his high-tech work. His case was featured on the CBS program *48 Hours*. Courtesy Todd Family.

said, mom, I might be paranoid, but I have the feeling that they are threatening my life if I don't stay."

In January 2012, immediately after he returned to Singapore from a trip to New Jersey, Shane told his parents he was being questioned at work not just by his own IME scientific team, but "separately and intensely by a set of Chinese businessmen."

Near the end of February 2012, Todd told his parents that he was quitting IME and had given notice. "At the time of his death," says Mary, "Shane had recently accepted a new job offer, had purchased his plane ticket back to Montana, and was in the process of washing and packing his clothes."

Bottom of Form

The coroner's inquiry into Todd's death ended messily. Todd family lawyers were not present in court because they had been dismissed by Todd's parents, who left Singapore after withdrawing from the inquest, saying they had no confidence in Singapore's legal process.

"We no longer have confidence in the transparency and the fairness of the system," the Todds said in a statement released to the press. "It appears to us that the outcome has been predetermined."

The Todds received support and assistance in the case from Montana's Democratic Senators Max Baucus and Jon Tester.

The Todds—who have been married for more than 40 years and raised four kids—have said that their next course of action will be to urge a U.S. congressional investigation into their son's death. "The implications are humongous," says Mary Todd. "It's frightening."

Shane Todd's case was featured on the CBS program *48 Hours* on October 5, 2013.

Investigation of Huawei Could Bring Justice

Huawei is currently under investigation by federal prosecutors for intellectual property theft and for violating sanctions on Iran. The investigation gives Mary Todd hope, after all these years, that she will see justice done for the death of her beloved son.

For years, the Todd family has been sending evidence and analysis reports to Singapore authorities and agencies of the U.S. government, trying to prove that Shane Todd was murdered in connection with a cover-up of Huawei's alleged theft of U.S. technology.

"We want a congressional investigation into the death of my son in relationship to Huawei," says Mary Todd.

41

A PUSHOVER FOR A HONEYMOON

Glacier National Park, 2013
Victim: Cody Lee Johnson
Case Status: Solved

WITH MORE THAN 700 MILES of hiking trails, Glacier National Park is home to some of Montana's steepest, rockiest, and most hypnotic terrain. Falls and accidents and even deaths from tumbles are not uncommon.

The U.S. National Park Service traces the park's first recorded death in Glacier National Park back to January 1913, "when a man froze to death while snowshoeing between Cut Bank and St. Mary." Of the approximately 260 people who died or are presumed to have died in the park during the first hundred years of its existence, most cases could be chalked up to clumsiness, recklessness, a lack of preparedness, or in some cases, all three.

When the body of Cody Lee Johnson, 25, was recovered below The Loop Trail on Going-to-the-Sun Road in Glacier National Park on Friday, July 12, 2013, it appeared as if the park had suffered another unfortunate accident—until investigators questioned his newlywed bride. She had called authorities to inform them that Cody was dead. The bride's inconsistent statements and a calloused, distant demeanor raised their skeptical antennas.

The victim, a Californian by birth who had moved to Montana with his mother as a young boy, hailed from nearby Kalispell. He was employed at Nomad Global Communication Solutions in Kalispell. His newlywed wife Jordan Linn Graham, 22, a Kalispell native, called dispatchers to report finding her husband's body at the bottom of a cliff below The Loop. Park rangers reported finding the body at 9:45 a.m. Autopsy reports detailed injuries consistent with a fall as being the cause of the young man's death.

Cody Lee Johnson and Jordan Linn Graham of Kalispell were married on June 29, 2013. Two weeks later Jordan confessed to pushing her new husband off a cliff in Glacier National Park. COURTESY FLATHEAD COUNTY SHERIFF'S OFFICE.

Cody had proposed to Jordan shortly before Christmas 2012, after a year of dating. They were married on June 29, 2013, only 14 days before he was found dead on July 12. Cody was reported missing by concerned friends July 8, 2013 when he did not report for work. At first, Jordan allegedly told Cody's relatives that on July 7, 2013, Cody was out joyriding and carousing with some of his friends. She later told law enforcement officers that she and Cody had been at dinner that same night with friends, yet afterwards she saw Cody "getting into a dark-colored vehicle with out-of-state plates."

It did not take long for the Kalispell Police Department to look askance at Jordan's story. When pressed harder, she admitted to shoving Cody off a cliff. She also admitted to making several false statements, including fabricating the timeline of events. She was caught in several acts of deception, including a bogus email account she had set up under the name "Tony," who was supposedly an out-of-town buddy of Cody's and who claimed that Cody had fallen during a hiking trip with him. She also told investigators that she had serious misgivings about their marriage from the very beginning. When questioned about her rationale for lying, she said that she only did so "because she was afraid she wouldn't be allowed to explain what happened on the cliff's edge."

In September 2013, Jordan Linn Graham appeared in U.S. District Court in Missoula on a charge of second-degree murder. According to published court documents, Jordan, who had a predisposition to melancholia, said that she never wanted to get married to Cody, and that immediately after they were married, she felt terrified of having any further sexual relations with him. Sex made her anxious, and even after only a few days together she felt trapped in a relationship that disgusted her as loveless and unfeeling. She said she was searching for an exit strategy. She fantasized about running away from Montana after their swift annulment.

During the trial, Jordan once more deviated from her initial deposition to investigators. Instead of seeing Cody leave in a vehicle with Washington plates, she said that she and Cody argued heatedly on the evening of July 7 and decided to travel to Glacier to cool things down.

"Once there, they walked on The Loop hiking trail for a while and were arguing," court documents state. "Then they walked to the other side of the trail to an area that was very steep and proceeded down the rocks near a stump. Graham stated their argument intensified."

According to available published accounts, Jordan told investigators that she turned to walk away but that her husband forcefully gripped her by her arm. Jordan stated that although she could have deescalated the argument by walking away, in a fit of blind anger she pushed Johnson "with both hands in the back, and as a result, he fell face first off the cliff."

After she pushed her husband to his death, she went home and slept through the night and did not report him missing; his co-workers called authorities on July 8 after he failed to show up at work. When interviewed by investigators on July 9, Graham said that she received a text that Cody was heading out of town with a friend.

Clearly, the guilt was weighing powerfully on her mind. On July 11, Graham walked up to a park ranger and reported that she had found Cody's body at "a place he wanted to see before he died." His body was recovered the next day with the assistance of a helicopter. On July 18, Graham admitted to authorities that she lied about the circumstances of Cody's death.

In March 2014, a federal judge sentenced Jordan Linn Graham to 30 years in prison for luring her new husband to Glacier National Park and pushing him to his death. She admitted that she acted rashly, though she stopped short of saying that the murder was an act of premeditation.

"It was a reckless act," Jordan told the judge after her abrupt change of plea from guilty to not guilty in the middle of the murder trial. "I just pushed.... I wasn't thinking of where we were."

The story of a short honeymoon and swift death attracted international media attention. Even though another suspicious fatality had occurred in Glacier National Park in 1983, Cody Lee Johnson's death was the first to conclude in murder charges, a park spokeswoman told Britain's *Daily Mail* in September 2013.

Jordan Graham appealed her conviction but hit a dead end in the appeals process. She is currently incarcerated at a federal prison in Alabama.

EPILOGUE

Tips, leads, or information significant to any of the open or unsolved cases profiled or referenced in this book should be directed to their appropriate local jurisdictions and municipalities. To direct comments or to address or share relevant information, or for suggestions as to additional future story ideas, the author may be reached at dambrosiobrian@hotmail.com

SELECTED BIBLIOGRAPHY

Books

Armbrister, Trevor, *Act of vengeance: The Yablonski murders and their solution*, Saturday Review Press; 1st edition 1975

Bosco, Antoinette, *Choosing Mercy: A Mother of Murder Victims Pleads to End the Death Penalty*, Orbis Books; 1st Edition 2001

Chase, Alston, *Harvard and the Unabomber: The Education of an American Terrorist*, W. W. Norton & Co Inc; 1st edition, 2003

Coston, John, *To Kill and Kill Again*, ONYX, The Penguin Group, 1st Edition, August, 1992

France, Johnny, *Incident at Big Sky*, Pocket; First Pocket Books Printing edition 1987

France, Johnny, with Malcolm McConnell, *Incident at Big Sky: The True Story of Sheriff Johnny France and the Capture of the Mountain Men*, W. W. Norton & Company, 1st edition, 1986.

Jaeger, Marietta, *The Lost Child*, Zondervan, June, 1983

Shors, Dave, Waits, Chris, Unabomber: The Secret Life of Ted Kaczynski, Farcountry Press, 1999

Swenson, Janet Milek, *Victims: The Kari Swenson Story*, Pruett Pubishing, 1989

Newspapers

Billings Gazette

Bozeman Chronicle

Casper-Star Tribune, March 4, 2004, and others

Great Falls Tribune, December 8, 1924, and others

Missoulian, March 29, 1969, and others

Montana Standard, March 12, 1930, and others

Spokesman-Review

INDEX